State and Society in Spanish America during the Age of Revolution

State and Society in Spanish America during the Age of Revolution

EDITED BY VICTOR M. URIBE-URAN

A Scholarly Resources Inc. Imprint
Wilmington, Delaware

Scholarly Resources Inc.
104 Greenhill Avenue
Wilmington, DE 19805-1897
www.scholarly.com

Library of Congress Cataloging-in-Publication Data

State and society in Spanish America during the Age of
    Revolution / edited by Victor M. Uribe-Uran.
        p. cm. — (Latin American silhouettes)
    Includes bibliographical references and index.
    ISBN 0-8420-2873-0 (alk. paper) — ISBN 0-8420-2874-9
(pbk : alk. paper)
    1. Latin America—History—18th century. 2. Latin America—
History—19th century. 3. Latin America—Social conditions.
4. Latin America—Economic conditions. I. Uribe-Uran, Victor.
II. Series.

F1412.S85 2001
980—dc21   00-058793

To Harold D. Sims, a great mentor

and superior human being

To Christopher D. Gray, an unforgettable colleague

and friend

About the Editor

VICTOR M. URIBE-URAN is director of graduate studies and associate professor of history at Florida International University, Miami. He is the author of *"Honorable Lives": Lawyers, Family, and Politics in Colombia, 1780–1850* (2000) and has published several articles and book chapters on legal history and the history of lawyers and legal education. His recent works, in *Comparative Studies in Society and History* (April 2000) and the *Journal of Social History* (forthcoming), explore the emergence of the public sphere during the Age of Revolution and deal with domestic violence in Mexico and Colombia during the late colonial and early postcolonial eras.

Along with Professor Luis Javier Ortíz, Uribe-Uran is co-editor of *Naciones, Gentes y Territorios. Ensayos de Historia e Historiografía Comparada de América Latina y el Caribe* (2000). He has been a Fulbright Scholar, received two Andrew Mellon fellowships, and was awarded a TIP Prize—a special honor recognizing Florida International University's best teachers. In addition, one of his articles was awarded the Antonine Tibezar Prize.

Acknowledgments

I wish to thank Arthur Herriott, dean of Florida International University's College of Arts and Sciences. The College's encouragement and financial support were vital to my ability to proceed with this endeavor and complete several pieces of the manuscript. I also acknowledge my colleagues Noble David Cook and William Walker III who, as chairs of the history department, offered me unwavering support during different stages of this project. As always, I am indebted to my wife, Valerie, for her patience and understanding. Her sense of humor was generous enough to deal with my anxiety and negativity in the long process leading to the completion of this book. It goes without saying that I am most grateful for the cooperation and patience of each of the contributors and the assistance of the editors and staff at Scholarly Resources Inc., particularly Linda Pote Musumeci. Finally, I acknowledge Alisa Newman's invaluable assistance in copyediting earlier versions of this manuscript.

Contents

Introduction—Beating a Dead Horse?

Victor M. Uribe-Uran

Alluding to the series of radical transformations, both political and economic, that occurred in different regions of the world between 1760 and 1850, over three decades ago historians R. R. Palmer and E. J. Hobsbawm called this era the Age of Democratic Revolutions and the Age of Revolution, respectively. Palmer referred to the years from 1760 to 1800 as a time of political transformations. A new feeling of equality came to the surface, and the rejection of public powers established upon the basis of privilege, status, or traditional rights became the norm. Hobsbawm saw the period as a combination of both political and economic changes, or a "dual revolution." The more political French Revolution and the Industrial Revolution in Britain resulted in the triumph of "capitalist industry" and the rise of the "conquering bourgeoisie." These events influenced profound changes in the shape of economies, societies, and polities throughout the rest of the world.[1] Several historians of Latin America have subsequently adopted the general concept of an Age of Revolution that bridges this region's colonial and early modern history.

As early as the 1970s some Latin Americanists not only borrowed the label but also endorsed the heuristic value of this "long period" in the region's history. They criticized the separation of Latin America's colonial from its modern history, arguing that this separation obscures significant economic, social, and even political continuities from one period to the next. More important, in addition to hiding continuities, the orthodox colonial-modern split also makes it difficult to evaluate historical changes—for instance, to appraise the true impact of political independence in a comprehensive manner. To facilitate the appreciation of economic, social, and political continuities and changes, these scholars proposed treating the second half of the eighteenth century and the first half of the nineteenth as a unified and distinct period.[2]

A decade ago Eric Van Young reminded us, for example, that "modes and social relations of production, family and gender relationship, certain characteristics of state structure and action, and so on, appear to have been substantially in place by the middle of the eighteenth century and to have altered more between 1700 and 1750, or between 1850 and 1900, than between 1750 and 1850." Van Young claimed that "recasting our work on the late colonial and early national eras into a single unit of study embracing the period 1750 to 1850, or some approximation thereto," would offer a number of new research possibilities, including the evaluation of the impact of political independence. He added that, although unconventional, this bracketing together of the late eighteenth and early nineteenth centuries would help raise important questions about this period's role as an epoch of "transition or proto-modernization."[3] Others argued that the historical events and social and political conflicts of this time were part of a "protracted bourgeois revolution" that cleared the path for capitalist development.[4] Still others indicated that the era was part of an even longer "middle period" important for understanding the *longue durée* of habits of mind and the generally slow change of mental dispositions, all of which are hard to make sense of when one follows the traditional periodization.[5]

Probably because these calls for an alternative arrangement of periods have been widely accepted, some colleagues now claim that to insist on the usefulness of this inclusive periodization is to beat a dead horse. The issue was allegedly resolved years ago in favor of research on the broader period.[6] Yet, except for important works addressing diverse, especially economic, dimensions of the long-term "heritage" or "persistence" from colonial to national Latin America, until recently it was rare to find studies bridging the late colonial and early postcolonial periods.[7] As recently as 1994, Lyman Johnson and Kenneth Andrien's volume on the political economy of Spanish America in the Age of Revolution reported that in general, "few monographic studies actually span the entire period 1750–1850." They went on to assert that "although some works dealing with the late colonial or early national period do address longer term continuities, few historians trace such changes systematically across the traditional chronological divide of independence."[8] Comprehensive research on Latin America's economy, society, and politics during the Age of Revolution, therefore, is still wanting.

The burden of tradition seems to have bolstered historians' conventional partition of periods and, over the last decade, to have impeded its advance in a comprehensive direction. It is also possible that some early objections raised to the adoption of a comprehensive periodization had an impact on the scholarly community, discouraged long-term research, and reinforced the conventional split of colonial from modern history. Among these objections was the argument that, although continuity in economic structures and modes of production makes the period relevant to the study of economic history, the long Age of Revolution is not so important for understanding social and political history. In support of this argument, over a decade ago William Taylor argued that the Independence Wars should be allocated a significant role in determining the chronology of Latin American social history because of their impact on such phenomena as migration, increased violent conflict in social relationships, and other equally important changes in social behavior.[9] At recent academic conferences, Susan Socolow and others have favored a similar interpretation.[10] Critics further pointed out that the traditional colonial-national periodization is, as Van Young put it, "predominantly political," making the Age of Revolution methodologically even less significant for understanding political history. After all, independence resulted in a clear political break, producing a series of legal and institutional changes that deserve separate treatment. Along these lines, Michael Costeloe has recently argued that it is wrong to underestimate or diminish the political effects of independence and the obvious political change it brought, which he describes as "the opening of the world of politics." Public political action and debate became significant for the first time after independence, making the colonial-postcolonial "continuity thesis" untenable for students of political history as well.[11]

Despite these objections, historical continuities and changes during the inclusive Age of Revolution are, at last, being uncovered by new research. Several recent anthologies that attempt to adopt this alternative periodization are collections of essays devoted separately to either the late colonial period, independence, or the postcolonial period.[12] Nevertheless, other monographs and articles on social and political history published during the 1990s have managed to address simultaneously the late colonial and early modern periods as well as the independence era.[13] A host of recent doctoral dissertations in the process of revision for publication have done the same.[14] This work joins this refreshing scholarly trend which, contrary to the objections alluded to above, underscores rather than neglects the significance of the deep social and political changes brought about by independence. It originated in a series of panels at the

American Historical Association's annual meeting and the Latin American Studies Association's international congress. Participants in the panels included some of the authors whose works are published here as well as historians Jeremy Adelman, Sarah Chambers, Arlene Díaz, Michael Ducey, Deborah Kanter, Frank Safford, Susan Socolow, and Charles Walker, whose contributions to the many lively discussions leading to this book are gratefully acknowledged.

This volume is divided into four parts dealing respectively with the political economy, business and political elites, gender and the family, and ideology, values, and culture. The eight essays included therein touch on the comparative history of all of Spanish America together with the specific cases of Chile, New Granada, Mexico, and Argentina. They are representative of a larger body of literature dealing with these and other cases throughout the region during the period in question.

The essays in Part I by Samuel Amaral and Richard Doringo, and Richard Salvucci, discuss aspects of the political economy of Spanish America from 1750 to 1850. To understand the unfolding of the economies of the Iberian peninsula and Latin America in the early nineteenth century, Amaral and Doringo look at underlying structures and the long-term development of the factors underpinning them. The authors consider trends in population, agriculture, commerce and industry, money, and credit. In addition to the Ibero-American cases, they include other European countries besides Spain and Portugal in their discussion. Their findings lend weight to the argument for economic continuity after independence. Indeed, the authors consider economic transformations not to have been the result of abrupt shifts derived from independence. Instead, they argue that economic changes during the Age of Revolution, some of which began as early as the 1770s and continued through the 1820s and beyond, resulted from the world economy's long-term evolutionary process.

In an effort to explain Latin America's unsatisfactory development and growth, Salvucci's essay also finds continuities in the nature of export economies throughout the region. His study of these continuities provides abundant empirical information to support the argument that Latin American economies suffered from a syndrome referred to by economists as "Dutch disease." This macroeconomic malaise results from an export boom, drawing especially on natural resources and leading to the decline of "traditional" exports. This trend ultimately brings about inflation of domestic prices, particularly for "nontradable" (no-import-competing) goods, as well as an appreciation or overvaluation of the real exchange rate and a reduction of other exports. Salvucci identifies this "disease" in diverse places and times ranging from late eighteenth-century Mexico to Peru in the 1840s. To demonstrate his findings, he runs a regression analysis using production, trade, and price figures for silver, maize, and cochineal in late colonial New Spain. Other cases that he analyzes include Peru's guano boom, begun in the 1840s. Here, Dutch disease is documented through rising export figures along with evidence of an increasing inflation rate. His research also touches on Brazil and, in passing, Costa Rica and Cuba. His overall conclusion is that the early commodity booms and recurrent Dutch disease in Latin America's resource-rich countries reflect continuities in economic behavior and responses. More important, they led to the neglect of manufacturing and thus hindered stable long-term industrial development throughout the region. Finally, Salvucci analyzes the economic discontinuities that resulted from the disruption of finance and internal and external trade during the Wars of Independence and the political and institutional instability brought about by the collapse of the Spanish empire. All of these factors augmented economic risks, reduced capital formation, and caused growth to lag.

The essays in Part II address issues concerning Latin America's entrepreneurial and political elites and state-building process. Marti Lamar finds some changes but more continuities in Chilean merchants' lives and ways of doing business before and after independence. Focusing on the thirty-three top import-export merchants of the 1795–1823 period, she notices their continuing interest in diversifying the nature of their trade and economic activities. Strategies for achieving this goal included selling a wide variety of commercial goods and investing in land, wheat production and ranching, urban real estate, and mining. Chile's merchants started to behave this way at least as early as the 1790s and continued to do so after independence. Similarly, both colonial and postcolonial merchants built networks of agents, assistants, and business partnerships that remained the accepted way to conduct business throughout the "middle period." The colonial patterns of familial participation in business also continued during the postcolonial era.

Lamar is not blind to major discontinuities in the merchants' business practices. In particular, she notices that some postcolonial merchants integrated family and business much less than their counterparts before independence. More important, she acknowledges that by the early 1820s the colonial generation of top import-export merchants had disappeared as a result of death, retreat from commerce, or political disgrace due to royalist sympathies. The overall emphasis of her work, however, is on continuities neglected by previous scholars. Her principal finding concerns the fact that merchants continued to do business much as they had done before the collapse of the colonial regime.

My own essay on late colonial and early postcolonial lawyers in New Granada provides evidence of another series of changes and continuities in the Age of Revolution. The main factors for change involved the regional and social origin of lawyers, state administrators, and politicians in the first three decades of the postcolonial period. A force for continuity was the undiminished importance of honor for both traditional and upwardly mobile elites after independence. Many of the lawyer-bureaucrats of the 1820–1850 period appear to have come from provincial and nonaristocratic families, yet these new attorneys and state officials kept striving for status-honor much like their competitors from traditional social groups. Over time, these elite sectors converged to become an economically homogeneous class, thus overcoming the status disparities typical of the colonial period. This convergence became especially urgent due to the common threat posed by insurgent groups of artisans in the midnineteenth century.

Both essays in Part III, which is dedicated to gender and family relations, address the case of Mexico. Elizabeth Anne Kuznesof, who has written extensively on the history of Brazil's urban families, provides insights into change and continuity in marriage, household and family life, standard of living, and occupational structures and opportunities in Mexico. Through a detailed examination of abundant secondary sources for the 1750–1850 period, Kuznesof links her findings to ideologies of gender and race, her main goal being to determine whether a trend toward greater autonomy, equality, and a better quality of life for women and castes occurred during this period. Among other findings, she concludes that women's education and legal rights for single women improved. There was also an expansion of female employment, although occupations for women of all races were limited to areas such as domestic service, production and sale of comestibles, and textile or tobacco production—tasks that were, as Kuznesof puts it, "at the level of the 'shifting proletariat.' " Furthermore, the autonomy of married women, minor daughters, and subordinate males was reduced as the power of the male head of household increased, the use of the dowry declined, and parental permission for marriage was required. Increased levels of poverty and unemployment also affected women's standard of living across social and racial boundaries. In sum, Kuznesof finds that even though new ideologies and laws may have favored women, women's real economic circumstances were far from positive.

Sonya Lipsett-Rivera focuses on a particular aspect of family relations in Mexico during the Age of Revolution: the ideas and expectations that men and women had of the "marriage bargain." Her main sources are documents concerning the Church's official policy toward "proper" married life, manuals written by sixteenth- and seventeenth-century moralists, late colonial clerical sources, and judicial and administrative records of marital disputes. All of these sources hint at slow and subtle changes in Mexicans' attitudes toward marriage and family life. One such change was the inclusion of children in divorce petitions, which became arguments over not only the conduct of wives or husbands as spouses but also as parents. A new emphasis developed on the education and upbringing of children as female education took on new importance in the late eighteenth century. Similarly, the rights of wives and their children started to gain precedence over those of fathers and husbands. One such change involved the practice of "depositing" women who filed for divorce or alleged mistreatment. Instead of being consigned to institutions such as convents and hospices, women were now to be deposited in honorable households. Overall, Lipsett-Rivera concludes that changes in the marriage bargain were sluggish; and, although women did gain some autonomy, marriage continued to be inequitable for wives.

The volume's final section, Part IV, deals with ideologies, values, and cultural practices in the Río de la Plata region. John Chasteen looks at dance in an effort to understand the relationship between popular culture and the state in late colonial and early postcolonial Buenos Aires. He reviews both the Church's and the state's reactions to fandangos and other "indecent" dances that afforded the possibility for gatherings of blacks, Indians, mulattoes, and mestizos in the post-1740 period. These prohibitions continued after independence, becoming even more absolute, yet by the midnineteenth century a series of both legal and illegal dance hall-like establishments, or *academias*, had spread throughout Buenos Aires. Chasteen notes that with independence, patriotic nativism caused the exaltation of dance as an expression of collective identity. Such was the case of the "*montonero*/National/Federal minuet," a popular dance that came to express an essential national spirit.

Other dances also acquired respectability as populist pride swelled in the postcolonial period. Chasteen concludes that the relationship between popular culture and the state experienced a long-term shift during the Age of Revolution.

Finally, Mark Szuchman discusses some political, ideological, and aesthetic dimensions of Buenos Aires's history during the colonial-republican transition. His major goal is to link the physical construction of the city to the ideational construction of the Argentine state. In the process, he examines four issues. First, he analyzes certain urban spaces, particularly the *pulperías*, which were key to both popular activities and the development of public opinion. Second, he examines mechanisms of social control, especially the *leva* and the military draft, both of which took advantage of crowded urban spaces, including cafés and the *pulperías* themselves. Third, he discusses the material bases of urban life, including the economic well-being of local elites and institutions, commercial and artisanal dynamism, and the fiscal powers and capacities of public utilities. And finally, he studies the connections between political beliefs and the urban aesthetic. Throughout his essay, Szuchman notices the coexistence of authoritarian colonial traditions, republican revolutionary rhetoric, and the enlightened plans of the republican era.

The book's conclusion, by Eric Van Young, examines insightfully some of the implications of this volume's periodization. It critically frames the periodization debate within the complex epistemological and methodological evolution (and the postmodern turn) of history as a discipline and Latin American history as a specialty. At first, turning away from his earlier position in favor of bridging the colonial and modern periods, Van Young seems to argue that our alternative periodization may blindly drag Latin America's historical experience along the lines of North Atlantic European history. It may also clash and be incompatible with the new developments ("downward displacement") in social and cultural history. Rather than sweeping syntheses of historical processes in large-scale periods, these new trends favor "microhistory" and "infrahistory," a concentration on processes at the private and local levels that may render periodization itself useless. As the conclusion unfolds, however, mounting evidence suggests that the conventional periodization of Latin American history is inconvenient, and that alternatives such as the one proposed in this volume, but others too, may constitute heuristic devices worth pursuing. Nonetheless, Van Young puts forward a salutary warning—namely, that periodizations are always tentative and fluid. They do not provide final answers in themselves, nor should they be reified. I believe this idea to be shared by each and all of the contributors to this volume.

Each of these essays invites us, in diverse ways, to reconsider economic, political, social, and cultural processes throughout the Age of Revolution. Whether their respective emphasis is on continuity or change may not ultimately be as important as the reminder they provide that as one leaves aside the traditional colonial-modern periodization, new avenues to the understanding of Latin American history open up. Other scholars may follow this lead and begin to appreciate the heuristic importance of this alternative periodization, providing us with new research on the series of slow changes and subtle continuities spanning the years from approximately the middle of the eighteenth to the midnineteenth century.

Notes

1. R. R. Palmer, *The Age of the Democratic Revolution: A Political History of Europe and America, 1760–1800*, 2 vols. (Princeton: Princeton University Press, 1959); Eric J. Hobsbawm, *The Age of Revolution [Europe], 1789–1848* (Cleveland: World Publishing Co., 1962). See also the subsequent works by Charles Breunig, *The Age of Revolution and Reaction, 1789–1850* (New York: Norton, 1970); and David Brion Davis, *The Problem of Slavery in the Age of Revolution, 1770–1823* (Ithaca: Cornell University Press, 1975).

2. See Woodrow Borah, "Discontinuity and Continuity in Mexican History," *Pacific Historical Review* 48 (1979): 1–25; Eric Van Young, "Mexican Rural History Since Chevalier: The Historiography of the Colonial Hacienda," *Latin American Research Review* 17, no. 3 (1983): 5–61, esp. 6–7; Eric Van Young, "Recent Anglophone Scholarship on Mexico and Central America in the Age of Revolution, 1750–1850," *Hispanic American Historical Review* 65 (1985): 725–43, esp. 730–33; Marcelo Carmagnani, "The Inertia of Clio: The Social History of Colonial Mexico," *Latin American Research Review* 20, no. 1 (1985): 149–66, esp. 157; and Mark D. Szuchman, ed., *The Middle Period in Latin American History: Values and Attitudes in the 18th and 19th Centuries* (Boulder: Lynne Rienner, 1988), 11–13, 18. See also Victor M. Uribe, "Continuity and Change in Latin American Political History, 1780–1850," paper presented at the annual meeting of the American Historical Association, January 1996, Atlanta, Georgia.

3. See Van Young, "Recent Anglophone Scholarship," 728–29, 741–44. Similar arguments on colonial-postcolonial economic continuities were advanced over a decade earlier by William P. McGreevey, "Tierra y trabajo en la Nueva Granada, 1760–1845," *Desarrollo Económico* 8, no. 30–31 (July–December 1968): 263–91; and by Charles H. Harris III, *A Mexican Family Empire. The Latifundio of the Sánchez Navarros, 1765–1867* (Austin: University of Texas Press, 1975), 311. For views on social continuities see Alida C. Metcalf, *Family and Frontier in Colonial Brazil: Santana de Parnaiba, 1580–1822* (Berkeley: University of California Press, 1992), 196–97.

4. These authors argued that "the wealth of empirical evidence garnered recently about both social structure and social movements in the 1780–1850 period can be interpreted as part of a long term process of both state formation and changes in political economy." See Peter Guardino and Charles Walker, "The State, Society, and Politics in Peru and Mexico in the Late Colonial and Early Republican Periods," *Latin American Perspectives* 19, no. 2 (1992): 10–43, esp. 13.

5. See Szuchman, *The Middle Period*, esp. 11–13.

6. In personal communications and at academic conferences both Professors Harold D. Sims and Frank R. Safford used this colloquialism to voice the opinion that the "periodization" dispute is irrelevant, as it was settled a long time ago in favor of long-term studies.

7. See especially Stanley J. Stein and Barbara Stein, *The Colonial Heritage of Latin America: Essays on Economic Dependence in Perspective* (New York: Oxford University Press, 1970); John Coatsworth, *Los orígenes del atraso: Nueve ensayos de historia económica de México en los siglos XVIII y XIX* (Mexico City: Alianza Editorial, 1990); Claudio Veliz, *The New World of the Gothic Fox: Culture and Economy in English and Spanish America* (Berkeley: University of California Press, 1994); Stephen Haber, ed., *How Latin America Fell Behind: Essays on the Economic Histories of Brazil and Mexico, 1800–1914* (Stanford: Stanford University Press, 1997); and Jeremy Adelman, ed., *Colonial Legacies: The Problem of Persistence in Latin American History* (New York: Routledge, 1999). See also several of the works cited in note 21 of the Conclusion, this volume.

8. See Kenneth J. Andrien and Lyman Johnson, eds., *The Political Economy of Spanish America in the Age of Revolution, 1750–1850* (Albuquerque: University of New Mexico Press, 1994), 6.

9. William Taylor, "Between Global Processes and Local Knowledge: An Inquiry into Early Latin American Social History," in *Reliving the Past: The Worlds of Social History*, ed. Oliver Zunz (Chapel Hill: University of North Carolina Press, 1985), 122–23, 171–72. For opposite views, see Van Young, "Recent Anglophone Scholarship," 725–43.

10. Panel on "The Economic, Social, and Political Historiography of Latin America during the 'Age of Revolution,'" annual meeting of the American Historical Association, January 1996, Atlanta, Georgia.

11. Michael Costeloe, *The Central Republic in Mexico, 1835–1846: Hombres de Bien in the Age of Santa Anna* (New York: Cambridge University Press, 1993), 3–4; "Hombres de Bien in the Age of Santa Anna," in *Mexico in the Age of Democratic Revolutions, 1750–1850*, ed. Jaime E. Rodríguez (Boulder: Lynne Rienner, 1994), 244. For an alternative view, see Victor M. Uribe-Uran, "The Birth of a Public Sphere in Latin America during the Age of Revolution," *Comparative Studies in Society and History* 42, no. 2 (April 2000): 425–57.

12. See, for instance, Antonio Annino et al., eds., *America Latina dallo stato coloniale allo stato nazionale*, 2 vols. (Milan: Franco Angeli, 1987); Rodríguez, *Mexico in the Age of Democratic Revolutions*; Mark D. Szuchman and Jonathan Brown, eds., *Revolution and Restoration. The Rearrangement of Power in Argentina, 1776–1860* (Lincoln: University of Nebraska Press, 1994); and François-Xavier Guerra et al., eds., *De los imperios a las naciones. Iberoamérica* (Zaragoza, Spain: IberCaja, 1995). For an exception, see the comprehensive essays in Andrien and Johnson, *The Political Economy of Spanish America*.

13. See Uribe-Uran, "The Birth of a Public Sphere"; Guardino and Walker, "The State, Society, and Politics in Peru and Mexico"; Thomas Whigham, *The Politics of River Trade. Tradition and Development in the Upper Plata, 1780–*

1870 (Albuquerque: University of New Mexico Press, 1991); and Andrien and Johnson, *The Political Economy of Spanish America*. Still longer-term studies include the excellent work by Neils Jacobsen, *Mirages of Transition. The Peruvian Altiplano, 1780–1930* (Berkeley: University of California Press, 1993); and Hans-Joachim König, *En el camino a la nación. Nacionalismo en el proceso de formación del estado y de la nación de la Nueva Granada, 1750–1856* (Bogotá: Banco de la República, 1994). See also Peter Guardino, *Peasants, Politics, and the Formation of Mexico's National State* (Stanford: Stanford University Press, 1996); Charles Walker, *Smoldering Ashes: Cuzco and the Creation of Republican Peru, 1780–1840* (Durham: Duke University Press, 1999); Silvia M. Arrom, *Containing the Poor: The Mexico City Poor House, 1774–1871* (Durham: Duke University Press, 2000); Sarah Chambers, *From Subjects to Citizens: Honor, Gender, and Politics in Arequipa, Peru, 1780–1854* (University Park: Pennsylvania State University Press, 1999); and Victor M. Uribe-Uran, *"Honorable Lives": Lawyers, Family, and Politics in Colombia, 1780–1850* (Pittsburgh: University of Pittsburgh Press, 2000).

14. See, for instance, Lee Michael Penyak, "Criminal Sexuality in Central Mexico, 1750–1850" (Ph.D. diss., University of Connecticut, 1993); Deborah Kanter, "Hijos del Pueblo: Family, Community, and Gender in Rural Mexico, the Toluca Region, 1730–1830" (Ph.D. diss., University of Virginia, 1993); and Martha Lamar, "The Merchants of Chile, 1795–1823: Family and Business in the Transition from Colony to Nation" (Ph.D. diss., University of Texas at Austin, 1993).

I
The Region's Political Economy

1

Latin America Was Behind
The Economic Background of Independence

Samuel Amaral and Richard Doringo

Samuel Amaral, a former professor of history at Northern Illinois University and currently at the University of Tres de Febrero, in Argentina, joins former Illinois graduate student, Richard Doringo, in a long-term comparative approach to Latin American history. Their essay focuses on demographic and economic trends that may explain material change in Latin America during the period discussed in this volume. Amaral's previous books include an anthology on the economic impact of independence and a major study of Buenos Aires estancias, or ranches, during the Age of Revolution. He is also the author of a number of published essays on related topics. He and Doringo, who is finishing a dissertation on collective welfare in Mexican economic thought from 1821 to 1917, engage here in a comprehensive discussion that includes Spanish America and European cases beyond Spain and Portugal. Their findings support the view that some economic trends persisted after independence, with changes occurring only gradually. Put differently, their contention is that Latin America's postindependence economic changes were not the result of radical shifts caused by independence. Economic transformations during the Age of Revolution, which Amaral and Doringo trace back as far as the early 1770s, derived rather from the cumulative evolutionary process of the world economy. To chart this long-term evolutionary process, they examine structural aspects pertaining to population, agriculture, trade and industry, and money and credit.

T he tumultuous character of Latin America's Age of Revolution makes it easy to be drawn to the dramatic events of war and the engrossing personalities entangled in the bedlam. In the economic sphere, it is just as tempting to focus on the immediate effects of this seemingly decisive historical event. The Latin American economies fared poorly amid the aftershocks of independence: the loss and displacement of human life led to labor shortages and disrupted commercial centers; war decimated plantation crops and livestock, mining was seriously damaged by either purposeful destruction or neglect, traditional trade and communication networks were disrupted, and the capital necessary to restore these losses was not readily available. These factors are, of course, important elements in understanding the region's economic history. More often overlooked, but no less crucial, are the underlying structures upon which these economies were built and their development in the long run.

Much of the recent research on the economic history of nineteenth-century Latin America concerns the debate over the continuities and disjunctures between the colonial period and independence. These studies aim their investigations at long-term trends in economic growth patterns, the evolution of political culture, and its impact on the economy as a whole.[1] This chapter looks at the Latin American economies focusing on the long-term evolution of the basic socioeconomic factors that were not immediately changed by the shocking political developments. We outline a general framework of long-term trends in four areas—population, agriculture, trade and industry, and money and credit—with the goal of facilitating the understanding of the conditions in which the economies of Latin America unfolded at the beginning of the nineteenth century. As Spanish America and Brazil were part of larger political structures that included the metropolitan areas of the Portuguese and Spanish empires, the same trends are observed for the Iberian peninsula.

Our discussion of population concentrates on a comparison of total growth, mortality rates, birth and infant mortality rates, and ethnic makeup. The section on agriculture looks at technological advances in each region, production methods, output, and the diversity of production. The dissolution of empire meant that trade between Latin America and Europe took on greater significance in the first decades of the 1800s. Consequently, we examine the changing nature of international trade during this period, with a special emphasis on the enhanced role assumed by Great Britain in the Latin American economies. And last, we look at money and credit to see how the presence, or absence, of necessary banking and financial institutions affected trade between these areas.

It has been suggested that following independence, Latin America had the potential to develop in much the same way as

Western Europe. This essay does not offer a clear answer to that counterfactual proposition, but the adoption of a comparative approach, measuring the four socioeconomic factors mentioned above in Latin America, Spain, and Portugal against events elsewhere in Europe, may help to illustrate the restrictions of such an argument.

Population

The population of Europe accelerated its growth in the second half of the eighteenth century due to causes that remain the subject of intense debate. In contrast to previous periods of growth, this expansion was no longer limited by hunger and the plague. At the beginning of the nineteenth century the total population of Europe was approximately 187 million. France, the most populous country, contained some 28 million people; Great Britain, almost 11 million; Spain, around 11 million; and Portugal, 3 million. Latin America was still an underpopulated continent: Mexico had 6.1 million people (1814); Peru, 1.2 million (1828); New Granada, 2.5 million; Central America, 1.2 million; Chile, 1 million; Río de la Plata, 0.5 million; Upper Peru, 1.1 million; and Brazil, between 3.5 and 4 million.[2]

A contemporary analysis of world population by Adrien Balbi offers a comparison by country. Although the accuracy of his study is open to question, Balbi's estimates reflect contemporary perceptions of global demographics. The Spanish and Portuguese monarchies (as they were designated) occupied the second and fifth places in terms of territorial expansion, a category headed by the Russian empire. The Chinese empire led the category of total population with 170 million; the English empire followed with 109 million; the Spanish came in fifth with 30.4 million; and the Portuguese, twelfth with 9.1 million. In the category of population density, the Japanese empire was first, with 185 persons per square mile, followed by the French empire with 151. The Spanish and Portuguese kingdoms occupied seventeenth and nineteenth place, respectively, with only 7 and 3 persons per square mile.[3]

In a more concrete comparison with other European countries, Spain and Portugal occupied sixth and tenth place in area (143,000 and 28,400 square miles) on a list headed by the Russian empire (1.5 million square miles). The Russian empire also came in first in terms of population quantity (48 million persons), while Spain (11.2 million) and Portugal (3.2 million) occupied fifth and thirteenth place, respectively. Smaller countries led the category of population density, with the Low Countries in eighth place (324 persons per square mile); England, thirteenth (243); France, thirtieth (181); Portugal, forty-sixth (116); and Spain, forty-ninth (78).[4]

The population revolution was then in its beginnings. Measures of birth rates and mortality as well as the distribution of population demonstrated parameters that, although changing, were still close to traditional norms. Mortality declined in Europe starting in the middle of the eighteenth century, a trend that contributed to population increases. England's mortality rate was between 26 and 27 per 1,000 people in 1800; in France it was 26 per 1,000 in 1811–1820; and in Sweden it was 28 per 1,000 in 1801–1810. Other regions of Europe recorded rates of more than 30 per 1,000; among these were Portugal, at 30.7 per 1,000; and Tuscany, with 30.6 per 1,000. Even in the first half of the nineteenth century, Spain was registering rates greater than 40 per 1,000.[5]

Birth rates, in the majority of cases, did not change perceptibly in the beginning of the nineteenth century. England's birth rate, however, rose from 30 to over 40 per 1,000 in a century's time. A decline in the French birth rate (to between 32 and 33 per 1,000) was accompanied by a drop in mortality, leaving a considerable balance of natural growth. Portugal's birth rate in 1801 was 33.9 per 1,000, but the difference in the mortality rate was minimal. This balance led to a population growth in Portugal of 0.3 percent, compared to 0.6 percent in France and 1.5 percent in England and Germany. Overall figures for Spain are not available, but the birth rate registered in one Castilian town in the first half of the nineteenth century was 45 per 1,000.[6]

The infant mortality rate in Sweden around 1800 was 178.5 per 1,000. In France between 1802–1811 it was 188 per 1,000; in Belgium, in the decade of the 1820s, 205 per 1,000; and in four Castilian towns in the first half of the nineteenth century, between 240 and 282 per 1,000. The life expectancy in Sweden in 1815 was 35.3 years for men and 38.4 years for women; in France between 1817 and 1831 it was 38.3 and 40.8 years, respectively. In the same Castilian towns, life expectancy was as low as 25 to 30 years, without distinction of gender.[7]

Only a few Latin American countries had statistics comparable to those of Europe. Birth and mortality rates were 47 and 21.5 per 1,000 in São Paulo, Brazil, in 1815. In Paraguay, in 1792, the rates were 40.3 and 35.6 per 1,000, respectively; if we exclude the Jesuit missions, however, the rates fall to 36.3 and 25 per 1,000. The figures for Lima in 1790 were 38 and 24 per 1,000. In 1822, Alexander von Humboldt estimated Mexico's birth and mortality rates at 59 and 33 per 1,000. Figures varied considerably between cities; however, in Querétaro the rates were 72 and 38 per 1,000; and in Guanajuato, 67 and 33 per 1,000. Minas Gerais in 1815 registered rates of 37 and 32 per 1,000, but with considerable ethnic differences: the rates for whites were 37 and 27 per 1,000; for slaves, 33.4 and 32.9 per 1,000; and for free blacks and mulattoes, 42 and 34 per 1,000. The infant mortality rate in São Paulo was 288 per 1,000 in 1798, while in Acatzingo, Mexico, in the second half of the eighteenth century it was 231 per 1,000 for the indigenous population and 221 per 1,000 for the rest of the city's residents.[8]

These figures do not show a remarkable difference in basic population trends between Europe and Latin America in the Age of Revolution. Incomplete data prevent a closer comparison of these trends, but from the previous picture more striking differences emerge within each continent due to specific conditions in each region than from a comparison between continents. However, one significant difference that does emerge is the ethnically heterogeneous population of Latin America. In Europe the massive movements of peoples had ended many centuries earlier, resulting in a homogenization of the region's population. In Latin America, in contrast, the ethnic mixture of Indians, Europeans, and Africans was at its highest point. The major European migrations of the eighteenth century took place from Great Britain and Germany to North America, and from Ireland to Great Britain. In Latin America the forced migration of Africans ceased only with independence (with the exception of Brazil, which continued to import slaves until 1850). At the time of independence, only 23 percent of the population of Brazil was of European origin; 54 percent were black slaves and mestizos, seven percent were Indian, and the remaining 16 percent were mulattoes or free blacks.[9]

Spanish America had comparable concentrations of peoples of African origin in some regions: blacks and mulattoes counted for 64 percent of the population in Tucumán, 54 percent in Santiago del Estero, 52 percent in Catamarca, 46 percent in Salta, 44 percent in Córdoba, and 24 percent in Buenos Aires around 1778.[10] In the Río de la Plata region the population of European origin ranged between 68 percent in Buenos Aires and 5 percent in Jujuy, where 82 percent of those counted were classified as *naturales*.[11] A similar proportion or even greater could be found in Upper Peru and the Peruvian highlands. In contrast, in Lima in 1790, 38 percent of the population were of European origin, 17 percent Indians and mestizos, 36 percent blacks and mulattoes, and the rest *castas*.[12] In New Spain, 60 percent of the population were Indians, 22 percent *castas*, and 18 percent of European origin.[13] Regional differences were evident in this case as well. The concentration of *naturales* varied between 40 percent in the Valley of Mexico and 88 percent in Oaxaca.[14] In Mexico City, 49 percent of the residents were classified as criollos, 2 percent as Spanish, 24 percent as Indian, and 25 percent as mestizos.[15]

The population of Europe in 1800 was principally rural. Scarcely 10 percent lived in cities of more than 10,000. Only twenty-three cities had more than 100,000 inhabitants; together, they housed 5.5 million people, only 3 percent of the total population of Europe. London was the largest city with 1.3 million, followed by Paris with 700,000 and Naples with 350,000; Lisbon at that time had 260,000, and Madrid between 150,000 and 200,000 (Joseph Townsend estimated Madrid's 1786 population at 147,000, while Balbi guessed the figure to be 168,000 in 1822). In Italy, the region with the most urban development, the nine cities that contained over 50,000 people constituted only 7 percent of the population.[16]

Latin America's population was also primarily rural. Mexico City and the provincial capitals held only 8 percent of the people of New Spain; a similar proportion existed between Rio de Janeiro and the provincial capitals with respect to the total population of Brazil. In 1828, Lima accounted for around 10 percent of the population of Peru, and Asunción for 9 percent of Paraguay's. Only Buenos Aires, whose countryside remained sparsely inhabited, contained 55 percent of the Argentine population in the midnineteenth century, but this figure fell to 47 percent two decades later. A similar trend characterized most of the Argentine interior, where small cities contained relatively high percentages of the population.[17]

Alone among the Ibero-American cities, Mexico City, with 168,000 in 1811, was comparable to second-level cities in Europe— Madrid, Marseilles, Berlin, Rome, or Milan with between 100,000 and 200,000 people. Lima and Rio de Janeiro approached this level, with populations of nearly 100,000. Very few cities ranked with those of the third European level (Florence, Bologna), with between 50,000 and 100,000. Buenos Aires contained 40,000 or 50,000, while Salvador, Bahia, held 60,000. In Mexico, Puebla also had a population of 50,000 or 60,000, until the epidemic of 1813 initiated a significant decline. In Upper Peru (today's Bolivia), Potosí, which at the beginning of the seventeenth century had more than

100,000 people and was rated then among the major cities of the Western world, scarcely conserved one-fourth of this number at the beginning of the nineteenth century.[18]

Any generalization about birth and mortality rates or life expectancy is dangerous, considering the marked regional and social differences both in Europe and in Latin America. However, it is possible to note some apparent similarities and differences. At the beginning of the nineteenth century the Latin American population was, at most, one-tenth of that of Europe. The population of Europe, like much of Latin America, was still overwhelmingly rural, but Europe had more large- and moderate-sized cities. The birth rates were similar, but in northwestern Europe the mortality rate had already begun to fall, a condition that produced the great climb in population during the nineteenth century. The infant mortality rate and life expectancy in Europe were still within traditional bounds, but in the first decade of the nineteenth century they began to improve.

Population trends were changing in Europe during the Age of Revolution, but for most of the continent the pace of change was very slow or nonexistent. These changes—mainly increasing urbanization and declining mortality rates—accelerated in Europe during the nineteenth century, partially as a consequence of industrialization and technical innovation. As these factors were missing in Latin America, population trends there remained largely unchanged for most of that century.

Agriculture

At the beginning of the nineteenth century, Europe was feeling the effects of the Industrial Revolution, but the effects of the previous century's agricultural revolution were even more pronounced. The introduction of new agricultural methods engendered a significant growth in productivity. That revolution, initiated in the Low Countries and transplanted to England by 1700, propagated itself in the second half of the eighteenth century in France, the United States, Sweden, Germany, and Denmark as well as regions such as the Po Valley and Catalonia. Paul Bairoch has stressed the fact that for the first time in history the threat of hunger had been largely overcome.[19]

This revolution involved new methods, such as crop rotation to eliminate fallow land, more intensive use of fertilizers, the incorporation of iron into agricultural tools, the use of the plow horse, and the removal of the feudal regime and forms of collective property. At the time of Latin American independence these innovations were slowly gaining ground in Europe. In the north of France, where measurements are available, the advance of intensive agriculture was carried out at a rhythm of some 60 km. every thirty years. Similarly, the disappearance of the fallow system in Germany took all of the eighteenth century.[20]

These transformations indicate certain limitations. The most notable example is agricultural machinery, which was introduced in the nineteenth century but did not have real importance until the twentieth. The first innovations were limited to the use of iron instead of wood in parts of the plow, and substituting the horse for the ox in providing draft power. Another limitation was the absence of a permanent international market for agricultural products. Agricultural goods crossed borders, but this trade was sporadic and designed primarily to make up for drops in regional production. Some regions imported goods on a regular basis, but such imports were of little economic importance. The Low Countries, for example, imported 14 percent of their agricultural consumption, while between 1811 and 1830 imported wheat accounted for only 3 percent of British consumption. Between 1831 and 1840 that share grew to 13 percent, but only with the repeal of the Corn Laws in 1846 did this proportion increase, turning England into a market for overseas agricultural products.[21]

Modern agricultural methods were not easily introduced into Spain, Portugal, and Latin America in the late eighteenth and early nineteenth centuries. Joseph Townsend's travels through Spain in 1786 and 1787 give an excellent account of the state of agriculture in that country. In Catalonia he encountered plows with iron parts, draft teams of oxen or mules, triennial rotation of cultivation without fallow land, irrigation, and use of fertilizer. Near Toledo the rotation was quadrennial and the plows were more primitive than those of Catalonia. Townsend made the same observation various times in his travels from Madrid to Asturias. Power was supplied in general by oxen, and horses and mules were used for threshing. Farm carts only occasionally had an iron cover on their axle, but even in England the wooden axle was in universal use until a few years earlier. In Avila, Townsend encountered wooden carts and plows drawn by pairs of oxen. In La Mancha, mules were used for all purposes, while in Asturias and in Granada oxen prevailed. In Cartagena he found a triennial rotation with wheat, barley, and fallow land; there, farmers used oxen for cargo and mules and donkeys as draft animals. Cereal yields varied notably: in Valencia, wheat yielded between 20 and 40 seeds for each seed sowed; in Lorca the ratio was 100:1, but at only seven leagues, in La Penilla, 8:1; in the area around Barcelona, 10:1 and 15:1; and in Añover, between Aranjuez and Toledo, 50:1. The average wheat yield in Aranjuez between 1768 and 1795 was around 8.2:1, ranging from 13.15 to 4.79.[22] This disparity may look confusing, but it was due perhaps to the type of information that did not differentiate averages from an occasional bumper crop.

Spanish agriculture mixed traditional and modern features. A modern trait stressed by Townsend was the uniformity of grain prices, a consequence of the removal of barriers to internal trade, initiated in Spain in the middle of the eighteenth century. Market unification was hindered, however, by the poor state of Spanish roads and by outdated regulations. Prices were controlled, the supply of meat was a municipal monopoly, and the privileges granted to the *mesta* (the sheepowners' guild) still existed. In contrast to England, property rights were not fully respected. In Carmona, Townsend talked with a Frenchman whose land, improved through diligence and skill, had been expropriated only to be handed over to negligent cultivators.[23] In this way, the lack of juridical security discouraged agricultural enterprise.

Balbi presented a less detailed but no more encouraging view of Portugal around 1820. Agriculture did not prosper in spite of government efforts in the second half of the eighteenth century. The government had created the Academy of Sciences in Lisbon to improve knowledge of agricultural matters and established the Alto Douro wine company to control the quality of wine production. The state expropriated lands in the south and even obtained authorization from the pope to work on holy days.[24] But the primary encumbrances remained: tax exemptions for land belonging to the Crown, corporations, and large proprietors; excessive tributes and *corveés* imposed on the peasantry; and too much uncultivated land belonging to communities, nobles, entailed estates, religious corporations, and the Crown. Other problems included the lack of roads and population scarcity, which accounted for the high cost of labor and frequent absenteeism. In general, Balbi associated the causes of the decline of Portuguese agriculture with the immobility of factors of production, although he followed a mercantilist logic in blaming cheap cereal imports for lowering the price of local grains and reducing farmers' profits.[25] Imports represented barely 7 percent of consumption, so the effect on profits should not have been so great. But this factor explains why in Spain and Portugal, in contrast to England, the nobility resided at court and not on their estates: it was more convenient to be near the distribution of privileges than to agricultural production.

Louis-François de Tollenare, who traveled mostly through the north of Portugal in the late 1810s, found a state of affairs that contradicted Balbi's picture to some extent. In Vinta, two leagues from Porto, he saw fields that yielded two annual harvests of oats or wheat and maize. Agriculture developed there thanks to irrigation, made possible by simple and rustic but well-built machines. The oats and wheat were of superior quality to those produced in France, but restrictions on exports, the tithe, and chaotic property rights discouraged agricultural activity.[26]

As a territory much more vast than either Spain or Portugal, the Americas exhibited more extreme variations in production. The most salient feature was the massive production of sugar in the Brazilian northeast for export to the European markets. Sugar was, indeed, the first agricultural product exported on a massive scale to an overseas market. It also gave rise to a society completely distinct from that of the Old World or other parts of Latin America. The same type of production was reproduced in the Antilles from the middle of the seventeenth century onward, resulting in a plantation society comprised of an extensive mass of African slaves at the base and a few European masters at the top.

The plantation was not the only model of social and economic organization found in Latin America at the beginning of the nineteenth century. Another important economic activity was cattle raising, practiced extensively in very different geographical contexts such as Durango, the plains of the Orinoco, the *sertão* and Rio Grande do Sul, and the pampas of Argentina. Cattle raising evolved in Brazil to meet the needs of the northeastern sugarcane region. Livestock ranches also expanded in the south prompted by demand from Rio de Janeiro, Minas Gerais, and São Paulo at the end of the eighteenth century.

Sugarcane plantations and cattle-raising haciendas were characteristic of some regions, while in others agricultural haciendas prevailed. In Cuba, sugarcane and coffee were "watered with the sweat of African slaves," but in the interior of Mexico, according to Humboldt, the word "agriculture" evoked a more benevolent image: "The Indian cultivator is poor, but he is free. His state is even greatly preferable to that of the peasantry in a great part of the north of Europe. There are neither *corveés* nor villenage in New

Spain; and the number of slaves is next to nothing."[27] Mexico's main crops were not luxury export products but rather cereal, edible roots, and agave. The principal source of its wealth was not its mines, Humboldt noted, but agriculture. The state of Mexican agriculture had gradually improved since the end of the eighteenth century. Contrary to the common opinion that the mineral wealth impeded the development of agriculture, Humboldt indicated that the areas of Mexico that most resembled the beautiful plains of France were those that surrounded the richest mines of the world, including the region around Salamanca, Silao, Guanajuato, and León.

New Spain's torrid zone produced bananas and manioc, but it was maize—cultivated from sea level to elevations as high as 2,800 meters—that accounted for most consumption. A year in which the maize harvest failed was, according to Humboldt, a year of hunger and misery for Mexico's people. Maize output was extraordinary: the sowing of a fanega could produce as much as 800 fanegas, while fertile lands in a common year produced 300 or 400 fanegas. In the area around Valladolid the harvest was considered poor when the seed ratio was 130:1 or 150:1. Even in sterile ground, planters in New Spain produced from 60:1 to 80:1. Humboldt estimated the average output as even 150:1, but the missions of New California were producing between 70:1 and 80:1 around 1800.[28]

European cereals (wheat, rye, barley) were also grown in Mexico at elevations of between 800 and 900 meters above sea level. Wheat production was astonishing in carefully cultivated lands; the more fertile parts of the plateau, between Querétaro and León, yielded between 35 and 40 seeds for each seed sowed, and in some great haciendas output rose to 50:1 or 60:1. Production in the Valley of Mexico reached between 18:1 and 20:1. The average calculated by Humboldt for the whole country was from 22:1 to 25:1. The average for the missions of New California was 17:1 in 1791, and 18:1 in 1802, with extremes of 3:1 in San Carlos and 50:1 in San Diego.

Humboldt compared this output with figures calculated for Europe: 5:1 or 6:1 in France (although as much as 15:1 in some sections); and 8:1 to 10:1 in Hungary and Croatia. Other parts of Latin America, such as Buenos Aires and Montevideo, attained 12:1 to 16:1, while levels in Cajamarca, Peru, reached 18:1 or 20:1.[29] Although these yields seem much greater than those of Europe, three main factors account for the difference. First, since Latin American land had not undergone long periods of intensive cultivation, it was more productive than European acreage. Second, Latin

American cultivators used a type of cereal that had a smaller seed and was perhaps more productive than the kind used in Europe. And third, the high outputs reflected bumper crops rather than average yields, as shown by the fact that, when available, Latin American averages were near those of Europe.

Spanish American agriculture was affected by restrictions that were absent in Spain. Key crops, such as grapes and olives, were banned. Chile and Peru had been authorized to grow these products only because they could not be obtained from Spain. Only a few remote areas—the central valley of Chile; San Juan and Mendoza, which were integrated into the viceroyalty of Río de la Plata in 1776; Arequipa, in Peru; and Cinti, in Upper Peru—had vineyards that supplied regional markets. There were vineyards in Mexico as well, but during Humboldt's residence there the viceroy received orders to destroy the vines after the Cádiz merchants complained of the decline in consumption of Spanish wines.[30]

At the end of the eighteenth century the spread of commercial agriculture in Mexico began the process of proletarianization of the peasantry. Quantitative changes, more than qualitative ones, produced this transformation. Eric Van Young has shown that technical backwardness and declines in productivity made Mexico's agricultural expansion similar to that of Europe before 1300. One aspect of this expansion was the elimination of the rights of common usufruct and internal colonization. Lands already claimed but not exploited for lack of labor and demand were placed in production. Due to demographic factors (the increase of workers in the face of inelastic resources), institutional structures (the land was nominally possessed by landowners), and economic limitations (the high investment required by cereal production for the urban market), peasants did not benefit from this expansion.[31]

The process of proletarianization in Mexico differed from that in England and France in that there were no feudal rights that could be turned into individual rights, nor were there independent peasants from the manor to serve as rural workers. As Van Young points out, independent peasants were already integrated into the Spanish monetary economy,[32] and yet the situation he describes for Guadalajara should not be generalized for all of Mexico. At the end of the colonial period, regions such as Oaxaca remained largely indigenous, while in the Bajío, where indigenous identity had been lost, leasing and sharecropping were more advanced. This different evolution depended principally on the characteristics of the urban markets that the haciendas of each region supplied. The growth in agricultural production helped strengthen the hacienda, later limited by war and political disorder.

The first decades of the nineteenth century in Spain saw the dissolution of noble rule, along with the end of communal, corporate, and noble property in western Europe. The mobilization of agrarian property went hand in hand with the disentailing of land.[33] This same process had different characteristics in Spanish America. There, private appropriation of land commenced in the late sixteenth and early seventeenth centuries. Latin America had no landed nobility similar to that of Spain, but it did have communal and corporate property. These did not disappear with independence, but in the second half of the nineteenth century the triumph of liberalism produced the disentailing of corporate property in Mexico, the suppression of the entailed estate in Chile, and in general the advance of private property over ecclesiastical and indigenous communal property. This phenomenon was a manifestation of the liberal notion of state-building based on a citizenry equal before the law, and not on the power of corporations.

The agricultural methods used in Europe and Latin America at the beginning of the nineteenth century did not differ greatly. The abundance of land in the Americas conspired against the adoption of intense cultivation methods, but productivity kept pace with European ratios. The Latin American agricultural enterprise differed from the European principally by the existence of plantations and cattle-raising haciendas, although the advance of commercial agriculture in Latin America resulted in a process of rural proletarianization that contained more similarities than differences with European trends. These generalizations do not account for the extreme differences that existed within Latin American agriculture, but European agriculture itself was far from homogeneous. Independence ignited forces in Latin American that emerged in the second half of the century due to the combination of particular national difficulties and the realities of the world economy. Not only did European demand for Latin American products fluctuate, but the new countries faced heightened regionalism, capital flight, and political and judicial instability.

After independence, the agricultural sector demonstrated more continuities than ruptures with the colonial period. This statement is qualified by the fact that the sector was transforming itself in the late colonial period through crops such as cotton in Brazil, coffee in Cuba, cacao in Venezuela, and hides in Río de la Plata. These export commodities were encouraged by the process of commercial liberalization, which allowed Latin American agricultural products to enter European markets directly. In this regard, independence proved to be a decisive step.

Trade and Industry

The influence of external demand on the Industrial Revolution is still being debated, but there is little doubt that England dominated trade in the Western world at the beginning of the nineteenth century. British foreign trade grew at a rhythm of 5 percent per year after 1780. The composition of that trade changed at the end of the eighteenth century; instead of exporting manufactured goods and primary products, England began exporting industrial products and importing grain. The structure of British exports varied between the end of the eighteenth century and the beginning of the nineteenth, in a sense in harmony with the Industrial Revolution. Textile raw materials went from representing 16 percent of imports in 1770 to 26 percent in 1820. Food imports (besides grain) rose from 32 percent to 41 percent during the same period.[34]

British exports to Latin America passed from an insignificant level to 5 percent of the total in 1815 and 13 percent a decade later. In the same manner, British imports from the region moved from negligible levels in the last decades of the eighteenth century to 9 percent in 1815 and 5 percent in 1825. England's leading exports to Latin America were manufactured cotton goods (55 percent in 1815, 56 percent in 1825), while principal imports included raw cotton (48 percent in 1815, 42 percent in 1825) and hides (32 percent in 1815, 21 percent in 1825), supplied mainly by Brazil and Río de la Plata. Although Britain's high expectations for the potential of Latin American markets were not fulfilled, exports to the region at midcentury represented 16 percent of total British goods shipped overseas.[35] England went from having a negative balance of trade with Latin America in 1815 to a favorable one in 1825, but, as Ralph Davis notes, this fact did not preoccupy more than the handful of people who made decisions concerning exports and imports.[36]

This trade existed, nevertheless, in a context of deteriorating terms of trade for England due to the cheapening of the manufactured goods that it produced. Estimates of England's balance of trade in the first half of the nineteenth century are negative; only if we add income from services, interest, and dividends does this balance appear positive between 1816 and 1850 (there are no estimates for 1800–1815).[37] Income from interest and dividends corresponded to foreign investments (discussed in the following section). Income from services originated from maritime insurance, the financing of international trade, and maritime transport—carried out, with few exceptions, in British vessels. If it is not possible to compare the dimensions of this merchant fleet with the other fleets of Europe, comparison of their war fleets shows the distance between England and its competitors: 458 ships in 1820 against 98 for Russia, 79 for France, 32 for the Low Countries, 13 for Spain, and 8 for Portugal.[38] British maritime predominance, a result of the Navigation Acts of the midseventeenth century, was a manifestation of English mercantilism.

British manufacturing favored mercantilism over free trade. Far from a coherent policy intended to maximize national wealth, mercantilism was the result of policies designed to provide income to the government and enrich special-interest groups. The world of empire and of imperial preferences was highly beneficial for the particular interests that sustained and profited from the government. The extension of free trade meant more goods for more people at lower cost. Its arrival cannot be attributed to a decision by merchants or high-ranking members of government but rather from a growing competition for privileges. The appearance of a market of privileges in this system marked the point of departure from freedom of trade. The competition for protection carried over to competition in the market for goods. This process was not completed even in England. As Karl Polanyi has noted, the substitution of the market for the sovereign in deciding how to assign resources is one of the great transformations of the nineteenth century.[39] But in spite of Adam Smith and the political economists who followed in his footsteps, international trade in the years of Latin American independence was still constrained by mercantilist restrictions. The Corn Laws of 1815 are an example; only after 1820 did London businessmen begin to press Parliament in favor of free trade. Although some liberalizing measures had been introduced previously (such as the end of the East India Company's monopoly over trade with India in 1813), ideas of free trade did not predominate until the 1840s, when the Corn Laws and the Navigation Acts were abolished.[40] In the following decade, imperial preferences in favor of sugar, wood, and coffee were repealed, and in 1860 England and France signed a commercial treaty that marked the predominance of free trade.[41]

Within the Spanish American empire, regulations declined in the late eighteenth century once it became clear that they were no

longer producing fiscal revenue. Reforms favoring free trade, initiated in 1765 in the Caribbean, extended to most areas of the empire
in 1778, culminating in New Spain in 1789. In conjunction with
other measures, these reforms produced the fiscal results desired.
They also whetted the appetite of colonial merchants for greater
commercial freedom. The reform process was not counterproduc-
tive for Spain nor contradictory with the existence of empire, but
the course of events showed that the necessary flexibility for such
adaptation did not exist. If this absence was characteristic of abso-
lutism in Spain, in Portugal it was representative of the liberal government. The Napoleonic invasion changed economic relations
between Portugal and Brazil; the flight of the court from Lisbon in
1807 immediately opened Brazilian ports to English commerce. Two
years later, Brazil signed the "fatal treaty with England," as Balbi
called it,[42] and in December 1816 the colony was put on the same
political level with the metropolis. At the time, Brazilians considered these measures to be their true declaration of independence:
Brazil was more important for Portugal than vice versa. In the late
eighteenth and early nineteenth centuries, Brazilian products such
as sugar, cotton, and hides accounted for almost two-thirds of Portuguese exports. Portugal in those years generally maintained a favorable balance of trade with England, but an extremely unfavorable
one with Brazil.[43] Direct access to British and continental markets
meant for Brazil, as it had for Spanish America, the elimination of
an unnecessary intermediary and access to new commercial practices and sources of financing.

More than twenty years ago, D. C. M. Platt began his study of
Latin American and British trade by indicating the limited importance of independence to this relationship.[44] From the point of view
of British trade it is difficult not to agree with his argument. From
the perspective of Latin American consumers, however, the changes
were notable. The most immediate consequence was the sudden
availability of new, cheap manufactures. It has been argued that
imports of European manufactured goods resulted in the destruction of local industries based on primitive technology.[45] This view
is based on the implicit counterfactual hypothesis that the high tariffs or import prohibitions that might have rescued these industries
would have been more beneficial to these economies than access to
new goods at lower prices. The same hypothesis implies that the
transfer of revenues to producers as a result of protective measures
would have resulted in a process of modernization. In spite of the
lack of protection, some of these primitive industries demonstrated

a remarkable resistance to imports, as proved by the survival of coarse native textiles. Other local industries, such as wine production, suffered less from imports than from the political and social disorders that followed independence.

After comparing the first and second halves of the nineteenth century, Platt argued that there was significant demand in Europe for raw materials from Latin America. These years of modest expansion (as Platt characterized the period following independence) were extremely significant for Latin America. Goods, commerce, and capital arrived as never before, and in the same manner goods produced in the region gained direct access to European markets. That many business operations failed does not obscure the importance of that point of departure.

Money and Credit

At the time of Latin American independence, the world relied on one medium of payment: specie. This does not mean that there was only one currency or that there were no substitutes. The most common alternative to cash was the bill of exchange, which avoided the transfer of specie by relying on the credit and debit balances of merchants in distant markets. At the end of the eighteenth century this instrument of exchange was perfected through the generalized use of endorsement and discounting, despite persistent penalties for usury in many European countries as well as in Latin America. Checks issued against previous deposits, as is done today, also existed, but their use was not yet widespread. More common were bank notes issued by the discount of bills, but this instrument was unknown in Latin America. Paper money had resulted in unsuccessful experiments, such as that of John Law in France in the 1710s.[46] In a world in which specie was frequently scarce, titles of public debt also acquired monetary functions. Again, in this case the experience of the French *assignats* served as a warning to imaginative public officials.[47] The idea of assigning a value to a piece of paper was very tempting, but making people accept that value proved more difficult. Chinese emperors in the fourteenth century successfully achieved this goal, but at a cost of the heads of whoever questioned them. Even European absolutist governments were more tolerant of dissent than the Mongol emperors of fourteenth-century China.[48]

The metallic content of money merited its acceptance as a means of payment. Nevertheless, there was always the temptation to vary the metal content—diminishing the quantity of gold or silver and increasing the amount of copper without varying the nominal value, as was done in Rome in the third century and in Spain in the seventeenth. All over Europe, sovereigns were ready to take the short step from mere seigniorage to the fraudulent diminution of the precious metal content. Only in the nineteenth century was value standardized, allowing Manuel Colmeiro to say that "the advice of the most discreet authors" who recommended assigning monetary values founded on good judgment and law had finally prevailed.[49] But at the time when the basis for the future gold standard was established, there were also successful experiments with inconvertible paper money—most notably, the British pound from 1797 to 1821.

In Latin America at the time of independence, the means of payment was specie. Silver produced by the New Spain and Peruvian mines was coined in the mints of Mexico City, Lima, and Potosí. The silver peso of eight reales was effective as the money of account as well as the means of payment. However, imperfect monies still existed at the lower levels of circulation, such as the Upper Peruvian *macuquina*, which due to its defects circulated at less than nominal value. In Brazil at the end of the eighteenth century, two-thirds of the coins in circulation were gold and one-third silver. Gold coins were destined for foreign trade, while provincial transactions involved silver and copper.[50]

Latin America had also known other mediums of exchange called "currencies of the land," including cacao seeds, woven cotton, and yerba maté. These currencies were primitive but effective. The monetization of goods did not imply the existence of barter, which means the absence of markets and price structures. Barter was common in sixteenth-century Latin America, but by the beginning of the nineteenth century only very remote regions remained unaffected by the monetary economy.

International payments took place by means of shipments of specie or bills of exchange traded between Spanish and American markets. Within Spanish America, drafts substituted for bills of exchange, since no change of currency was necessary. Drafts were used to cancel balances after occasional operations; accounts for long-standing commercial relationships were usually settled by balancing credits and debts in the ledgers.

The principal monetary and financial development of the eighteenth century was the monetization of credit, as a consequence of two institutions created in the 1690s: the Bank of England and the public debt. The Bank of England monetized the private credit by means of bank notes that entered circulation when discounting bills, and the public credit was monetized by means of government bonds placed among voluntary investors. After the Napoleonic Wars, continental Europe followed the English financial model (which actually had originated in the Netherlands). Around 1820, according to Balbi's estimate, England had a public debt of 20 billion francs; the Netherlands, 4.2 billion; the Russian empire, 4 billion; Spain and France, 3.8 billion each; and Portugal, 0.2 billion. If we correlate these figures to the annual income of each country, it would take England 13.5 years to pay its public debt, compared to 24.6 years for the Dutch, 3.8 years for the Russians, 23.3 years for the Spaniards, 4.2 years for the French, and 5.3 years for the Portuguese.[51]

The discount of bills in England began in the seventeenth century. It was originally handled by the Bank of England but was eventually practiced by an increasing number of country banks: 12 in 1750, 370 in 1800, and 780 in 1810.[52] The development of England's financial institutions had no parallel in continental Europe, where the great banks were more at the service of governments than individuals. Such banks were managed by families or societies; they did not have the privilege of issuing notes and attended primarily to the needs of large commerce. A singular experience was that of the English colonies of North America, which at the end of the seventeenth century already circulated letters of credit issued by both the colonial authorities and private companies. The former issued letters of credit for payment of expenditures and for advance payment of funds for mortgages, while private institutions issued funds for mortgages only. Colonial titles were originally convertible, but an inability to maintain this status or prevent forgery resulted in their depreciation and the decision of the London government to return the colonies to specie circulation. The Continental Congress began issuing notes in May 1775, more than a year before independence; if the colonies still had doubts about political independence, they did not hesitate with regard to monetary independence. (Its meaning would be known soon when those notes—called "continentals"—depreciated.) After independence, and especially after Jeffersonian individualism gained ascendancy, the United States experienced a notable banking expansion. By the time of Latin American independence, between 250 and 300 banks operated in the United States, thus strengthening the nation's agricultural and industrial activities.[53]

Financial institutions developed much more slowly in Spain and Portugal. Spain created the Banco de San Carlos in 1782, with the primary aim of financing government deficits, which function eventually led to the bank's insolvency.[54] Similarly, the Banco do Brasil was established after the arrival of the Portuguese court in Rio de Janeiro, also with the purpose of acting as a financial agent for the government; it, too, failed.[55] Colonial Latin America lacked institutions to fulfill the credit, monetary, and productive investment functions that English banks accomplished in the middle of the eighteenth century, or that North American banks did at the end of the century. It took some time for such institutions to develop after independence. With the exception of some failed experiences, including one in Buenos Aires in the 1820s, banks that carried out these functions only appeared in Latin America in the latter half of the nineteenth century. The main sources of private credit in the colonial era were religious institutions, which provided loans drawn on rural properties bearing fixed interest rates. In colonial Spanish America, the financial needs of the government were satisfied by transfers between different types of fiscal income and extraordinary contributions.

The tax structure of Spain and Portugal, as well as of Spanish America and Brazil, was antiquated and rigid. Townsend, awed by the confusion of the Spanish tax system, discussed the bewildering range of taxes alphabetically.[56] Regarding Portugal, Tollenare, a Frenchman of the Restoration, reported that feudal duties were still paid on the land and that the principal source of income remained customs duties, whose burden fell on imports as much as exports. The financial necessities of the war against Napoleon, he said, had been covered by borrowing within Portugal itself and by issuing paper money that circulated with a discount of 15 percent.[57]

At the end of the eighteenth century, Spain's currency consisted of gold, silver, copper, and royal notes called *vales reales*. These notes, issued from 1780 onward to finance the costs of war, were in fact titles of debt drawing an annual interest of 4 percent. They functioned as a partial substitute for money, since they could be used to cancel debts with the state and between individuals. The need to obtain funds for halting the depreciation of royal notes in 1799 gave rise to the disentailing of ecclesiastical property in Spain and the Americas.

In 1778 the income of the Spanish Crown reached some 417 million *reales de vellón*, of which 9.6 percent originated from the Indies, 16.1 percent from the tobacco monopoly, 16.8 percent from customs revenues, and 22.1 percent from provincial revenues. In 1801 a total of 880 million *reales de vellón* entered the royal treasury. Remittances from the Indies accounted for 17.8 percent of this amount, but their average for 1792–1807 was around 9 percent. Humboldt estimated Spain's 1804 income at 35 million pesos, compared to around 36 million for Spanish America. Of this total, 56 percent pertained to New Spain, 11 percent to Peru, another 11 percent to New Granada, 5 percent to Caracas, 6 percent to Cuba, and another 11 percent to other regions. The Spanish treasury received 8.2 million pesos per year from America; 73 percent originated in New Spain, 12 percent in Peru, 9 percent in Buenos Aires, and 6 percent in New Granada.[58]

Of the 20 million pesos that entered the Real Hacienda of New Spain, 27.5 percent came from taxes on mining, 20 percent from the tobacco monopoly, 15 percent from sales taxes, 6.5 percent from Indian tribute, 4 percent from the tax on pulque, 2.5 percent from import and export duties, and the rest from many other minor taxes. In New Spain, as in the rest of the empire, the tax structure was complex and included taxes collected for a common fund used to meet the regular expenses of each royal treasury; taxes that should be sent to Spain; taxes for some particular purposes; and still others, called *ajenos*, which, although collected by the royal treasuries, were not proper taxes but income corresponding to corporations. Although from the accounts of 1784–1789 it appeared that the cost of tax collection was reaching 30 percent of its gross product, Humboldt estimated the proportion at a more realistic 16 to 18 percent, explaining the difference as a result of the mixing of accounts.[59] Officials endeavored to manage this fiscal complexity by introducing the double-entry system in 1785, but two years later it was abolished. The state continued a system of *cargo* and *data* that further obscured rather than simplified the true state of the Real Hacienda (for its administrators as well as for present-day historians). This tortuous accounting system lasted longer than the empire. In Buenos Aires it was replaced in 1821, but the rest of the Río de la Plata provinces continued to use the old system for more than three decades. In Mexico it remained in use into the 1840s, when the government ordered the publication of Fabián de Fonseca and Carlos de Urrutia's still useful description of the late colonial Real Hacienda.[60]

Finally, the period of Latin American independence saw Europe's leading financial center shift from Amsterdam to London. Both financial markets had been closely integrated during the eighteenth century, but the Napoleonic Wars led to London's preeminence.[61] As London demonstrated its vitality and stability, foreign funds flowed there to be invested in the public debt or in shares of joint-stock companies. The financial market that emerged after the Napoleonic Wars was characterized by a wide variety of options, many of which were attractive but risky projects to be implemented outside of England. London was not the world's first financial market, but it was the first capital market, since there was a massive investment in foreign bonds (even those issued by nonexistent countries, such as Poyais) and in a multitude of local and foreign projects (most of them unsuccessful, such as the Río de la Plata Mining Company).[62] In these turbulent waters, some Latin American agents, such as Antonio José de Irisarri and Francisco Antonio Zea, personally benefited from placing government loans that Chile and Colombia paid for but did not enjoy. Other enterprises, such as the Real del Monte Company, were at least real, if not extremely successful.

Widespread speculation in these projects led to the collapse of the market in December 1825.[63] This failure cannot be attributed to Latin American factors but rather to British investors' excessive expectations and their ignorance regarding overseas political and economic conditions. The recently independent Latin American countries did not profit much from that first contact with international finance (as did the British promoters of such schemes), but they did not suffer much, either. The tie between these countries and the London financial market was established in that awkward way, but in most cases there were no new attempts for the next three decades. A worthy by-product of this experience was the proliferation of descriptions of diverse Latin American regions written by restless diplomats, bankrupt businessmen, and unsuccessful mining engineers. This period marked the incipient opening of the new continent to European capital and labor.

Finance is, consequently, the area in which more obvious differences existed between Europe and Latin America in the Age of Revolution. The discount and endorsement of the bill of exchange, the monetization of credit and the circulation of bank notes, the regularization of the public debt, and the development of capital markets were all signs of a mobilization of economic resources that, although not homogeneously achieved across Europe, was completely absent in Latin America.

Conclusion

Many similarities existed between Europe and Latin America in the late eighteenth and early nineteenth centuries, but there were key differences as well. Birth, death, and infant mortality rates were comparable, as was the ratio of rural to urban populations. However, Latin America's population was much more dispersed and more ethnically diverse than that of Europe, accounting for greater internal disparities. Agricultural methods and output were also similar, but cultivation was much more intensive in Europe than in Latin America, where plantations and cattle-raising haciendas were a distinctive characteristic of the agricultural landscape.

Disparities are more obvious when trade, industry, and finance are considered. The gap between the two regions cannot be reduced to the industrialization of Europe. The mobilization of economic resources that had been taking place there had not yet reached Latin America. Banking, capital markets, and nonmetallic (but still convertible) currencies were long established in Europe but remained unknown to Latin Americans at the time of independence. These disparities were sufficiently marked to explain the different pattern of economic performance in Europe and Latin America in the nineteenth century.

Latin America's postindependence economic development did not follow Western European patterns. While Europe saw an expanding industrialization, Latin America turned into a supplier of raw materials and agricultural products. This statement does not mean that there were two models of economic growth to choose from; rather, there was a process of specialization due to the comparative advantages of different regions in an increasingly integrated world. The study of the long-term evolution of basic socioeconomic foundations makes clear that the key difference between the two regions was a different institutional history. Technical innovation could eventually be exported from Europe to Latin America, but institutions—as the product of a different historical evolution—could not be successfully reproduced, in spite of the efforts made in that direction by enlightened Latin American liberals.

There were no missed opportunities in Latin America. Although fashionable until very recently (and perhaps not completely gone), the idea that all nations undergo the same pattern of economic development or political organization at different stages of their history is clearly wrong. On the one hand, long-term trends cannot be easily reversed, since they are the outcome of a particular institutional evolution. On the other, the increasing integration of the world economy does not mean similar patterns of change.

Values and preferences do play a role in policymaking, in a way that may preclude a better economic performance. But even dismissing that situation and assuming the right values and preferences are present, a government capable of enforcing the law is necessary to make them effective. The newly created Latin American countries were far from model law-enforcing agencies. The political legacy of the Age of Revolution was the Age of Caudillos. It is hardly a coincidence that until this age was overcome, growth was so elusive. It was the unfortunate, but not unparalleled, fate of Latin America that the very movement that helped the region to catch up with a changing world unleashed forces that marred its future.

Notes

1. See the essays in Reinhard Liehr, ed., *América Latina en la época de Simón Bolívar* (Berlin: Colloquium Verlag, 1989); Leandro Prados de la Escosura and Samuel Amaral, eds., *La independencia americana: Consecuencias económicas* (Madrid: Alianza Universidad, 1993); and Kenneth J. Andrien and Lyman L. Johnson, eds., *The Political Economy of Spanish America in the Age of Revolution, 1750–1850* (Albuquerque: University of New Mexico Press, 1994).

2. For European countries, see Andre Armengaud, "Population in Europe, 1700–1914," in *The Industrial Revolution, 1700–1914*, ed. Carlo M. Cipolla (London: Harvester Press/Barnes & Noble, 1976), 29; for Mexico, Timothy Anna, "The Independence of Mexico and Central America," in *The Cambridge History of Latin America*, ed. Leslie Bethell (New York: Cambridge University Press, 1985), 3:51; for Peru, Heraclio Bonilla, "Peru and Bolivia from Independence to the War of the Pacific," ibid., 3:539; for New Granada, Malcolm Deas, "Venezuela, Colombia, and Ecuador: The First Half-Century of Independence," ibid., 3:508; for Central America, R. L. Woodward, Jr., "Central America from Independence to c. 1870," ibid., 3:478; for Chile, Simon Collier, "Chile from Independence to the War of the Pacific," ibid., 3:584; for Río de la Plata, John Lynch, "The River Plate Republics from Independence to the Paraguayan War," ibid., 3:627; for Upper Peru, Bonilla, "Peru and Bolivia," ibid., 3:564; and for Brazil, Maria Luiza Marcílio, "The Population of Colonial Brazil," ibid., 3:63.

3. Adrien Balbi, *Essai statistique sur le Royaume de Portugal et d'Algarve* (Paris: Rey & Gravier, 1822), 2:259–60.

4. Ibid., 2:260–63.

5. For England, France, and Sweden, see Armengaud, "Population in Europe," 44–45; for Portugal, Nuno Alves Morgado, "Portugal," in *European Demography and Economic Growth*, ed. W. R. Lee (London: Croom Helm, 1979), 334; for Italy, Lorenzo del Panta, "Italy," ibid., 226; for Spain, Vicente Pérez Moreda, *Las crisis de mortalidad en la España interior (siglos XVI–XIX)* (Madrid: Siglo XXI, 1980), 211.

6. For England and France, see Michael Anderson, *Population Change in North-Western Europe, 1750–1850* (London: Macmillan, 1988), 30; for Portugal, Alves Morgado, "Portugal," 334; for population growth rates, Anderson, *Population Change*, 25; for Spain, Pérez Moreda, *Las crisis de mortalidad*, 137.

7. For Sweden, see Armengaud, "Population in Europe," 47–48; for France, Etienne van de Walle, "France," in Lee, *European Demography*, 143; for Spain, Pérez Moreda, *Las crisis de mortalidad*, 141, 148.

8. For Brazil, see Nicolás Sánchez Albornoz, *The Population of Latin America*, trans. W. A. R. Richardson (Berkeley: University of California Press, 1974), 117; for Paraguay, Pedro A. Vives Azancot, "Demografía Paraguaya, 1782–1800. Bases históricas y primera aproximación para su análisis, sobre datos aportados por Félix de Azara," *Revista de Indias* 40 (January–December, 1980): 193; for Lima, María Pilar Pérez Cantó, *Lima en el siglo XVIII* (Madrid: Universidad Autónoma de Madrid Cantoblanco, 1985), 63–64; for Mexico, Alexander von Humboldt, *Political Essay on the Kingdom of New Spain* (1822; reprint, New York: AMS Press, 1966), 1:105; for Minas Gerais, Marcílio, "Population of Colonial Brazil," 62; for São Paulo, Sánchez Albornoz, *Population of Latin America*, 118; for Acatzingo, Thomas Calvo, "Démographie historique d'une paroisse méxicaine: Acatzingo (1606–1810)," *Cahiers des Amériques Latines* 6 (1972): 25.

9. Sánchez Albornoz, *Population of Latin America*, 138–39.

10. Jorge Comadrán Ruiz, *Evolución demográfica argentina durante el período hispánico (1535–1810)* (Buenos Aires: Eudeba, 1969), 81.

11. Ibid.

12. Pérez Cantó, *Lima en el siglo XVIII*, 50.

13. Anna, "Independence of Mexico and Central America," 54.

14. Humboldt, *Kingdom of New Spain*, 1:131.

15. Ibid., 209.

16. Armengaud, "Population in Europe," 32, 34; Joseph Townsend, *A Journey through Spain in the Years 1786 and 1787* (London: C. Dilly, 1791), 2:209; Balbi, *Essai statistique*, 2:266.

17. Ernesto J. A. Maeder, *Evolución demográfica argentina desde 1810 a 1869* (Buenos Aires: Eudeba, 1969), 33–61.

18. Anna, "Independence of Mexico and Central America," 51; Sánchez Albornoz, *Population of Latin America*, 83, 128; Maeder, *Evolución demográfica argentina*, 33; Leslie Bethell and José Murilo de Carvalho, "Brazil from Independence to the Middle of the Nineteenth Century," in Bethell, ed., *The Cambridge History of Latin America*, 3:679; Guy P. C. Thomson, *Puebla de los Angeles: Industry and Society in a Mexican City, 1700–1850* (Boulder, CO: Westview Press, 1989), 159.

19. Paul Bairoch, "Agriculture and the Industrial Revolution, 1700–1914," in Cipolla, ed., *The Industrial Revolution, 1700–1914*, 453.

20. B. H. Slicher van Bath, *Historia agraria de Europa occidental (1500–1850)* (Barcelona: Península, 1974), 243.

21. Bairoch, "Agriculture and the Industrial Revolution," 477. On the repeal of the Corn Laws see Knick Harley, "Foreign Trade: Comparative Advantage and Performance," in *The Economic History of Britain since 1700* (2d ed.), ed. Roderick Floud and Donald McCloskey (New York: Cambridge University Press, 1994), 1:309–18.

22. Townsend, *Journey through Spain*, 3:117, 118, 179, 269, 296; Gonzalo Anes Alvarez, *Las crisis agrarias en la España moderna* (Madrid: Taurus, 1970), 194.

23. Townsend, *Journey through Spain*, 2:218–40, 286.

24. Balbi, *Essai statistique*, 1:144–45.

25. Ibid., 1:162–65.

26. Louis-François de Tollenare, *Notes dominicales prises pendant un voyage en Portugal et au Brésil en 1816, 1817, et 1818*, ed. Léon Bourdon (Paris: Presses Universitaires de France, 1971), 1:31.

27. Humboldt, *Kingdom of New Spain*, 2:403–4.

28. Ibid., 2:442–43.

29. Ibid., 2:461–77.

30. Ibid., 2:517.

31. Eric Van Young, *Hacienda and Market in Eighteenth-Century Mexico: The Rural Economy of the Guadalajara Region, 1675–1820* (Berkeley: University of California Press, 1981), 351–53.

32. Ibid.

33. Angel García Sanz, "Crisis de la agricultura tradicional y revolución liberal (1800–1850)," in *Historia agraria de la España contemporánea*, ed. Angel García Sanz and Ramón Garrabou (Barcelona: Crítica, 1985), 1:21–39.

34. Richard Brown, *Society and Economy in Modern Britain* (London: Routledge, 1991), 172–73.

35. Ralph Davis, *The Industrial Revolution and British Overseas Trade* (Leicester, UK: Leicester University Press, 1979), 88–125.

36. Ibid., 53–59.

37. Brown, *Society and Economy in Modern Britain*, 176.

38. Balbi, *Essai statistique*, 2:266.

39. Karl Polanyi, *The Great Transformation* (New York: Rinehart & Co., 1944).

40. Stanley L. Engerman, "Mercantilism and Overseas Trade, 1700–1800," in Floud and McCloskey, eds., *The Economic History of Britain*, 1:197–203.

41. Brown, *Society and Economy in Modern Britain*, 181.

42. Balbi, *Essai statistique*, 1:410.

43. Fernando Novais, "Notas para o estudo do Brasil no comércio internacional do fim do século XVIII e início de século XIX (1796–1808)," in *L'Histoire quantitative du Brésil de 1800 à 1930*, ed. Fernando Novais (Paris: CNRS, 1973), 59–75.

44. D. C. M. Platt, *Latin America and British Trade, 1806–1914* (London: Adam & Charles Black, 1972).

45. Stanley J. and Barbara H. Stein, *The Colonial Heritage of Latin America* (New York: Oxford University Press, 1970).

46. Larry Neal, *The Rise of Financial Capitalism: International Markets in the Age of Reason* (New York: Cambridge University Press, 1990), 72–76.

47. Thomas J. Sargent and François Velde, "Macroeconomic Features of the French Revolution," *Journal of Political Economy* 103 (1995): 474–518.

48. Gordon Tullock, "Paper Money: A Cycle in Cathay," *Economic History Review* 9 (1957): 393–407.

49. Manuel Colmeiro, *Historia de la economía política en España* (Madrid: Taurus, 1965), 2:1063–83.

50. Maria Bárbara Levy, "Elementos para o estudo da circulação da moeda na economia colonial," *Estudos Econômicos* 13 (1983): 837.

51. Balbi, *Essai statistique*, 2:263–64.

52. Charles P. Kindleberger, *A Financial History of Western Europe*, 2d ed. (London: George Allen & Unwin, 1993), 81.

53. Ibid., 145.

54. Miguel Artola, *La hacienda del antiguo régimen* (Madrid: Alianza, 1982), 382–88.

55. Carlos Manuel Peláez, "The Establishment of Banking Institutions in a Backward Economy: Brazil, 1800–1851," *Business History Review* 44 (1975): 446–72.

56. Townsend, *Journey through Spain*, 2:218–20.

57. Tollenare, *Notes dominicales*, 1:220.

58. Humboldt, *Kingdom of New Spain*, 4:240–42.

59. Ibid., 4:223.

60. Fabián de Fonseca and Carlos de Urrutia, *Historia general de real hacienda*, 6 vols. (Mexico City: Impr. por V. G. Torres, 1845–1853).

61. Neal, *Rise of Financial Capitalism*, 223.

62. Poyais was a fake kingdom, but a loan was granted to it anyway. See Thomas Strangeways, *A Sketch of the Mosquito Shore, including the Territory of Poyais, Descriptive of the Country, with Some Information as to Its Productions, the Best Mode of Culture, &c., Chiefly Intended for the Use of Settlers* (Edinburgh: Sold by W. Blackwood, 1822). The scheme was exposed in *The Quarterly Review* 28, no. 55 (October 1822): 157–61.

63. On the London financial market boom and collapse in the 1820s, see Frank Griffith Dawson, *The First Latin American Debt Crisis: The City of London and the 1822–25 Loan Bubble* (New Haven: Yale University Press, 1990).

2

"Dutch Disease" and Other (Dis)Continuities in Latin American History, 1780–1850

Richard J. Salvucci*

After writing extensively on the economic history of colonial and nineteenth-century Mexico, and especially on its textile industry, economic historian Richard Salvucci engages here in an ambitious comparative discussion of the political economy of several Latin American countries in the 1750–1850 period. To explain the region's less than satisfactory economic performance, Salvucci—a professor at Trinity University in San Antonio, Texas— points out continuities in the character of export economies. His study relies on abundant empirical evidence that Latin America suffered from what economists call the "Dutch disease." This macroeconomic problem results from an export boom, drawing especially on natural resources. This phenomenon ultimately causes inflation—that is, a rapid increase of domestic prices— particularly for "nontradable" (no-import-competing) goods. It also causes an overvaluation of the real exchange rate (the value of local currencies relative to foreign currencies) and the consequent reduction of traditional and other exports.

Salvucci documents this situation for diverse places and times, particularly in late eighteenth-century New Spain (today's Mexico), for which he runs statistical tests using production, trade, and price figures for silver, maize, and cochineal. He also discusses Peru during its midnineteenth-century guano boom, Brazil, and, in passing, Costa Rica and Cuba. Salvucci concludes that early commodity booms and the recurrent Dutch disease in nations rich in natural resources, such as the ones addressed in this essay, are indicative of continuities in economic practices. Yet, more significant, those booms contributed to the disregard

*I am grateful to Debra Patterson, Eric Van Young, and Victor Uribe for their comments on this essay.

of manufacturing and impeded stable long-term industrial development in the region. Salvucci also takes into account the economic discontinuities derived from the disruption of finance and
trade (both internal and external) during the wars of independence as well as the political and institutional instability brought
about by the collapse of the Spanish empire. All of these factors
augmented economic risks, reduced capital formation, and
caused negative growth.

For reasons too obvious to bear much analysis, historians have
always been deeply interested in manifestations of stability
within larger patterns of change. Such an interest can take many
forms, including but not limited to matters of politics, social structure, or economic change. To draw on relatively recent work, for
example, Norman Davies's history of Europe from the Creation, so
to speak, argues that "for more than five hundred years the cardinal
problem in defining Europe has centered on the inclusion or exclu-
sion of Russia."[1] David Hackett Fischer, a late bloomer in these
matters, has recently examined the history of price inflation since
the twelfth century, a "great wave," as he puts it, whose meanings
and consequences "are limited only by the reach of our imagination."[2] A detailed study by Joshua Goldstein reaching back to the
fifteenth century has done much to recast and reinterpret the study
of Kondratieff waves.[3] And then there were Braudel and the
Annalistes, now in eclipse, but once the defining school of modern
socioeconomic history and deeply influential in Latin American
history because of the work of François Chevalier, Pierre Goubert,
Ruggiero Romano, and others—Woodrow Borah, Stanley and Barbara Stein, David Brading, Enrique Florescano, and Tulio Halperín,
to name a few. The attempt to find patterns of coherence within
masses of data, often quantitative but sometimes not, was (and is,
in a few cases) the hallmark of a historical imagination of a very
high order. For historians interested in economic history, but not
necessarily in cliometrics, this scholarship offers a challenge as well
as a model. The challenge is to incorporate this large body of socioeconomic work into a modern synthesis, as yet incomplete. The
model, of course, is to go and do likewise, whatever else current
fashion in historical writing might dictate.

When asked to write an essay on continuity and change in Latin
American economic history during the era of independence (1780
to 1850), I considered ways in which independence did or did not
make a difference in economic performance. While the approach
adopted is eclectic and intuitive, it nevertheless draws on the sys-

tematic findings of a body of economic analysis, much of it macroeconomic in orientation, intended to explain the stylized facts of economic development. The best of this literature is associated with economists such as Jeffery Sachs, Robert Barro, and others involved in the study of economic growth and development. It is to an important topic in this literature, "Dutch disease," that we now turn.

Dutch Disease and Export Economies

For some thirty years, economists have been interested in what an export boom, and especially a boom in natural resource exports, does to a country's macroeconomic performance.[4] Different commodities will have different effects, but there is some consensus about the general features of what happens. The volume of the new export increases, but the share of "traditional" exports declines. Domestic demand rises as income from exports grows. The demand for tradable goods (that is, goods that have imported counterparts) is satisfied by rising imports, so prices for these goods cannot rise much. The demand for nontradable goods (that is, goods that have no competition from imports) has to be satisfied domestically. The prices of these goods must rise to attract the labor and capital necessary to expand their production. If the nominal exchange rate is fixed, the rise in the price of nontradables will increase domestic prices and produce an appreciation in the real exchange rate.

Even if the nominal exchange rate is flexible, the problem does not disappear. A sudden increase in the export of natural resources can generate a rapidly increasing supply of foreign exchange. This supply grows so quickly that it outstrips demand. What is commonly called "overvaluation" results—the home currency can buy more goods overseas than domestically. A rise in imports, which are now artificially cheap, depresses the production of tradables. The high exchange rate of the home country's currency will also discourage other exports. In macroeconomics, the syndrome is called "Dutch disease" after its appearance in the Netherlands in the 1960s. There is no point in starting a priority debate—no one is about to rebaptize "Dutch disease" as *mal latino*—but Dutch disease afflicted Latin America as early as the eighteenth century, if not before.

Dutch disease is emphatically not a modern malady. The silver boom in late eighteenth-century Mexico produced a version of Dutch disease, as did the guano episode in Peru in the 1840s. A number of other commodity booms in Latin America did so as well, although there is not room here to describe them all. It is perhaps best to start with the Mexican case because it is familiar, but nevertheless germane.

Mexico

If the silver boom of the late eighteenth century caused Dutch disease, we should be able to detect its traces. For example, the rise in silver exports should have depressed "traditional" or competing exports. A rise in silver production should have driven up the real exchange rate of the peso as well as the price of nontradables. However, eighteenth-century data are not very good by the standards of modern economic analysis. One must be pragmatic in the choice of variables, and it is impossible to test them all. One must also be cautious in interpreting the results of these tests. The data are usually not well specified, which means that they do not always measure what one wants them to measure. The tests are also apt to be crude and do not (and cannot) always meet modern standards of proof.

In this case, the test for Dutch disease involves regressing the production of cochineal, Mexico's second largest export (defined as a "traditional" or competing exportable) against the production of silver. The price of maize is included as a wage good that could affect the supply of cochineal, because food prices obviously affect costs. The sign on both variables should be negative. If Dutch disease occurred, rising silver production and export should have displaced cochineal exports. The remainder of changes in supply should have the usual sign: rising input prices shift the supply curve to the left.

The figures for cochineal are based on Brian Hamnett's series on the registration of cochineal in Veracruz between 1756 and 1810. Silver production is measured, imperfectly to be sure, by mint figures from Mexico City that Lucas Alamán compiled. Enrique Florescano's series of maize prices for Mexico City is included in the regression as well. All variables are expressed in rates of change, or logarithms, and the results have been corrected for first-order positive serial correlation. The regression estimates appear in Table 1.

The results of the regression are about what one would expect, even though the model and the data are not tightly specified. An increase in silver output depressed the production of cochineal for export, as did rising maize prices.[5] Maize prices and silver production account for about one-half of the variance in cochineal exports. Viewed purely in statistical terms, the silver boom tended to displace cochineal production on a nearly one-for-one basis (-.95).

Table 1. Regression Analysis of Three Commodities

Dependent Variable: Log. Cochineal
Independent Variables

Constant:	29.89[a]
Log. Silver:	−.95[a]
Log. Maize:	−.26[b]
Adjusted R:	.53
D-W:	2.07
SEE:	.33

[a]Significant at 99 percent.
[b]Significant at 90 percent.

Another viewpoint is to consider what happened to the real exchange rate of the Mexican peso. Dutch disease should entail some real appreciation of the home country's exchange rate. In this instance, the nominal exchange rate was the international price of silver, which did not change much in the late eighteenth century. The real exchange rate basically depended on what happened to the Mexican price level in terms of its trading partners' price levels. We have a crude index of the real exchange rate of the peso in terms of the pound sterling. These results, modified somewhat from their original form, appear in Table 2.

Table 2. Silver Production and Median Real Exchange Rate

Years	Silver Production (000,000 kilograms)	Median Real Exchange Rate
1761–1780	7.328	100
1781–1800	11.249	83
1801–1820	8.658	135

Sources: Silver Production: *Estadísticas históricas de México*, 2 vols. (México: INEGI, 1985), 1:437; Median Real Exchange Rate: Richard J. Salvucci, "The Real Exchange Rate of the Mexican Peso, 1760–1812: A Research Note and Estimates," *Journal of European Economic History* 23:1 (1994): 139.

An appreciation of the real exchange rate corresponds to a lower index number. It takes fewer pesos to purchase British output (which is the exchange rate computed). By this standard, the real exchange rate appreciated 17 percent between 1761–1780 and 1781–1800. It depreciated sharply after 1801, although the measure continues no further than 1812.

What transpired during the Mexican silver boom of the late eighteenth century makes for a plausible Dutch disease story. We are accustomed to thinking about the price of maize mostly in terms of supply, but demand must have played a role as well. The population was growing, so there were more mouths to feed. The price of other nontradables, such as land, was rising as well. Anecdotal evidence collected in the early nineteenth century suggested that the price level of wage goods had doubled between 1786 and 1806.[6] On the other hand, the prices of tradables, such as woolen textiles, declined. As they fell, the production of the long-established Mexican *obrajes* collapsed. Employment in the *obrajes* suffered too.

For silver producers, rising costs were of limited concern. Mexico did not monopolize world silver production in the late eighteenth century, but it did account for two-thirds of Spanish American silver output.[7] For cochineal, the story was a bit different. The regression in Table 1 shows that rising maize prices depressed cochineal production. In fact, the largest fall in supply took place in the 1790s, caused at least in part by surging maize prices that raised labor costs. Silver came mostly from Mexico, but one could obtain cochineal from Guatemala, where export levels had begun to rise very rapidly by the late 1820s, as well as from the East Indies and the Canary Islands. Mexican exports of cochineal to Britain and France were still a very substantial 450,000 pounds as late as 1839. Within two years, they had fallen by nearly one-half.[8] According to Jeremy Baskes, the abolition of the *repartimiento* drove one nail into the coffin of the Oaxacan cochineal industry in the 1780s.[9] The rising cost of living associated with Mexican silver was another blow.

Since silver mining did not employ many people, the peasants who tended the *grana cochinilla* in Oaxaca were not likely to strike out for Guanajuato in search of better jobs. The transition for textile workers might have been somewhat easier in principle, but much of the *obraje* work force was essentially unskilled. Because nonexport agricultural productivity was apparently rather low, it is easy to understand why late colonial Mexico had a problem with income distribution. Where exactly were people supposed to find work as their old jobs disappeared?

Ironically, the growing demands of the Spanish Crown for revenue may have mitigated the effects of Dutch disease. By 1805, Carlos Marichal estimates that the Crown was raising about 10 million pesos per year in Mexico, "a large part of which was destined to cover the international financial obligations of the Crown that resulted from the Napoleonic Wars."[10] That sum was a lot of money, probably close to 4 to 5 percent of the Mexican GDP. We often think of the Crown as killing the goose that laid the golden egg in Mexico by taxing it to death. But since Dutch disease is basically the result of a rapid rise in domestic demand, the rising tax burden may have actually cut domestic inflation and kept the collapse of domestic industry and secondary exports from being even worse.

Peru

The Mexican silver boom is a clear case of Dutch disease, albeit a rather awkward one. One could argue that exporting silver mattered less than mining it. Just digging it out of the ground drove up domestic demand, since silver was money, and high-powered money at that. As Pedro Pérez has astutely observed, silver balances supported bills of exchange that were money as well.[11] The guano boom that began in Peru in the 1840s produced a textbook example of Dutch disease, at least in the regional economy in which Lima was situated. Great amounts of labor or capital were not necessary to "mine" guano, but the impact of the export boom on government spending (guano was a state monopoly) and, hence, on domestic demand was quite large. The speed of the guano boom was stunning, as the data in Table 3 show. Exports averaged 17,206 metric tons in 1841–1845; ten years later, they had increased to 354,612 metric tons. At the same time, "traditional" silver exports were still significant, but they were falling. Silver exports stood at 482,430 marks in 1841–1845 but had fallen nearly 25 percent to 367,144 marks in 1851–1855. The stability of the unit value of guano exports underscores the strength of international demand. No wonder an overvaluation ensued. It was possible to generate foreign exchange with a shovel—literally.

Table 3. Peruvian Economic Indicators, 1841–1855 (Annual Means)

Years	COL	Guano (metric tons)	Unit Value	Silver (marks)	Terms of Trade
1841–1845	100	17,206	28.50	482,430	100
1846–1850	100	115,668	27.55	383,635	103
1851–1855	103	354,612	28.08	367,144	117

Sources: (*COL*=Cost of Living): Paul Gootenberg, "*Carneros y Chuño*: Price Levels in Nineteenth-Century Peru," *Hispanic American Historical Review* 70:1 (1990): 26; Guano, Unit Value, Silver: Paul Gootenberg, *Between Silver and Guano: Commercial Policy and the State in Postindependence Peru* (Princeton: Princeton University Press, 1989), 162–63. Guano unit values and terms of trade are the author's calculations.

Guano comprised upwards of one-half of Peru's exports by 1850.[12] An estimate of Peru's net barter terms of trade suggests an improvement of about 17 percent, or more if falling transportation costs are considered. This trend continued into the 1870s. Inflation between 1841–1845 and 1851–1855 was mild, under the circumstances. Since guano production did not require much labor or capital, factor markets did not tighten. It also did not bid labor or capital away from other activities. The rise in income that guano could generate must have weighed most heavily on domestic demand. And since guano was a state monopoly, one naturally wonders why there was so little inflation to begin with.

The answer, logically enough, is that guano produced little income at the outset. From 1841 to 1849, according to Shane Hunt, the Peruvian government struck "generally poor bargains" with "generally foreign contractors." Only after the Gibbs Contract of 1849 did returned value from guano, which had previously been 33 percent, double to 65 percent. The rate of inflation confirms Hunt's analysis. In 1856–1860 the index of domestic prices hit 113; by 1861–1865 it had reached 127. Prices, in other words, rose only after the Peruvian state captured a bigger share of guano revenues. Moreover, there was lots of slack in the economy. Paul Gootenberg argues that "until 1845, political-military instability kept Peru in deep economic recession." He suggests that severe Guano-Age inflation erupted only after 1855.

The rise in government spending was the key to the Dutch disease episode in Peru. As Hunt remarks, "the guano bonanza transformed the Peruvian fiscal system. . . . In 1857, the income from guano alone was greater than total government revenue only three years earlier." However, only about 20 percent of the increase in government spending could plausibly be considered as contributing to an increase in the supply of capital. The remainder financed tax relief, an expanded bureaucracy, and transfer payments. It is not surprising that there was not much real growth between 1845 and 1870. Real wages in Lima rose only 11 percent, which corresponds to Hunt's conclusion that "any growth experienced by the Peruvian economy during the guano age was slow at best." It is hard to avoid the conclusion that Peru in the Guano Age sounds like Mexico in the Silver Age; to paraphrase Gootenberg, these are countries stuck between silver and guano.

Why did this happen? Hunt's answer is striking: "Peru became a rentier economy, exporting guano and importing virtually all manufactured products. . . . Foreign exchange earnings are so abundant that the exchange rate cannot depreciate. . . . Caught between increased import competition and irreducible costs, import-substituting industries are squeezed and no other sector can expand employment to take up the slack." In other words, rising domestic prices pushed up the real exchange rate and imports surged. This is Dutch disease in a slightly different form.

Moreover, the evidence suggests that Peru "deindustrialized"; in other words, a fall in textile production was offset in part by a rise in agricultural production. Among the increase in nontradable production, the relative price of food fell in 1854–1870 while urban rents nearly quadrupled. Clearly, the increase in supply occurred in foodstuffs. In the face of stagnant real incomes, this implies a change in the relative shares of agriculture and industry in domestic product. It can be characterized as ruralization—or moving backward, if you prefer—to no growth and increased "underdevelopment."

Brazil, With Some Account of Costa Rica and Cuba

According to Nathaniel Leff, the *mil-reís* value of Brazilian exports rose at a rate of 4.5 percent yearly between 1822 and 1913. The net barter terms of trade improved by about 80 percent between 1826 and 1850, or some 2.0 percent per year. The growth in the purchasing power of exports was even larger, about 2.3 percent per year, which Leff terms "respectable."[13] And yet Leff also describes the rate of real per capita growth as moderate: "On a per capita basis, income in Brazil does not seem to have risen at a high rate." By way of conclusion, he writes that "the growth of Brazil's foreign trade during the nineteenth century clearly did not lead the country to generalized economic development."[14]

In accounting terms, Leff believes that the reason for Brazil's mediocre performance was largely—although not completely—due to the poor performance of the country's Northeast.[15] "In part," he writes, "the poor aggregate experience of the Brazilian economy during the nineteenth century reflects the especially dismal performance of the country's large Northeast region, where almost half of Brazil's population resided. A rough estimate suggests that real per-capita income in the Northeast *fell* by approximately 30 percent between 1822 and 1913."[16] Leff regards this decline as "astonishing," because it meant that the Northeast could not increase its share of sugar and cotton on the world market at a time when international demand for these commodities was growing.[17] While the trend rate of growth of coffee exports in 1822–1850 was 5.7 percent, the

value of sugar exports grew at only 1.5 percent for most of the nineteenth century. Cotton exports in 1824–1848 actually *fell* at a trend
rate of 4 percent. In other words, regional income differences expanded between the Southeast (coffee) and the Northeast (cotton
and sugar).[18]

While Brazil experienced sustained inflation after 1822, its
exchange rate, which was free to float, experienced what Leff terms
"a strong trend to depreciation." After 1822 and until 1913, the trend
rate of currency depreciation was 1.4 percent per year, but there
was a big difference in the annual rate of price increase between
tradables (5.1 percent) and nontradables (1 percent).[19] This difference signals a substantial appreciation of the real exchange rate.
The nominal rate fell in proportion to the rise in the price of
tradables. Here again is the pattern discerned for Mexico and Peru:
a large shift toward nontradable goods and a decline in the "traditional" exports of sugar and cotton in favor of coffee. This is Dutch
disease, and that is what Leff calls it: "The decline of the Northeast's
sugar and cotton exports reflected the fact that nineteenth-century
Brazil had a stronger comparative advantage in coffee than sugar
or cotton. . . . Because the domestic resource cost of foreign exchange was much lower in coffee than in sugar or cotton, the Northeast experienced a nasty case of 'Dutch disease.' "[20] The real
exchange rate increasingly reflected the cost of producing coffee,
not cotton or sugar.

The twist that Leff gives the story is striking. It holds interesting possibilities for the rest of Latin America. Leff proposes that
Brazil's Northeast would have been better off on its own—as an
independent country, with its own currency. If labor and capital
cannot be smoothly reallocated from less to more productive activities, the appreciation of the real exchange rate remains a problem, for costs are irreducible. A region populated enough to offer
potential economies of scale but with higher than usual costs under
the existing exchange regime might be better off as an independent
country whose currency can depreciate. Real wage costs can fall
and the economy can begin to grow once more—hardly a far-fetched
idea. (A comparable case might have been California in the early
1990s. The state, now growing once more, might have recovered
more quickly if it had had its own currency.)

Leff gives a number of reasons for thinking that reallocation in
Brazil was not plain sailing. Regional differences in geography and
climate as well as the cost of migration blunted the market signals
responsible for the reallocation of labor and capital.[21] There is no

reason why these explanations should apply only to Brazil. They could just as well describe any large and regionally diverse eighteenth- and nineteenth-century economy in which intersectoral mobility was limited. Mexico, Colombia, Peru, and Argentina are only the most obvious examples. Leff's analysis goes to the heart of the economic content of regionalism. His argument explains why falling transportation costs produced spectacular, and sometimes revolutionary, changes in patterns of regional comparative advantage later in the nineteenth century.

The patterns of Dutch disease discernible in Mexico, Peru, and Brazil were evident elsewhere in Latin America, especially in Cuba and Costa Rica. For instance, the quantum of Cuban sugar exports to the United States trebled between the 1820s and the 1850s. At the same time, the quantum of coffee exports fell 47 percent despite the rise in the demand for coffee in the United States. Spanish commercial policy, which drove up the price of foodstuffs imported into the island from the United States, probably made matters worse.[22] Oddly enough, Puerto Rico does not seem to have gone through a similar episode.

In Costa Rica the coffee boom of the early 1840s all but obliterated previously large exports of sugar, not to mention brazilwood and tobacco.[23] By 1855 coffee accounted for 90 percent of Costa Rican exports. A steep inflation ensued in the price of nontradables, such as foodstuffs. The cost of eggs, maize, and beans all rose sharply, as did the price of horses, mules, and oxen. The complaints of foreign visitors are classic: "The cost of living in San José is very high, just as it is in other cities of Costa Rica. Most food is expensive. . . . House rentals are constantly rising. Getting clothes washed is very expensive." In short, the price of nontradables had risen dramatically. And despite complaints that even the prices of tradables were out of line, there was what one historian calls "massive import of cheap foreign goods of the widest variety." The wages of carpenters and masons rose but—also a classic symptom— employment of spinners and weavers fell, since domestic production could not compete with imports. The Costa Rican coffee boom, therefore, also seems like a good example of Dutch disease.

Patterns of Continuity in the
Development of Resource-Rich Economies

There are, to repeat, many continuities in the pattern of economic change in the period between 1780 and 1850 from which to choose.

We could, for instance, point to the apparent stagnation in the growth of productivity of what Victor Bulmer-Thomas calls "domestic use agriculture."[24] Bulmer-Thomas correctly concludes that the stagnation of domestic use agriculture represented a drag on the growth of the export sector and, more important, on overall growth. Unfortunately, we know virtually nothing about agricultural productivity outside the export sector, which represents a serious gap in the historical literature.[25] Yet the prevalence of Dutch disease in the export booms of Mexico, Peru, Brazil, Costa Rica, and Cuba points to the subtle continuity of a common response to an essentially uniform economic impulse across countries, colonies, and commodities. Economists and political scientists have concluded that it is hard for resource-rich countries to achieve stable patterns of long-term development.[26]

A recent paper by Jeffrey Sachs and Andrew Warner has set down some of these findings in a coherent, systematic way.[27] The long-term economic performance of resource-rich countries seems generally inferior to countries with fewer natural resources—or at least it seems so in the twentieth century, now that transportation costs do not impede trade as they once did. Countries with lots of human capital do better than countries with abundant resources. One culprit that Sachs and Warner point to is Dutch disease. In countries suffering from Dutch disease, manufacturing shrinks because of the appreciation of the real exchange rate. Structural transformation is reversed, or at least delayed. As a result, the economy remains vulnerable to commodity price shocks, much as did Latin America through the 1940s. It can further be argued that the roots of this phenomenon go back to the eighteenth century in Latin America and that they attended many of the region's commodity booms. Short of taxing away export income and spending it countercyclically—pursuing a modern fiscal policy, in other words—it is difficult to see how the problem could have been avoided. But this is a silly counterfactual; what is surprising is not that Latin America's experience with the international market spawned "export pessimism," but that it took until the middle of the twentieth century for export pessimism to appear.

Discontinuities: Some Economic Consequences of the Imperial Finale

The collapse of empires inevitably creates costly disruptions. There is no need to draw on examples from Rome or the Ottoman empire;

the fall of the Soviet empire offers abundant examples. In economic terms, the Soviet collapse produced supply shocks—unpredicted and unpredictable changes in costs—whose consequences for real domestic product were nothing if not catastrophic. A Cuban could testify to the implications of regime change as well.[28] If the end of empire brings disruption to trade and finance, shocks to aggregate supply and demand inevitably follow. It might help to give a few concrete examples of what happened in the former colonies of Spain's American empire.

Cuba and the Spanish Caribbean: Situados *and Fiscal Shocks*

The end of empire forced a major economic adjustment in Spain's remaining Caribbean colonies, Cuba and Puerto Rico. There could be no further financial subsidies, known as *situados*, from New Spain. These remittances had been enormous. Between 1720 and 1800, *situados* to the Caribbean totaled more than 218 million pesos—about equal to New Spain's annual GDP at the end of the eighteenth century.[29] In the 1750s the subsidy was equivalent to over 10 percent of Cuba's domestic product; this is only an estimate, for it takes no account of respending effects. Previous estimates of per capita income in Cuba in 1750 (around 90 pesos) seemed very high, but the size of the Mexican subsidy makes the estimate somewhat more credible. Mexican silver bankrolled the building of battleships, the construction of fortifications, and the payment of troops, adding to Cuban expenditures in the eighteenth century. Is it any wonder that Cuban income seems so high? The Spaniards were carrying out income redistribution on a massive, intercolonial scale.[30]

Cuba received no further subsidies after 1811, presumably because of the outbreak of civil war in New Spain. It is difficult to imagine that the cutoff did not produce a substantial contraction in demand. In fact, some estimates of per capita income growth in Cuba between 1750 and 1850 have suggested very little growth, a finding consistent with a shock to demand.[31] Moreover, efforts to compensate for the fall in demand by loosening constraints on supply were not completely successful. Despite the declaration of "free trade" for the island in 1818 and the continuing (illicit) import of large numbers of African slaves, Spain's fiscal demands seem to have grown more quickly than the tax base. In 1846 the island's intendant, the Conde de Villanueva, put the per capita tax burden at 20 pesos, or 40 pesos if only the white population was considered.

This figure implies an average rate of taxation of an astronomical 20 percent or more, depending on how one treats the issue of slavery and its effect on per capita income. But the effect of taxation is to restrain the growth of both aggregate supply and demand—and Villanueva thought that Cuba in 1846 was taxed more heavily than Great Britain, a mild understatement.[32] The first Cuban sugar boom looks a little different from this perspective: it was either a complex balancing act or an effort to run in place, depending on how one views the evidence. The situation is not unlike what had occurred in New Spain a century earlier, where silver miners were blessed with subsidies and cursed with taxes and "loans." No wonder some authorities called Cuba's sugarcane plantations its "mines." The analogy was uncomfortably accurate.

Discontinuities in Trade

We could well imagine that the collapse of the American empire both created and destroyed opportunities for trade and exchange. On the one hand, independent countries conduct an autonomous commercial policy. Their consumers are no longer—at least in theory—constrained to take only what the mother country offers. They buy what they want from whom they want. On the other hand, the empire was either a customs union or an economic union, depending on how the function of its larger units is understood. Erecting national trade restrictions between what had once been integral parts of a customs or economic union makes people worse off. The empirical issue would seem straightforward enough. Did the benefits of autonomy or the costs of (literal) disintegration predominate?

Intuition suggests that the benefits of commercial autonomy prevailed, but intuition is not proof. On the one hand, the Spanish empire never interfered much with intercolonial trade. The seventeenth-century prohibition of intercolonial trade between New Spain and Peru affected the production of woolens around Puebla; however, trade between New Spain and Venezuela and Guatemala, between Peru and Chile, or, most famously, between Córdoba and Potosí, in Bolivia, suffered no similar interference.[33] On the other hand, the volume of this trade did not amount to much overall. Trade between the newly independent nations was small, and it remained so until World War II. As late as 1938, Latin American exports to destinations in the region were a scant 6.1 percent of exports, or little more than the overall volume of exports to France.[34] One suspects that imperial restrictions did not greatly affect patterns of trade. Factor endowments, transportation costs, and trade complementarities were what really mattered.

Still, trade and exchange, either between countries or between regions, did reflect the impact of political factors and administrative changes on the supply of exportables. Historians have long emphasized the consequences that the creation of the viceroyalty of La Plata had for Lima after 1776, but that is hardly the only example. Where the struggle for independence affected silver production, existing patterns of trade were disrupted well into the 1830s and 1840s. For instance, the late colonial silver boom in Potosí provided both the capital and the market for the expansion of the coca-producing valleys of the district of Chulumani.[35] When the mines of Potosí and Oruro went into decline in the early nineteenth century, so too did the demand for coca and the population of the coca-producing valleys (Herbert Klein dates the contraction to 1786–1838). Sempat Assadourian argues that the collapse of Bolivian silver production after independence literally annihilated the mule trade between Córdoba and Upper Peru (Bolivia). It still had not recovered by 1850.[36]

Yet independence brought commercial autonomy, and commercial autonomy had its compensations. Consider Cochabamba. Under the Bourbons, its economy was connected to the Peruvian and Bolivian *altiplano*. Cochabamba kept shipping grains and cloth to its former markets into the 1820s, although at reduced levels. But in the 1840s the expansion of Peruvian exports helped reorient southern Peru toward the Pacific coast and international markets.[37] Independence did not cause this shift but made it and other such readjustments possible. Moreover, independence had little effect on the cattle trade between Córdoba and Chile. In fact, it gave Córdoba the chance to adjust to the shock of losing silver from Potosí by exporting wool, pork, and hides through Buenos Aires to the international market.[38] In light of these developments, it is hard to see exactly which commercial advantages were sacrificed to independence.

In some instances, the Wars of Independence altered patterns of internal trade, or at least accelerated changes that were already under way. For instance, the Crown opened the Mexican port of Tampico to direct trade with Spain in 1814, inevitably increasing Tampico's share in international trade. Yet the emergence of Tampico also depended on the continuing productivity of the mines of Zacatecas, which, unlike those of Guanajuato, had not been affected by the insurgency. Comparative advantage—here, under the guise of resource endowments and transportation costs—favored Tampico.[39]

Something similar happened in San Blas, on the west coast of Mexico, a port whose growth took off during the insurgency in the 1810s. Eustace Barron wrote in 1824 that "San Blas may be ranked one of the first Ports of the Mexican Dominions; a very large district of the Country depends upon it for its support, it being the channel through which all Merchandise pass to the Interior of the Provinces of Jalisco, Sinaloa, and Sonora. . . . The Chief imports of British goods consist in cotton and linen manufactures which have hitherto been introduced from Panama, Peru, and Chile; a considerable trade exists with Calcutta, principally reduced to the coarse cotton manufactures of Asia." Barron thought that the "returns" from San Blas to India, and for British goods imported, "may be calculated, net returns, to amount to one Million of Dollars yearly, although last year [1823] it exceeded that sum considerably."[40] Independence fostered commercial autonomy, and commercial autonomy fostered regional development.

For its part, northern Mexico was deeply affected by the westward and southward expansion of the U.S. economy. To some extent, this development was economically "exogenous": it depended on the pace and pattern of economic growth in the United States, something over which Mexico had no control. Yet, as David Weber has argued, the loosening of political ties between central Mexico and northern Mexico after 1821, and the erosion of institutional controls over the frontier (such as the missions and the system of presidios), facilitated the pull of commercial attraction from the United States and strengthened the demographic weight of Anglo settlement.[41] As Charles Harris III noticed in his study of Coahuila, these same factors disrupted colonial patterns of commerce and hastened the emergence of regional markets in the north in the 1820s and 1830s.[42] Political shocks certainly did not "cause" regionalism, but they profoundly altered its long-term meaning and implications.

The larger trade flows with Europe and the United States are harder to sort out. There is an understandable temptation to seize on the rise of direct trade with Britain, France, or the United States as a clear "discontinuity." National independence, commercial treaties, commercial policy, the exchange of ambassadors and ministers—all these factors encourage the impression of a very new world, even if it had been called into existence, as George Canning famously (and fatuously) remarked, to redress the balance of the old. But trade is not about flags, bureaucrats, merchants, or memoranda.

It is about merchandise flows, and these are notoriously difficult to get right.

It is also possible to exaggerate the novelty or discontinuity that independence brought. Latin America's commercial autonomy *was* new, but the underlying composition of its trade probably was not. One small but, as Leandro Prados calls it, "expressive" bit of evidence is the pattern of trade between Great Britain, its West Indian colonies, and Latin America from the 1780s through the 1820s (see Table 4).[43]

Table 4. British Exports to British West Indian Colonies and to Latin America
(Thousands of £)

Years	British Antilles	British Antilles Share (percent)	Latin America
1784–1786	1,428	99.5	7
1794–1796	4,490	98	79
1804–1806	7,260	87	1,125
1814–1816	6,906	74	2,476
1824–1826	4,126	45	5,009

Source: Leandro Prados de la Escosura, "El comercio hispano-británico en los siglos XVIII y XIX," *Revista de Historia Económica* 2:2 (1984): 125.

British exports in current prices to British West Indian colonies and to Latin America after 1800 are in the range of £8.4 to £11.3 million. But notice the steadily falling share of exports to the West Indies: 99.5 percent in 1784–1786; 98 percent in 1794–1796; 87 percent in 1804–1806; 74 percent in 1814–1816; and 45 percent in 1824–1826. Prados notes that Javier Cuenca discovered that Spain's trade with its American colonies (1790–1820) fell just as Great Britain's share rose. It is not easy to fix precise dimensions to clandestine events, but the overall trends suggest that the ostensible surge in British trade with Latin America in the mid-1820s owes more to the redirection of existing flows of cloth and silver than it does to a "calling forth" of new trade. If there was a discontinuity, it was produced by the decline in silver production that constrained the growth of international trade.

Institutional Discontinuities

Several recent anthologies on the economic consequences of Latin American independence emphasize the role that institutional factors played in constraining growth in the nineteenth century.[44]

Political transitions naturally create institutional uncertainty. Issues such as the definition of property rights and their adjudication; the legitimacy of the state, and of claims against it; the creation (or restoration) of a functioning bureaucracy; the relation of the state to civil society; the distribution, exercise, and limits of coercive power—all these must be definitively resolved. If they are not, uncertainty continues. Uncertainty constrains growth because it increases the variability of return on investments. It is, in other words, a source of increased risk.

Explanations that depend on institutions are often substitutes for explanations, not explanations themselves. Economic growth and structural change do not depend on institutions per se but rather on increasing the supply and productivity of labor and capital. Institutions have an indirect effect, albeit an important one. However, it is difficult to know how they affect such measurable factors as the productivity of labor and capital by altering incentives, labor intensity, relative prices, and the diffusion of technology.

Contemporary events, for instance, show that the collapse of the Soviet empire has had high costs. In places such as the former Soviet republic of Georgia, which has exhibited extreme instability, the costs have been astounding,[45] but arguing by analogy at such a high level of generality is not very helpful. A rose may well be a rose, but the costs of political and economic instability will change with the evolving character of the political and economic systems themselves. Supply in the Soviet Union was arguably better integrated than in the Spanish empire. There is no reason to suspect that the costs of disintegration in Latin America were as high—but then again, we really do not know one way or another. Did creating new institutions or adapting old ones to a new situation really exact substantial costs?

Institutional change or discontinuity may affect the distribution of wealth. As Peter Guardino argues for Chilapa (now in the state of Guerrero, Mexico), the abolition of colonial village governments after 1820 left the Indian peasantry increasingly vulnerable to the appropriation of their land and water by the white and mestizo elites who controlled the new municipalities. The ascendancy of the centralists in 1836 led to further political and economic change, which "exposed peasant resources to the local wealthy in ways the introduction of municipalities had not."[46]

When institutional change and transition led to armed conflict, the costs of uncertainty and the destruction of assets could be considerable. In Mexico, the outbreak of civil war created an excess demand for draft animals. This demand drove up the cost of transportation, cut internal trade, and reduced economic efficiency. The evidence for this trend is indirect, but compelling nonetheless. During periods of civil strife in Mexico, the export of animals overland to the United States disappeared. The price of draft animals in Mexico rose relative to the price prevailing across the border. As a result, the previous outflow of animals was reversed.[47] Foreign observers described the problem in detail. Charles O'Gorman, for example, wrote to the British government in 1825 that "great inconvenience is felt from the frequent embargo of mules by the government and local authorities whenever it is necessary to transport troops, military stores or government property; in such cases the rate of freight becomes excessively high, either from the scarcity of animals or from the muleteer being obliged to lay out for the risk he may incur of being forced into such temporary employment for account of the government at an inferior rate, which he, with difficulty, gets paid."[48] Instability does not merely destroy productive assets. In nineteenth-century economies, instability reduced productivity by interfering with trade and exchange and by making economies of scale impossible to capture.[49]

Héctor Lindo Fuentes has looked at the destruction of reproducible capital caused by civil strife in El Salvador in the nineteenth century.[50] The destruction was severe, and military finance absorbed funds that would have otherwise been used for productive investment. As a result, the stock of assets that could support growth was eroded. In El Salvador, too, endemic instability disrupted the supply of animals for transportation. Lindo Fuentes also emphasizes the effects of constant warfare on the labor supply, although its effects are difficult to measure and interpret. Still, his conclusions are clear enough. Twenty years of warfare between the 1820s and the 1840s goes some way toward explaining the "weak foundations" of economic growth in independent El Salvador.

Nevertheless, as Lindo indicates, the real problem was not so much the destruction of physical assets or the military demand for labor as it was the pervasive climate of uncertainty: in a preindustrial society, physical capital plays a smaller role in production than does working capital. Physical capital can also be repaired. Historians have suggested that even the severe losses of the Mexican insurgency were made good in short order. Doris Ladd believes that the Bajío had recovered by the 1820s,[51] and Margaret Chowning's careful survey of data on loans, personal wealth, urban and rural prices, and rental transactions points in much the same direction. After a catastrophic collapse in the 1810s and 1820s, when Chowning estimates that growth fell by 40 to 50 percent, "the per capita performance of the nonsubsistence sector of the economy [of the Michoacán region] had exceeded the levels measured during 1800–1810 by the early 1850s."[52] By any reasonable standard, the impact of fighting on the aggregate labor supply of El Salvador appears rather modest—less than 1 percent. The physical effects of warfare alone did not impoverish Latin America in the early nineteenth century.

Conclusion

In his *Economic History of Latin America since Independence*, Victor Bulmer-Thomas describes the failure of export-led growth in Latin America in the nineteenth century. Export-led growth failed for a couple of reasons: the export sectors were not large enough to offset the massive weight of slowly growing domestic agriculture, and commodity prices never stayed up for very long. Boom and bust cycles could bring an opera house to the Amazonian jungle, but they could not bring prosperity to impoverished masses. The routine performance of the export economies was pedestrian. Only Argentina and Chile grew enough from exports to double standards of living every fifty years. As Bulmer-Thomas concludes, "Export performance during the golden age of growth left much to be desired."[53]

True enough, one could say. But why exactly did export sectors remain small if exports were profitable? And why was it so difficult for the export sectors to transmit productivity gains to the rest of the economy? Bulmer-Thomas's answer is elegant, complex, and nuanced, but in the final analysis it comes down to a (neo)structuralist emphasis on the inadequacies of factor markets in general, and labor markets in particular, to allocate resources to their most productive uses. He adduces the usual causes: high transportation and transaction costs, muddled institutions, and the uncertainty that poor economic policy often created. Much potential income was lost as a result.[54]

It is hard to imagine that most historians could find fault with Bulmer-Thomas's analysis. However, he underestimates the prevalence and seriousness of what he terms "destructive" export expansion, something that sounds a lot like Dutch disease. The Mexican silver boom, the Peruvian guano boom, the coffee booms in Brazil and Costa Rica—all had what Bulmer-Thomas calls "destructive" consequences. Their direct impact was bad enough, for it led to a shrinkage of domestic industry and to monocultural exporting, so that vulnerability to external shocks remained a serious problem. Yet the rise in costs produced by the increase in the prices of nontradables also implied a loss of potential income—how much, exactly, no one can really say at the moment. The vulgar model of export-led growth that dominates contemporary discussion in the popular media is a demand-side model in which supply passively responds to changes in demand. But if this is merely unreasonable in the twentieth century, it is utterly fantastic for the eighteenth and nineteenth centuries, when the production bottlenecks that Bulmer-Thomas so ably describes existed. No wonder export booms could not easily transmit productivity gains to the rest of the economy— and no wonder the export sectors themselves did not grow as much as they could have.

This finding is important. It helps explain why dependency thinking found such a favorable audience among Latin American historians for nearly twenty years. Anyone could see that most of the nineteenth-century export economies failed to deliver generally higher levels of welfare, but not everyone could see why. A lot of sensible historians seized on the notion of unequal trade as an explanation, although even very liberal economists (and High Church *dependentistas*) had their doubts about whether this was the answer.[55] A terms-of-trade argument looks improbable even for open economies such as Cuba, which came to depend on monoculture.[56] The "institutions" story has more potential, for it addresses both questions of growth and distribution. Where conventional historians want to blame international trade, or, failing that, capitalism itself for unequal distributions of wealth and income, economic historians are more inclined to look at the way in which property rights are defined and assigned. Dependency and its dimmer offspring may be dead, but it is not clear what will replace them. The putative criticisms of "neoliberalism" on offer thus far are pretty weak.

Finally, we need to put some empirical flesh on the elegant but largely dry bones of the new institutional economics. When all is said and done, what Shane Hunt calls the "institutional" confusion that reigned in much of Latin America for the half century after 1800 will play a larger part in explanations of unsatisfactory growth than we have generally assumed. It remains to be seen whether historians of Latin America, who regard "institutional history" as an oxymoron, will have any role to play in telling this story. In the current intellectual climate, there is little cause for optimism. Magic realism and critical theory are great fun, but differences in productivity growth ultimately pay the rent.

Notes

1. Norman Davies, *Europe: A History* (New York: Oxford University Press, 1996), 10.

2. David Hackett Fischer, *The Great Wave: Price Revolutions and the Rhythm of History* (New York: Oxford University Press, 1996), xiv—*a vox clamantis* in a postmodern wilderness, to be sure.

3. Joshua S. Goldstein, *Long Cycles: Prosperity and War in the Modern Age* (New Haven: Yale University Press, 1988).

4. Jeffrey D. Sachs and Felipe Larraín B., *Macroeconomics in the Global Economy* (Englewood Cliffs, NJ: Prentice-Hall, 1993), 668–72, for the characteristics of Dutch disease.

5. It would be nice to know what happened to the price of mules, another nontradable good whose demand undoubtedly increased along with silver production. Mules were one of the major goods distributed in the *repartimiento* to peasants in Oaxaca. See Jeremy Baskes, "Indians, Merchants, and Markets: Trade and Repartimiento Production of Cochineal Dye in Colonial Oaxaca, 1750–1821" (Ph.D. diss., University of Chicago, 1993), 74.

6. Richard L. Garner with Spiro E. Stefanou, *Economic Growth and Change in Bourbon Mexico* (Gainesville: University of Florida Press, 1993), 3.

7. Peter Bakewell, "Mining in Colonial Spanish America," in *The Cambridge History of Latin America*, 8 vols., ed. Leslie Bethell (Cambridge, UK: Cambridge University Press, 1984–1995), 2:147.

8. I calculated the quantities by adding the volume of exports to Great Britain as cited in United Kingdom, Parliament, House of Commons, *Mexico* (1842), 2; and to France as cited in *Tableau général du commerce de la France avec ses colonies et les puissances étrangères, 1839, 1840* (Paris: Impr. Nationale, 1840–1841), "Mexique." See also Ciro F. S. Cardoso and Héctor Pérez Brignoli, *Centro América y la economía occidental (1520–1930)* (San José, Costa Rica: Universidad de Costa Rica, 1977), 172–74; Miles Wortman, *Government and Society in Central America, 1680–1840* (New York: Columbia University Press, 1982), 258–59; and Murdo MacLeod, *Spanish Central America. A Socioeconomic History, 1520–1720* (Berkeley: University of California Press, 1973), 174–75.

9. Baskes, "Indians, Merchants, and Markets," 52. There is another possibility that I have not considered in the text. The growth of silver mining was not apt to lure away labor from cochineal, but it could have drawn away credit. Baskes emphasizes the critical role played by merchant credit financing cochineal. D. A. Brading's argument in *Miners and Merchants in Bourbon Mexico, 1763–1810* (Cambridge, UK: Cambridge University Press, 1971), is exactly that. Because of the new system of *comercio libre*, "Manuel Ramón de Goya, for example, changed from backing magistrates in the Indian south to financing a silver miner in Zacatecas" (Brading, *Miners and Merchants*, 116). The expansion of silver mining thus implied a contraction of cochineal. International trade theorists have a name for this effect: the Rybczynski theorem. It makes sense in this context.

10. Carlos Marichal, "La bancarrota del virreinato: Finanzas, guerra y política en la Nueva España, 1770–1808," in *Interpretaciones del siglo XVIII mexicano*, ed. Josefina Zoraida Vázquez (Mexico City: Nueva Imagen, 1992), 164.

11. Pedro Pérez Herrero, *Plata y libranzas. La articulación comercial del México borbónico* (Mexico City: El Colegio de México, 1988).

12. For this and subsequent paragraphs, see Shane J. Hunt, "Growth and Guano in Nineteenth-Century Peru," in *The Latin American Economies*, ed. Roberto Cortés Conde and Shane J. Hunt (New York: Holmes & Meier, 1985), 258, 270, 285, 287–88; Heraclio Bonilla, *Un siglo a la deriva. Ensayos sobre el Perú, Bolivia y la Guerra* (Lima: Instituto de Estudios Peruanos, 1980), 34; Paul Gootenberg, "*Carneros y Chuño*: Price Levels in Nineteenth-Century Peru," *Hispanic American Historical Review* (hereafter *HAHR*) 70:1 (1990): 29.

13. Nathaniel H. Leff, *Underdevelopment and Development in Brazil*, 2 vols. (London: George Allen & Unwin, 1982), 1:79, 82.

14. Ibid., 1:37, 90.

15. Ibid., 1:41–43.

16. Nathaniel H. Leff, "Economic Development in Brazil, 1822–1913," First Boston Working Paper Series, Graduate School of Business, Columbia University, FB-92-02, January 1992, 1–2. Italics in original.

17. Leff, *Underdevelopment*, 2:12.

18. Ibid., 1:85.

19. Ibid., 1:97–98.

20. Leff, "Economic Development in Brazil," 2.

21. Ibid., 3.

22. Linda Salvucci and Richard Salvucci, "Price and Quantum Indices of U.S.-Cuba Trade." Paper presented to the Annual Meeting of the Economic History Association, Cincinnati, 1994.

23. Iván Molina Jiménez, *Costa Rica (1800–1850). El legado colonial y la génesis del capitalismo* (San José, Costa Rica: Universidad de Costa Rica, 1991), 199–206. The quotations in the paragraph are my translation and come from pages 206 and 208.

24. Victor Bulmer-Thomas, *The Economic History of Latin America since Independence* (Cambridge, UK: Cambridge University Press, 1994), 121–30.

25. Richard Salvucci, "Agriculture and *The Colonial Heritage of Latin America*: Evidence from Bourbon Mexico," in *Colonial Legacies. The Problem of Persistence in Latin American History*, ed. Jeremy Adelman (New York: Routledge, 1999), 107–33; and Leff, "Economic Development in Brazil," 29.

26. For instance, see Gustav Ranis, "Contrasts in the Political Economy of Development Policy Change," in *Manufacturing Miracles: Paths of Industrialization in Latin America and East Asia*, ed. Gary A. Gereffi and Donald Wyman (Princeton: Princeton University Press, 1990), 218, 224; and Stephen Haggard, *Pathways from the Periphery: The Politics of Growth in the Newly Industrializing Countries* (Ithaca: Cornell University Press, 1990), 35.

27. Jeffrey D. Sachs and Andrew M. Warner, "Natural Resource Abundance and Economic Growth," unpub. ms., Harvard University and Harvard Institute for International Development (September 1995).

28. Stephen Fidler, "Castro Keeps Reform on the Leash," *Financial Times* (October 27, 1995), 19, repeats the oft-cited estimate that Cuban gross domestic product fell an estimated 50 percent between 1990 and 1994.

29. Carlos Marichal and Matilde Souto Mantecón, "Silver and Situados: New Spain and the Financing of the Spanish Empire in the Caribbean in the Eighteenth Century," *HAHR* 74:4 (1994): 612–13; and my calculations.

30. The estimate is based on Marichal and Mantecón's figures. Their *situado* figures are almost twice as high as Leví Marrero's in *Cuba: Economía y sociedad*, 14 vols. (Madrid: Editorial Playor, 1972), 12:319. I am not certain about the source

of the discrepancy. Marichal uses Mexican sources, while Leví Marrero draws on materials from the Archivo General de Indias in Seville. But even if Mexican *situados* accounted for 5 percent of per capita income in Cuba, it is a substantial amount. For Cuban income see Pedro Fraile Balbín, Linda K. Salvucci, and Richard Salvucci, "El caso cubano: Exportación e independencia," in *La independencia americana: Consecuencias económicas*, ed. Leandro Prados de la Escosura and Samuel Amaral (Madrid: Alianza Editorial, 1993), 97.

31. Pedro Fraile et al., "El caso cubano," 98–101. It is worth mentioning that Bill McGreevey and Rob Tyrer put per capita GDP in Cuba in 1825 at $170 (prices of 1950). In current (that is, 1825) prices, that would be about $76. If McGreevey and Tyrer were correct, per capita income in Cuba *fell* from $90 in current prices in 1750 to $76 in 1825, rising again to about 100 pesos in 1850. The pattern sounds familiar and is by no means inconsistent with the story we outline here. For the 1825 estimate, see William Paul McGreevey and Robson B. Tyrer, "Recent Research on the Economic History of Latin America," *Latin American Research Review* (hereafter *LARR*) 3:2 (1968): 98.

32. Leví Marrero, *Cuba*, 12:356. The average rate of taxation on income in Great Britain in 1846 was 7d to the pound, or 2.9 percent. See D. E. Schremmer, "Taxation and Public Finance: Britain, France, and Germany," in *The Cambridge Economic History of Europe*, 8 vols. (Cambridge, UK: Cambridge University Press, 1941–), 8:342.

33. The classic account of intercolonial trade in the empire, with abundant illustrations drawn from the "Peruvian space," is Carlos Sempat Assadourian, *El sistema de la economía colonial. Mercado interno, regiones y espacio económico* (Lima: Instituto de Estudios Peruanos, 1982).

34. Bulmer-Thomas, *Economic History*, 240.

35. Herbert S. Klein, *Haciendas and Ayllus: Rural Society in the Bolivian Andes in the Eighteenth and Nineteenth Centuries* (Stanford: Stanford University Press, 1994), 36, 84–85, 90.

36. Sempat Assadourian, *El sistema de la economía colonial*, 229–35.

37. Robert H. Jackson, *Regional Markets and Agrarian Transformation in Bolivia: Cochabamba, 1539–1960* (Albuquerque: University of New Mexico Press, 1994), 45–46.

38. Sempat Assadourian, *El sistema de la economía colonial*, 235–76.

39. Jackie R. Booker, *Veracruz Merchants, 1770–1829: A Mercantile Elite in Late Bourbon and Early Independent Mexico* (Boulder, CO: Westview Press, 1993), 132–33.

40. Eustace Barron to Consul Staples, Tepic, August 10, 1824, United Kingdom, Public Record Office, Foreign Office 203/3 (hereafter UK, PRO, FO). See also Eric Van Young, *Hacienda and Market in Eighteenth-Century Mexico: The Rural Economy of the Guadalajara Region, 1675–1820* (Berkeley: University of California Press, 1981), 145–46.

41. David J. Weber, *The Mexican Frontier, 1821–1846: The American Southwest under Mexico* (Albuquerque: University of New Mexico Press, 1982).

42. Charles H. Harris III, *A Mexican Family Empire: The Latifundio of the Sánchez Navarro Family, 1765–1867* (Austin: University of Texas Press, 1975), esp. 231–70.

43. Leandro Prados de la Escosura, "El comercio hispano-británico en los siglos xviii y xix," *Revista de Historia Económica* 2:2 (1984): 124. Javier Cuenca's piece is "Statistics of Spain's Colonial Trade, 1792–1830: Consular Duties, Cargo Inventories and Balances of Trade," *HAHR* 61:3 (1981): 381–428.

44. Mostly Prados de la Escosura and Amaral, *La independencia de América*, with its relentlessly Douglass Northian subtext. But see also Kenneth J. Andrien and Lyman L. Johnson, *The Political Economy of Spanish America in the Age of Revolution, 1750–1850* (Albuquerque: University of New Mexico Press, 1994).

45. Georgia's projected output in 1995 was 17 percent (!) of its level in 1989. This is an extreme case, but by no means unique. See Kevin Done and Anthony Robinson, "EBRD Praises 'Fast Track' Countries," *Financial Times* (November 2, 1995), 2.

46. Peter Guardino, "Barbarism or Republican Law? Guerrero's Peasants and National Politics, 1820–1846," *HAHR* 75:2 (1995): 195.

47. Richard J. Salvucci, "The Origins and Progress of United States-Mexican Trade, 1825–1884: 'Hoc opus, hic labor est,' " *HAHR* 71:4 (1991): 720.

48. Charles T. O'Gorman, "Transport of Merchandise," Mexico, 1 March 1825, UK, PRO, FO 203/3.

49. The basis for most contemporary speculation about the effect of political instability on economic growth is Robert Barro's "Economic Growth in a Cross Section of Countries," *Quarterly Journal of Economics* 106:2 (1991): 432. Barro interprets his measures of political instability as "negative influences on property rights, and thereby as negative influences on investment and growth."

50. Héctor Lindo Fuentes, *Weak Foundations: The Economy of El Salvador in the Nineteenth Century* (Berkeley: University of California Press, 1990), esp. 49–60, for what follows.

51. Doris M. Ladd, *The Mexican Nobility at Independence, 1780–1826* (Austin: University of Texas Press, 1976), esp. 134.

52. Margaret Chowning, "The Contours of the Post-1810 Depression in Mexico: A Reappraisal from a Regional Perspective," *LARR* 27:2 (1992): 125.

53. Bulmer-Thomas, *Economic History*, 47–82. The quotation is lifted from page 67.

54. Ibid., 83–118.

55. See Shane Hunt's review of Pedro-Pablo Kuczynski, "Peruvian Democracy under Economic Stress: An Account of the Belaunde Administration, 1963–1968," *Journal of Economic History* 38:2 (1978): 576: "Terms of trade don't convince me . . . institutional confusion . . . is the proximate cause of underdevelopment." See also Samir Amin, *La acumulación a escala mundial. Crítica de la teoría del subdesarrollo* (Mexico City: Siglo Veintiuno, 1974), 97, for a much more nuanced view of the terms-of-trade story than one finds, say, in André Gunder Frank.

56. See Linda Salvucci and Richard Salvucci, "Cuba and the Latin American Terms of Trade: Old Theories, New Evidence," *Journal of Interdisciplinary History* 31:2 (2000): 197–222.

II
Elites, State Building, and Business

3

The Changing Meaning of Honor, Status, and Class

The *Letrados* and Bureaucrats of New Granada in the Late Colonial and Early Postcolonial Period

Victor M. Uribe-Uran

Victor M. Uribe-Uran teaches history at Florida International University in Miami. His publications concern the history of Latin American lawyers, justice, and legal systems. Building on his research into the legal profession in New Granada (present-day Colombia), this essay addresses major changes in the regional and social origins of lawyers, state administrators, and politicians in the three first decades after independence. Uribe finds that, in contrast to the colonial period, many of the lawyer-bureaucrats of 1820–1850 came from provincial and nonaristocratic families. Despite these changes, however, larger cultural concerns remained fundamentally unaltered. Honor, for instance, had major significance for both traditional and upwardly mobile elite figures. Following their colonial predecessors, the new attorneys and state officials continued to strive for status-honor, as did their competitors from more traditional social backgrounds. These two segments of the elite came to converge over the years, ultimately becoming an economically homogeneous ruling class. Over time, the status disparities typical of the colonial period and the early postindependence years declined and were for the most part put to rest. This cultural convergence was facilitated by the common threat faced by elite groups from insurgent artisans in the

This article includes material from Victor M. Uribe-Uran, *"Honorable Lives": Lawyers, Family, and Politics in Colombia, 1780–1850* (Pittsburgh: University of Pittsburgh Press, 2000). © 2000 by the University of Pittsburgh Press. Reprinted by permission of the University of Pittsburgh Press.

midnineteenth century, a challenge that required the united reaction of a ruling group whose privileges were at stake.

By using information on the late colonial and early postcolonial
letrados (lawyers) and bureaucrats of New Granada and their
families, this chapter revisits the nature of social stratification in
the late colonial and early postcolonial period, a topic that remains
confusing and little studied.[1] Furthermore, it suggests considering
the culture-driven concept of status—understood, in the Weberian
sense, as "social esteem" or "social prestige" flowing from the honor
attached to a particular style of life—as a notion required for understanding some of the social hierarchies in those societies. In this
sense, status becomes a notion supplementary or alternative to the
economy-centered one of social class, or the race- and ethnic-
centered ones of estate and caste.[2]

In addition, the chapter argues that one of the changes Latin
American societies underwent as they experienced the transition
from the colonial to the national period was that different groups
(in this case, elites) ceased to be regarded (and to regard themselves) as socially diverse status fractions. Instead, as market relations expanded they became more unified, letting economic factors
dictate their social homogeneity or the lack thereof. In other words,
determinations of social location based on colonial-like status considerations gave way to determinations based on economic identity, a "modern" perception.

Finally, the essay concludes that the transition from "status" to
"class" among some elite segments, which paralleled the switch
from the colonial to the national period, allows us to make sense of
certain otherwise incomprehensible postcolonial political conflicts.
Although such conflicts were not strictly class (that is, economic)
conflicts, they did follow a social logic of a cultural kind, involving
clashes between economically homogeneous groups that carried over
status-honor rivalries and differences from the colonial period. It
took time before such disputes could be relegated to a secondary or
marginal place.

The Colonial State

Spanish America's colonial state was basically an intermediary in
efforts aimed at occupying, conquering, and exploiting new territories for the benefit of a foreign power. Furthermore, it was the
administrative arm of a system in which general policies, key deci-

sions, significant appointments, and important issues were resolved in a faraway metropolis. The colonial state sought the Christianization of the native populations and their social control through a segregationist caste regime. It dealt with the arbitration of judicial conflicts and the military protection of territory against foreign invasions and guarded against the illegal penetration, through smuggling, of foreign commodities. It was charged with the organization of local forms of labor (by slaves, Indians, and wage-laborers) to benefit white *peninsular* and American-born mine-owning, merchant, agrarian, manufacturing, and bureaucratic elites. Moreover, the colonial state was responsible for the control and taxation of all sorts of economic endeavors (commerce, mining, agriculture, and some limited manufacturing), so that key activities in the metropolis remained sheltered while ensuring a constant flow of economic surplus from the colonies. It was, in sum, a highly tributary and interventionist state.

Politics, rather than market forces, was thus to a large extent the determining factor for economic dynamism within the Spanish colonies, which meant that the precapitalist features of those social formations were more accentuated than the capitalist ones.[3] The state closely regulated the provision of labor and all types of economic activities. In addition, it appropriated for itself a significant share of the surplus produced by slaves, Indians, and peasant workers toiling in mines, on haciendas, plantations, ranches, and in textile workshops, independent agriculture, and crafts. It also ensured that another substantial share went to white mine owners, ranchers, hacendados, and plantation owners. However, the state's interventionist role also extended to all social sectors, including the elite.

In representing the interests of the Spanish monarchy, and paralleling the somewhat contradictory forces of patrimonial and legal domination that it embodied, the colonial state had a contradictory relationship with the highest social strata of the different territories.[4] On the one hand, it sought to regulate and limit them; and in so doing its bureaucrats appeared to act in a technical and neutral fashion (at the service of and *por amor al rey*), which caused periodic clashes with local elites over such issues as Indian labor, tribute, economic restrictions, bureaucratic performance, and the treatment of the Church.[5] On the other hand, the state tended to fuse with these elites by granting all of them, with relatively equal largesse, honors, prestige, power, and economic prerogatives in exchange for political loyalty and economic support. The Crown received substantial tributes and backing from each and all of these groups and accorded them, in return, economic, social, political, and cultural privileges.

Among these privileges was the granting of access to intellectual professions, especially law and the priesthood. Depending on educational accomplishments, access to state service, whether of a patrimonial or a legal sort (tax-farming or professional bureaucratic service), was another key state-granted prerogative reserved for the elite. In fact, both the professions and state service became a vital way—as vital as any given trade or economic occupation—for the dominant social groups to maintain and increase their individual and familial opportunities and social status. These privileges, therefore, are particularly important for understanding the nature and sources of social stratification in the colonial period.

Honor, Status, and Class in a Colonial Setting

The importance of honor as an overall concern of Iberians and Latin Americans during the colonial period has been widely recognized in discussions concerning both attitudes toward manual and mercantile activities and the nature and evolution of gender roles.[6] Little has been said, however, about education and state service as sources of honor and status. Honor was not solely linked to noblemen's concerns with the demeaning character of manual labor or trade, nor was it chiefly a question of patriarchal preoccupations with promise-keeping, manliness, female sexual virtue, and purity. Rather, honor was a general pursuit of individuals and families looking for means to accumulate prestige, esteem, influence, and other related ways to improve their standing in society. That is why there were so many legal battles over *hidalguía* and the use of deferential expressions such as *don* and *doña*, which were intended to ensure social standing and public recognition of whiteness, or *limpieza de sangre*, and its associated privileges, including access to higher education, municipal government, and state jobs.[7]

Access to and graduation from academic institutions were a confirmation of honor and prestige. Since it facilitated entrance into both the Church and state ranks, education also constituted an avenue to raise one's social prominence. Racial purity, an appropriate religious background, legitimacy of birth, and membership in families headed by nonmanual workers were qualifications presumed of all college students, and consequently of all graduates. Students and graduates were visibly distinguished from the rest of society by strict dress codes. They also took part in pompous public academic ceremonies and processions, which gave them further opportunities to be honored and to display their superior social status.[8]

In addition to education, participation in the state bureaucracy—a little-investigated and infrequently acknowledged source of social preeminence—was a determinant of social superiority. In fact, being part of the state ranks was not merely a source of material benefits, such as stable income and power, but it also afforded prestige, deference, and honor. Honor, in turn, entitled its possessors to a higher status, or "right to pride."[9] This right was not strictly individual but was extended or passed on to family members. In other words, honor was both a personal and familial affair; bureaucrats not only achieved it but also passed it on to their kin.[10] Further, families and individuals also worried about getting closer to the state as a means to improve their status. They saw proximity and service to the Crown and Church as a convenient way to accumulate honor.

As anthropologists have argued, honor had an "intimate connection with the realm of the sacred" and was associated with the authority of the Church. However, it also emanated from the king; indeed, honor was attached to the authority of the state and its functionaries and was a result of the "power of rank."[11] The bestowing of honor upon state officials was a common practice in Anglo-Saxon and other cultures. Samuel Haber, for instance, has argued that as English kings gradually came to monopolize violence and civil affairs took precedence over military ones, honor was bestowed more and more upon civil functionaries rather than upon warriors. "Honor, therefore, became the reward of closeness to and assistance to the sovereign," as the king and the royal household became coveted "fountains of honor."[12] This same phenomenon also applied in France, in Hapsburg and Bourbon Spain, and, by extension, in colonial Latin America.[13]

Bureaucratic activities were therefore true sources of significant moral or cultural incentives. To be sure, royal service or government employment carried material benefits—in particular, job security and steady, sometimes high, salaries or other monetary returns—in addition to power and influence.[14] Yet, such service also offered other nonmaterial incentives, among them prestige, honor, and status. To paraphrase Max Weber, bureaucratic power was valued not just for its material benefits but also "for its own sake," for the social honor that it entailed.[15]

That bureaucratic careers were honorable positions was suggested by the fact that "service to the Crown in civil and military affairs could help one obtain noble status and the associated rewards."[16] Indeed, bureaucrats sought to acquire and were granted "aristocratic or semi-aristocratic symbols of status," especially noble titles and, more frequently, knighthood in the military-religious orders of Santiago, Calatrava, and Alcántara.[17] The honor springing from bureaucratic service was also implicit in late colonial writers' complaints about the predominantly ostentatious ends of many job seekers.[18] Public rituals, celebrations, and parades were a common occasion for display on the part of bureaucrats and their rivals.[19] Bureaucrats in general made it a point to draft and update their résumés, indicating their academic credentials and, most important, summarizing their personal and familial *méritos*, or worthiness. These *méritos* were essentially a series of services, ranging from nonremunerative employment in city councils to jobs in prestigious audiencias, rendered to the Crown or Church by individuals and their kin, including even their most distant relatives. In fact, as the abundant colonial *relaciones de méritos* make clear, individuals and families alike frequently boasted of the honor derived from Church and state service.[20]

Those observers judging the merits of Church and bureaucratic service naturally had to determine social differences between, on the one hand, insiders and their respective families—to whom honor and status were extended—and outsiders, on the other. Distinctions had to be made even among insiders and outsiders who belonged to relatively similar ethnic, religious, legal, and economic groups. Yet one cannot refer to such differences as class differences, for although they could have translated into economic advantages or disadvantages, they were not the result of economic factors, the source from whence class differences spring.[21]

In other words, if the concept of social class could, after all, be applied to groups in colonial settings in which social stratification responded to numerous noneconomic factors (religious antecedents, legitimate birth, ethnic origin, place of birth, noble titles, nonmanual occupations, service to the Crown), certainly one could not claim to find significant class differences between those in the state bureaucracy (and their respective families) and those outside of this bureaucracy.[22] For example, it is impossible to discern such differences between, on the one hand, certain bureaucrats and their landowning, mine-owning, merchant, or professional relatives and, on the other hand, nonbureaucrats and their similarly wealthy or

middling landowning, mine-owning, merchant, or professional relatives. Still, noneconomic factors—state service itself and its associated status-honor, especially—determined social differences
among such familial groups.

As mentioned, the existence of diverging status across elite
groups surfaced during public rituals, celebrations, and parades. In
such events, ceremonial display was of paramount importance. In
seventeenth-century Upper Peru at Potosí, for instance, religious
processions kept "the officers of law and justice" apart from artisans, tradesmen, and members of the *cabildo* and near the nobility
and the wealthiest members of society: the plutocracy of quicksilver refiners. Those officials wore particular attire and distinctive
headgear. Along with other royal and municipal dignitaries, such
as officers of the mint and treasury, they were afforded certain privileges, including personal meetings with the viceroy.[23] As a result
of the key value attributed to such rituals, seating arrangements
during ceremonies or dress codes caused frequent disputes over precedence between honor-conscious bureaucrats and honor-hungry
members of the secular city councils, or *cabildos*.[24]

Differences in status between bureaucrats and the rest of society were also noted in the self-perceptions of contemporary actors.
In his early nineteenth-century genealogical remarks, a late colonial bureaucrat who was part of a clan with a long history of bureaucratic involvement in the Viceroyalty of New Granada referred
to the "muy honoríficos" bureaucratic services of his ancestors and
boasted of the unspecified "honores" to which their appointments
entitled them and himself. The same bureaucrat noted that his father, *contador* of the Royal Treasury, was quite modest and tended
not to "exaltar sus méritos" (emphasize his merits) but instead
"procuraba rebajarlos o disimularlos para ponerse a nivel de todas
las gentes" (played them down or disguised them so as to be at the
same level as the rest of the people), which suggests that as a bureaucrat he was not at the same "level" with the rest.[25]

This perception of the honor of government service was also
reflected in restrictions on bureaucrats' social intercourse. Marriages were confined to their own circle, effectively limiting their
prospects to relatives of other bureaucrats, nobles, or *gentes
principales* (the leading local families).[26] These restrictions were
in part self-imposed by the bureaucrats' perception that alliances
with certain families would further their careers. However, some
rules were enforced and sanctioned by the Crown to avoid conflicts
of interest and corruption and maintain social prestige. The public's

perception of the honorable character of royal servants required that a superior supervise the choice of marriage partners for officials of all ranks.[27]

Finally, there were instances in which the higher honor and status of bureaucrats were apparent in more material terms. Previous works have demonstrated that preferential treatment for appointment and promotion were accorded to the aspiring sons and relatives of former bureaucrats who profited from the *servicios contrahidos* between the Crown and their ancestors or other kin.[28] This practice ultimately determined the establishment of a sort of dynastic succession. Officials continued to build family-bureaucratic networks even during the second half of the eighteenth century, when the bureaucracy became increasingly more professional.[29] This familial right to office denotes, but should not be confused with, the convertibility of honor and status into material advantages for family and self.[30] These advantages included both the direct economic benefit of having a bureaucratic job and those perks associated with access to office (for example, leverage for business deals, attractiveness for marriage into elite families, power to deliver patronage and receive allegiance in exchange). Material benefits, again, were undeniably linked to a superior status, but this status had clear moral repercussions and created major cultural differences.

Like other economic, social, and political features of the colonial period, the series of status disparities between state and Church insiders and outsiders did not magically disappear after independence. Their images were carried over to the postcolonial period, this time not confined to petty disputes over access to honor symbols and the appropriate etiquette but contributing to unleash military confrontations, regional rivalries, and political factionalism.

Status, Class, and Early Postcolonial Political Disputes

A new kind of society emerged in Latin America during the first half of the nineteenth century. Religious and ethnic background, noble titles, the manual character of one's occupation, the place and even the legitimate or illegitimate nature of one's birth ceased more and more to determine one's social standing.[31] But it was not just that these factors had gradually lost weight in determining social hierarchies and perceptions. Other factors also changed, causing significant transformations in social arrangements and stratification in the process. One such factor was elites' relationship with the state, in particular the social meaning and importance attributed to membership in the state bureaucratic ranks. These changes were slow to come and took place amid much social tension. Their impact is illustrated here by the particular case of New Granada.

New Granada's independence was led mostly by elite Creoles, including numerous high-ranking colonial bureaucrats and their upper-status families. These individuals resented the unwillingness of Spanish bureaucrats to conciliate and establish wider governing coalitions during the political crisis of 1808–1814. They were also deeply alienated by the bloody repression that followed the organization of cogovernmental committees, or juntas, in mid-1810.[32] Between 1810 and 1815 the same local elites who had led the revolution's Juntas Supremas and worked intensely to write constitutions and design institutional reforms also spent precious time settling internal quarrels.[33] The most critical dispute pitted the province of Cundinamarca—home of the most traditional and aristocratic families of the colonial period as well as of the most important central institutions of the Spanish colonial state—against the so-called Provincias Unidas de la Nueva Granada, a union comprising nearly all of the rest of the provinces.[34] The quarrel revolved around the Cundinamarcan elites' reluctance to give up the substantial resources of their region's (that is, Bogotá's) mint, and their desire that Cundinamarca continue to be the center of bureaucratic life, as it had been during the colonial period. They perceived this continuity as fundamental for the prolongation of their individual and familial status-honor.[35]

Some of these families had traditionally monopolized such key posts as treasurer of the mint. This monopoly was a result of the decision by their ancestors, founders of the mint in question, to turn it over to the Crown in exchange for perpetual annual payments to them and their descendants as well as other privileges, including control over the office of treasurer.[36] The leader of the Cundinamarca faction, Antonio Nariño Alvarez, belonged to one of the most traditional bureaucratic clans of the colonial period. In 1810 he still had uncles and cousins serving as members of Spain's Council of the Indies and as *oidores* in Latin American audiencias, not to mention close relatives and friends in the fiscal bureaucracies of Bogotá and Popayán.[37]

Members of commanding elite families such as the Nariños staffed the officer corps of the swelling armies engaged in both civil wars and revolutionary activities.[38] They recruited as soldiers the peons who worked on their ranches, the slaves who labored in their mines, and the peasants who paid tithes to their parishes. One leading officer was the "revolutionary" General José María Vergara y Lozano, a member of one of the most remarkable and resilient bureaucratic dynasties of the late colonial period.[39] General Vergara y Lozano became Colombia's diplomatic envoy to London in 1819, where he sought credits and support for the revolution. In 1820 he became alarmed by the fact that New Granada's traditional social order had been altered by the protracted war for independence, which threatened to bring "democracy" and elections to the country. In a pamphlet dedicated to Simón Bolívar, the general expressed his fears of democracy and proposed a system similar to the safer English aristocracy, which he praised.[40] At the time, his family continued to command bureaucratic prominence and status: his uncle Cristóval was administrator of the Zipaquirá salt mines, a large deposit near Bogotá; his first cousin, Estanislao Vergara Sanz de Santamaría, was secretary of the interior of the government organized by General Bolívar after the defeat of Spanish troops in Colombia; and several other family members held bureaucratic jobs in Cundinamarca and Popayán, including the post of treasurer of Cundinamarca's mint.[41]

Estanislao, continuing in the footsteps of several of his ancestors and relatives, was a *letrado*, or lawyer. Law was a more common background for elites joining the bureaucracy than theology or medicine, the other two intellectual careers then available to individuals of high social standing. General Bolívar, who was deeply conscious of the need to rely on influential local clans to consolidate power, handpicked Estanislao, then age 29, to be a minister in his government. He was joined by at least two other young lawyers, one of them from roughly the same social background.[42] Estanislao remained a member of the cabinet until the mid-1820s when—at the same time that his uncle was moving from the administration of the salt mines to the governorship of the key provinces of Cauca and Boyacá—he became a member of the Supreme Court. Much like his cousin the general and his other relatives, Estanislao opposed popular elections and feared a "tumultuous" democracy. In letters to General Bolívar, his friend and mentor, Estanislao insisted that a strong monarchical government was absolutely necessary for Colombia.[43] He was certainly concerned with stability and order, as were many men in those days, but the threat that free elections represented to his family's traditional bureaucratic share and long-established prominence must also have been on his mind. Along with a select clique of prominent families from Bogotá and the aristocratic regions of Popayán and Cartagena—two other traditional bureaucratic and religious centers of the colonial period—Estanislao did all he could to terminate the many elections and constitutional congresses held during the 1820s.[44]

Besides landowning, mine-owning, and commerce, leading families from these regions traditionally pursued Church service and state administration. These families (the Pey, Alvarez, Paris, Leiva, Caro, Sanz de Santamaría, Caicedo, Pérez de Arroyo, and Mosquera clans, for example) must have seen dominant positions in the bureaucracy as their rightful legacy and an exclusive source of social prestige and status-honor. To protect these privileges they tried to restrict access to the state and therefore promoted the suspension of the republican constitution adopted by Colombia in 1821. They also favored the "dictatorship" of General Rafael Bolívar in 1828 and subsequently launched the atypical 1830s "dictatorship" of General Urdaneta, which received strong support from Bogota's cabildo and high society. (Urdaneta himself was a former colonial bureaucrat and nephew of a high-ranking official in Bogotá's Tribunal de Cuentas.[45]) During the late 1830s and through the 1840s, these families also promoted a conservative system of government, widely perceived to be proclerical, aristocratic, and semicolonial. In all of these efforts they were opposed by another elite segment composed of provincial landed gentry, merchants, mine owners, lawyers, priests, and military officers who lacked the status attached to colonial bureaucrats and their relatives. These two opposite groups went on to fight each other in New Granada's first postindependence nationwide civil war. They struggled for control of the state apparatus in 1839–1841 and eventually became the social core around which the Conservative and Liberal parties of Colombia were founded during the late 1840s.

Politics: Class Conflict or a Mess?

In an attempt to make sense of Colombia's and nineteenth-century Latin America's political conflicts and history, scholars have tried to find links between political factions and parties and specific economic activities and social classes. Most of these attempts, however, have been proven wrong. Studies of various parts of Spanish America have concluded that the struggles between Conservatives and Liberals were not a confrontation between landowners and an emerging bourgeoisie. Among other reasons, there was not much specialization of economic activities in this region. It was common to find elite individuals in all political groups who were simultaneously lawyers, landowners, and merchants.[46] In the example above, for instance, the Vergaras were landowners, priests, and lawyers, and they had cousins involved in import-export activities, incipient industrial ventures, and mining.[47] This was also true of some of their postcolonial political rivals.[48]

As a result of these findings, the class nature of the liberal transformations, or "revolutions," of midnineteenth century Latin America, long alleged to have been liberal bourgeois movements against a dominant conservative landed aristocracy, also comes into question.[49] This trend is not confined to Latin America. Since at least the mid-1980s, Spanish, French, German, and Italian historians have been arguing the same for their regions, asserting that no revolutionary bourgeoisie distinct from the rest of the elite can be discerned in midnineteenth-century Europe.[50]

Given the lack of clear economic confrontations between factions, nineteenth-century Latin American politics (particularly during the first half of the century) appears to be a mess. Historians have seen this period as "utter chaos"—a meaningless, personal scramble for spoils. It was, as a typical textbook puts it, a period dominated by the rule of "force, no matter what the constitutional form; usually, he [the chief executive] ruled with the support of a coalition of lesser caudillos, each more or less supreme in his own domain. The supposed independence of the judicial and legislative branches was a fiction. As a rule, elections were exercises in futility."[51]

Due to these assumptions, the traditional view of Latin America during the first half of the nineteenth century emphasizes the barbarization, militarization, and ruralization of politics. These years have come to be seen as a "long wait"—a transition from colonial stability to the stability brought about by the agrarian export boom of the 1850s, when Latin America forged a new colonial pact with the major industrializing countries.[52] The time in between is characterized as one of political chaos punctuated by the periodic but futile exercise of holding elections and writing constitutions and laws obeyed by few people. Authority, according to these explanations, was not successfully embodied in Spanish America's many constitutions and laws but rested instead with a myriad of individual caudillos and local military chiefs.[53]

There are several problems with these interpretations. First, they are mostly a result of the "normal" periodization of Latin American political history—that is, the partition and separate study of the colonial and the postcolonial or national periods. This periodization leads historians of modern Latin America—those who start their works with the 1820s—to encounter individuals whose colonial social background and interests go unexplained in their investigations.

A second problem is the belief that once economic interpretations and class struggles are discarded, one is left without any coherent social explanation of postcolonial political confrontations. In other words, the period is reduced to a chaos of individuals, provincial military bosses, and meaningless laws. At least as influential historian Frank Safford suggests, in spite of the uselessness of class theories, a coherent explanation of postcolonial political affiliations and conflicts could be found in the "social location" of the members of diverse political factions. In other words, political factions reflect the rivalries between groups of individuals from administrative and educational centers of the late colonial period and those from marginal regions, where access to "structures of power" was negligible.[54] This same author adds that explanations founded on "status" differences and clashes should be ruled out as a valid alternative, since status is a concept characterized by "variability and relativity"; it is difficult to measure and can only be evaluated subjectively.[55] The criteria outlined by this author to explain political rivalries are important, and, in fact, the status differences discussed earlier overlap with differences in individuals' "social location." For the same reason, however, it is wrong to say that it is impossible to use status as a marker of social stratification. Like numerous other historical phenomena that may not be measurable in an exact way, status can and must be interpreted with some accuracy based on the incomplete historical evidence available. Interpretation of incomplete evidence is, after all, the essence of historical research.

Status Conflict and Political Struggles

Contrary to the views stated by the dominant orthodox Latin American historiography, a social pattern did in fact underlie political conflict in New Granada (and perhaps in other Latin American nations). It was not a pattern of class-conflict or conflict over the means of production, but rather a pattern of status-honor conflict and conflict over the means of administration. As Weber argued, individuals "do not strive for power only in order to enrich themselves economically . . . very frequently, the striving for power is also conditioned by the social 'honor' that it entails."[56] Colonial societies were to a large extent stratified by status considerations that went hand in hand with the monopolization of ideal and material goods and opportunities, including the opportunity to enter the high ranks of the bureaucracy.[57] Colonial status circles tended to practice endogamy and intermarriage.[58] In these increasingly closed groups, preferential opportunities for special employment grew into a monopoly of key offices for the network's members. These circumstances dictated that democratic forms of access to the state apparatus were not convenient to traditional (high-status) colonial groups such as the Vergaras. For them, "democracy" raised the threat of a free market in state jobs, leading to a breakdown of one of the main sources of traditional elite honor, prestige, and power. The new legal order that sanctioned this breakdown had to be resisted at all costs.

The Colombian movement for independence caused radical changes in the prevailing legal order and threatened to disrupt the traditional standing of some status groups. It meant the gradual transformation of the prevailing patrimonial-bureaucratic form of domination, in which families such as the Vergaras and the Sanz de Santamarías monopolized the symbols of power and honor. It also meant the gradual emergence of a predominantly legal (bureaucratic) form of domination in which the mechanisms for accessing the state, and the state itself, were substantially different. Elections, about which scholars of nineteenth-century Latin America know very little, and the constitutions and laws that regulated them were a substantial part of the new mechanisms.

Latin Americans in this period seem to have held elections and written laws and constitutions unceasingly. Colombians were no exception. If elections were exercises in futility and constitutions were mere forms, why did contemporaries care so much about them? And if power rested in the barrels of guns and on the backs of horses, why were the Vergaras, for instance, so worried about elections leading to a "tumultuous" democracy and about so many noisy constitutional congresses? As one of their descendants indicated, the Vergaras were concerned about the involvement of the "ignorant and irresponsible *populacho*" in politics. This concern was typical of Latin American elites;[59] however, the Vergaras and others like them were even more worried about the new "grammar" of politics reflected in the new constitutions, which dispersed political power and allotted it to provincial elites.[60] They also worried about the potential beneficiaries of elections—not so much the *populacho* itself, but rather the provincial elites who actively looked for, and seem to have commanded, the votes from their regions. These elites came from regions without a significant colonial bureaucracy and lacked a familial tradition of state or High Church service; Socorro and Neiva were two such regions in early postindependence Colombia.

The Rise of the Provincial Elites

An active group of lawyers from the province of Socorro, who came to be known as the Socorranos, led the antimilitary struggles of the 1820s and opposed the authoritarian (monarchical) projects of traditional clans such as the Alvarezes and Vergaras.[61] Antonio Nariño Alvarez's election as vice president was derailed in response to pressures from these provincial Jacobins; under pressure from the same sectors, he was tried by the Senate in the early 1820s on corruption charges springing from his activities in the colonial period.[62] Similarly, the leading member of the Vergara clan, Estanislao, was fired from the Supreme Court, expelled from Bogotá in 1831, and banned from participating in politics thereafter.[63] The Socorranos formed coalitions in the early 1830s with some moderate aristocrats from Popayán and Tunja, with whom they managed the state until 1837. At that point a former ally of theirs who went over to the most intolerant aristocracy won the presidency and began to push them aside. This lawyer, José I. de Márquez, was backed by aristocratic Bogotano families like the Vergaras. Popayán aristocrats such as the Mosqueras, whose uncle Joaquín had been an influential *oidor* and member of Spain's Council of the Indies, also supported him, as did the wealthy mine owners, landowners, and merchant families of Antioquia, Buga, Pamplona, and Girón. In the 1820s and 1830s these plutocrats joined the ranks of the high-status elite, repeating a pattern set during the colonial period and continued in New Granada and elsewhere.[64] During the second half of the 1830s the Socorrano group, fiercely opposed to the new government, was joined by another active cluster of upwardly mobile lawyers from the regions of Neiva, Mariquita (Ibague), and Casanare, and by several marginal figures from Bogotá and Tunja. The Neiva ones are worth discussing further.

The south-central region of Neiva, an intermediate point between the traditional urban centers of Bogotá and Popayán, had experienced the colonial bureaucracy only peripherally (it represented approximately 1 percent of total bureaucratic jobs in the entire viceroyalty).[65] The elites of Neiva, therefore, lacked a tradition of bureaucratic service. The province's main economic activities revolved around small-scale agriculture, ranching, and a little mining, which occupied elites and common folks alike.[66]

A good example of the late colonial generation of lawyers linked to this region is José María Lombana, the son of a small Bogotá-based merchant. Although Lombana's admission to one of Bogota's law schools was originally denied during the 1790s because of the alleged illegitimate birth of his mother,[67] he eventually entered law school and became a lawyer around 1805. After graduating, he settled in the thriving rural region of La Plata in a small town in Neiva not far from Popayán. Here he devoted part of his efforts to developing a cacao plantation. Cacao was a valuable commodity in affluent mining regions and other areas, and planters seem to have made a good living. Passing through Popayán, mules loaded with cacao traveled from La Plata all the way to gold-rich Antioquia, where hot chocolate made from cacao was an important staple of the local diet.[68] Lombana must have accumulated some wealth, which made him eligible to marry into an influential local family. His wife was a member of La Plata's landowning Buendía clan, which had ties with other local lawyers, including a leading member of the Céspedes family.[69] Lombana died in 1816 during the Wars of Independence but left offspring in Neiva.

Like an increasing number of individuals from provincial families in the 1830s, two of Lombana's sons, Ramón and Vicente Lombana Buendía, profited from the postcolonial boom in education resulting from the plan of legal studies sponsored by the provincial elites and adopted in 1832 and 1835. The plan promoted teaching law at the provincial level and allowed students to take as many courses during the academic year as they wished. The Lombana brothers both eventually became lawyers.[70] Subsequently, Ramón, like many other provincial lawyers, became a middling bureaucrat (*oficial tercero* at the Ministry of Economy) in 1837. Vicente, in addition to being a lawyer and active law professor, was a small shopkeeper, medical doctor, and opposition politician from the mid-1830s onward.[71] He fit perfectly the description of two-year *doctores* in both medicine and jurisprudence who were condemned in the aristocratic press of New Granada as part of its campaign to close the "excessive" numbers of provincial *colegios* in the early 1840s.[72]

Neiva also had a few aristocratic lawyers in the colonial period. Among them was Andrés José Iriarte Rojas, a native of Timana (Garzón) and son of a colonial governor of Neiva during the 1740s. After teaching law and serving in low bureaucratic jobs over the course of sixteen years, he became *fiscal* of the Royal Audiencia of Quito in 1799, where he died in 1809. Part of his family remained in Neiva and, much like Lombana's, his relatives—particularly his nephew, *doctor* Joaquín Gómez Iriarte—received legal training and became active politicians during the postcolonial period.[73] Gómez Iriarte's political views were very different from those of his *paisanos*. He was a *ministerial*, or supporter of aristocratic lawyer José Márquez's government in the late 1830s, whereas the rest of Neiva's lawyers were *progresistas* opposed to the regime.[74] In May 1837, Gómez Iriarte supported the law, resisted by the provincial elites, that cleared Márquez's recent election to the presidency from any constitutional defect, and in 1840 he opposed an important amnesty law proposed by the provincial elites. In both cases he went against Neiva residents, who were among the most active members of the *progresista* opposition.[75] Their social background helps to explain their political stance.

The majority of lawyers from Neiva in the late 1820s and 1830s seem to have come from families who tended more toward Lombana's upwardly mobile background than toward Iriarte's traditional roots. Prominent names included Domingo Ciprián Cuenca (1801–1850), a practicing lawyer of relatively modest origins in both Bogotá and the little town of Purificación, at the time part of the province of Neiva. Cuenca reinforced his social roots by marrying the sister of fellow Socorrano lawyer Angel María Flórez (1802–1836), a former governor of his native Vélez and an active supporter of Francisco de Paula Santander's 1832–1837 provincial-staffed administration.[76]

Other leading Neiva lawyers included Bernardo Herrera Buendía (1812–1887), an 1834 law graduate who came from an apparently affluent family of landowners from the towns of Palermo, Tello, and Villavieja. Herrera was a first cousin of the Lombana Buendía brothers, and in 1838 he served alongside his cousin Ramón as *oficial segundo* at the Ministry of Economy. That same year he married a daughter of the high-ranking and authoritarian-minded Antioqueño bureaucrat José Manuel Restrepo, a match that might have kept him from joining at least one of his cousins in the civil war of the late 1830s.[77] Perhaps following in his father-in-law's footsteps, Herrera ran an unspecified business in Bogotá and became an astute practicing lawyer, but he was not co-opted by the aristocrats; he supported provincial General José María Obando's presidential candidacy in 1837 and gravitated toward the *progresista* group (later the Liberal Party) in the 1840s and beyond.[78]

The Manrique Gaitán brothers, Eladio and Eloi, their brother-in-law Gaspar Díaz (1810–1878), and Andrés Durán González, all of them young law graduates, were also part of Neiva's provincial elites. They all came from families of middling provincial proprietors lacking in aristocratic credentials or high bureaucratic colonial backgrounds. They seemed to have represented a sort of middle class from which some prosperous landholders were not altogether absent. Little is known about their family strategies, but we do have some information about their careers. All four became practicing lawyers in Bogotá and Neiva as well as active politicians, congressmen, law professors, and bureaucrats during the 1830s.[79] More important, they opposed the aristocratic Márquez government, which was supported by the traditional elites of Bogotá, Tunja, Popayán, and Cartagena and by plutocrats from Antioquia, Buga, Pamplona, and Girón.

Thirty-year-old Vicente Lombana Buendía was part of the provincial group that requested Márquez's impeachment in 1837 and was a member of the 1838 opposition group, Sociedad Democrática Republicana de Artesanos i Laboradores Progresistas. Lombana Buendía worked as assistant director of Bogotá's Colegio del Rosario in 1840 while managing a pharmacy that he owned in Bogotá and some lands in Neiva. He was forced to abandon his jobs and possessions in 1841, when the Conservative government expelled him from Bogotá.[80]

The social and political trajectory of these men from Neiva applies to some of their fellows from towns in the neighboring province of Mariquita. Examples include Manuel Murillo Toro, Eujenio Castilla, and Patrocinio Cuellar, modest provincial students from a little place called Chaparral, which only became an official town (*cantón*) of the province in 1837, perhaps thanks to their influence.[81] Castilla's family activities are obscure; all we know is that the Castillas lived and married in rural Chaparral, and that one of Eujenio's uncles was for a long time a parish priest in Neiva, where he was active in raising funds for the creation of a local *colegio* and probably contributed to the education of his nephew.[82] Murillo, who had served during his adolescence as a scribe for aristocratic families, was referred to as "hijo de padres escasos en bienes de fortuna" (offspring of a modest family) or "de modesta cuna" (from a poor cradle). He was educated in a provincial *colegio* under the sponsorship of another local priest. Like Castilla, he later moved to Bogotá, where both men became lawyers, bureaucrats, and active opposition politicians during the late 1830s and 1840s.[83]

Lawyers from marginal regions in neighboring Bogotá also belonged to this upwardly mobile group. Here we find the cases of Romualdo Liévano and Rafael María Vásquez. Liévano, a native of the little town of Fusagazuga near Bogotá, was described by a contemporary as a "man of modest origins." After returning from exile in the early 1830s, he occupied high judicial positions, owned a small shop, and practiced law in Bogotá.[84] Vásquez, an Indian native of the town of Funza, was considered by his contemporaries to be an individual of "modest fortune." He escaped persecution during the political upheavals of the late 1820s by becoming a priest. He later became a lawyer and, as was common among provincials, a bureaucrat and professional full-time educator during the early 1830s.[85]

Upward Mobility and Conflicts over Control of the State Apparatus

Provincial lawyers gained access to state positions and actively participated in politics in the early 1820s and 1830s. They attained such positions partly because of their connections to strategically located provincial military leaders. They also benefited from the networks knitted by their peers within the national, regional, or local bureaucracy. However, their upward mobility was at least partially due to the changes in the character and mechanics of the distribution of bureaucratic power. These changes were worked out through a body of laws and constitutions that valued the revolutionary merits and the intellectual achievements of these individuals or their ancestors.[86] The laws and constitutions also sanctioned the fact that these provincial figures were "popularly" elected or collectively nominated (by the *cámaras provinciales*) to the Congress and other positions. The "election" of provincial figures was something that traditional Bogotano clans were not willing to stomach, a position leading inevitably to conflict.

Provincial elites naturally opposed the anti-electoral pretensions of aristocratic clans such as the Vergaras, Caicedos, and Sanz de Santamarías. Their disputes involved which social sectors were to be enfranchised and how elections were to be conducted.[87] To the annoyance of the aristocrats, provincial elites succeeded in promoting local, regional, and national elections to the Congress, provincial assemblies, and other governmental bodies. They also sought a new model of legal education oriented toward the training of a new type of bureaucrat. Their proposed curriculum emphasized subjects such as administrative science, constitutional science, the science of legislation, and political economy, disciplines that reinforced belief in the convenience of republican forms (for example, competitive elections) for the selection and management of the state bureaucracy.[88]

These republican activities and disciplines threatened the status of traditional families from Popayán, Cartagena, and Bogotá. The socially and regionally heterogeneous Congress and provincial assemblies—the results of constant electioneering—actively intervened in the selection of candidates for high-ranking state jobs. In the past, these jobs had been the almost exclusive monopoly of the traditional clans of these regions.[89]

Disputes over the control of the state bureaucracy, the definition and practice of elections, and the orientation of legal education were behind some of the skirmishes and civil wars of the nineteenth century.[90] But why did provincial elites fight so hard to gain access to the state and to shape its management? Did they want to use the bureaucracy, education, and elections to advance the interests of a particular social class? It seems that this was not overtly the case. Whenever they managed to control the state apparatus, the provincial figures did not promote economic policies very different from those pursued by the Vergaras or other traditional groups. Both groups agreed, for instance, on the need to maintain a pragmatic protectionist policy and to preserve the state monopoly over certain economic activities (for example, tobacco trade and cultivation) during the 1820s, 1830s, and part of the 1840s. Provincials and aristocrats alike advocated tariffs and monopolies to alleviate the chronic fiscal crisis of an emerging state whose main sources of revenue were fees and customs duties. These protectionist policies were intended to guarantee the subsistence of the state itself; they were not industrial or mercantile policies, but rather fiscal policies.[91]

Furthermore, during the midnineteenth century these two opposing groups clearly agreed on the need to open up Colombia to foreign manufactures and to direct its economy to the export of raw materials and agrarian commodities, mainly tobacco. By this time, thanks to a long process of intermarriage and business combinations, status disparities between aristocrats and provincials were fading away and class identity was beginning to play a dominant role.[92] Neither group appears to have used the state as a means to further the economic interest of a particular social class, such as merchants or landowners. Rather, they appear to have fought to maintain or increase their social status—their chance to hold onto power or honor or, as Richard Graham puts it in the case of nineteenth-century Brazil, the chance to dispense or seek patronage.[93] Finally, even these fights tended to decline. As class identity became central and abundant opportunities to accumulate wealth opened up, the conviction that taking part in the state's administration was vital for one's individual and familial status declined. As a result, elite social groups began to criticize *empleomanía*, or the obsessive quest for a bureaucratic position. Such critiques were unheard of in the colonial period. By the midnineteenth century, instead of a source of prestige, the pursuit and attainment of state jobs began to be viewed as an activity for unproductive hangers-on.

Conclusion

Lawyers and their families represented an important segment of Latin American colonial and early postcolonial societies. They played central roles in the liquidation of the colonial regime, the rise of a public sphere during the Age of Revolution, and the parallel emergence of a system of political parties through the second quarter of the nineteenth century. Since many members of the legal profession strove to follow bureaucratic careers, their activities allow us to link state service, political confrontations, and social transformation or, in other words, state-society interactions.

Judging from the history of Colombian lawyers' involvement in society and politics, many of the political conflicts in Latin America during the period after independence were over who would control the state and its resources. At least during the first half of the nineteenth century, the state continued to be first and foremost a source of jobs that provided honor, power, prestige, and patronage. To be sure, honor, power, and patronage are ultimately linked to a class situation, for they can lead (in the last instance) to the accumulation of wealth and the promotion of policies beneficial to a particular regional or familial network, economic group, or social class. Yet the pursuit of status-honor accruing from state service seems to have had a dynamic of its own or at least did not always have overt links to the pursuit of economic wealth.

In any event, the connection between bureaucratic service, honor, and economic gain is still mysterious. More work is required to understand the ways in which bureaucratic power was exerted during Latin America's colonial period and to discern the social differences among the groups linked to or excluded from that exercise.

The same is true for the postcolonial state. Otherwise, it will be difficult to interpret the nature and meaning of Latin America's nineteenth-century intra-elite conflicts, some of which appear to have been primarily status conflicts for the control of the means of administration.

Notes

1. The best work may still be that of Mario Góngora, *Encomenderos y estancieros* (Santiago, 1970), and "Estratificación social urbana en Chile (Siglos XVI, XVII y primera mitad del XVIII)," University of Wisconsin-Milwaukee, Center for Latin American Studies, Center Discussion Paper No. 30, December 1971. See Hugo Nutini, *The Wages of Conquest: The Mexican Aristocracy in the Context of Western Aristocracies* (Ann Arbor, 1995), 1–52, 269.

2. Max Weber, "Class, Status, and Party," in *Class, Status, and Power: Social Stratification in Historical Perspective*, ed. Reinhard Bendix and Seymour Lipset (New York, 1946), 21–28. A more or less similar definition refers to honor as "the value of a person in his own eyes, but also in the eyes of his society. It is his estimation of his own worth, his *claim* to pride, but it is also the acknowledgment of that claim, his excellence recognized by society, his *right* to pride." See Julian Pitt-Rivers, "Honor and Social Status," in *Honour and Shame: The Values of Mediterranean Society*, ed. I. G. Peristany (Chicago, 1966), 21–77; and Julian Pitt-Rivers, "Honor," in *International Encyclopedia of the Social Sciences*, 6:503–10.

3. See Karen Spalding, ed., *Essays in the Political, Economic and Social History of Colonial Latin America* (Newark, DE, 1982), xi. On politics as essential dynamics of pre-capitalist societies see Perry Anderson, *Lineages of the Absolutist State* (London, 1974); and Douglas Friedman, *The State and Underdevelopment in Spanish America: The Political Roots of Dependency in Peru and Argentina* (Boulder, 1984).

4. The most descriptive work on patrimonial and legal-bureaucratic features is by Magali Sarfatti, *Spanish Bureaucratic-Patrimonialism in America* (Berkeley, 1966). See also Richard M. Morse, "The Heritage of Latin America," in *The Founding of New Societies: Latin America, South Africa, Canada, and Australia*, ed. Louis Hartz (New York, 1964), 123–77; Fernando Uricoechea, *The Patrimonial Foundations of the Brazilian Bureaucratic State* (Los Angeles, 1980); and Reinhard Bendix, *Nation Building and Citizenship* (Berkeley, 1964), esp. 39–65. For some "traditional domination" features see also John L. Phelan, *The Kingdom of Quito in the Seventeenth Century: Bureaucratic Politics in the Spanish Empire* (Madison, 1967), esp. chap. 17.

5. See, for instance, Steve J. Stern, *Peru's Indian Peoples and the Challenge of the Spanish Conquest: Huamanga to 1640* (Madison, 1982); and Ramón Gutierrez, *When Jesus Came, The Corn Mothers Went Away* (Stanford, 1991).

6. On honor and gender see Patricia Seed, *To Love, Honor, and Obey in Colonial Mexico* (Stanford, 1986), esp. chaps. 6 and 9; Ann Twinam, "Honor, Sexuality, and Illegitimacy in Colonial Spanish America," in *Sexuality and Marriage in Colonial Latin America*, ed. Asunción Lavrin (Lincoln, 1989), 118–55; Gutierrez, *When Jesus Came*, chaps. 5–8. On honor, nobility, and mercantile activities see William J. Callahan, *Honor, Commerce, and Industry in Eighteenth-*

Century Spain (Boston, 1972). On the general importance and medieval roots of honor in Iberian and Mediterranean society see Frederick Robertson Byron, *The Point of Honor in Sixteenth-Century Italy: An Aspect of the Life of a Gentleman* (Chicago, 1935); Alfonso García Valdescasas, *El hidalgo y el honor* (Madrid, 1948); Julian Pitt-Rivers, *The Fate of Schechem or the Politics of Sex: Essays in the Anthropology of the Mediterranean* (Cambridge, 1977), esp. 1–47; and Catherine Lafages, "Royalty and Ritual in the Middle Ages: Coronation and Funerary Rites in France," in *Honour and Grace in Anthropology*, ed. J. G. Peristany and Julian Pitt-Rivers (Cambridge, 1992), 19–49.

7. García Valdescasas, *El hidalgo y el honor*; Jaime Jaramillo Uribe, "Mestizaje y diferenciación social en el Nuevo Reino de Granada en la segunda mitad del siglo XVIII," *Anuario Colombiano de Historia Social y de la Cultura* 2, no. 3 (1965): 21–48; Beatríz Patiño Millán, *Criminalidad, ley penal y estructura social en la Provincia de Antioquia, 1750–1820* (Medellín, 1994), 197–253.

8. John Tate Lanning, *The University in the Kingdom of Guatemala* (Ithaca, 1955), chaps. 10–11; Richard Kagan, *Students and Society in Early Modern Spain* (London, 1974); Renán Silva, *Universidad y sociedad en el Nuevo Reino de Granada* (Bogotá, 1992).

9. Julian Pitt-Rivers, "Honor and Social Status," 22. Weber, in fact, utilized the concept "status honor" in one of his main articles on the subject. See Weber, "Class, Status, and Party."

10. Mark Burkholder, "Bureaucrats," in *Cities and Society in Colonial Latin America*, ed. Susan M. Socolow and Louisa S. Hoberman (Albuquerque, 1986), esp. 96–99; Victor M. Uribe, "The Lawyers and New Granada's Late Colonial State," *Journal of Latin American Studies* 27, no. 3 (October 1995): 517–49.

11. Peristany and Pitt-Rivers, *Honour and Grace*, 2–3, 5.

12. Samuel Haber, *The Quest for Authority and Honor in the American Professions, 1750–1900* (Chicago, 1991), part 1. For public service, even undertaken by men of modest origins, as involving unmistakable signs of social distinction see Jonathan Powis, *Aristocracy* (New York, 1984), 69, 72, 78. See also Hans Speier, "Honor and Social Structure," in *Social Order and the Risks of War*, ed. Hans Speier (New York, 1952), 36–52.

13. See Emmanuel Leroy Ladurie, "The Court Surrounds the King: Louis XIV, the Palatine Princess, and Saint-Simon," in Peristany and Pitt-Rivers, *Honour and Grace*, 51–78; Powis, *Aristocracy*, 21; Callahan, *Honor, Commerce, and Industry*, 3; García Valdescasas, *El hidalgo y el honor*, 193; Mark Burkholder, *Politics of a Colonial Career: José Baquíjano and the Audiencia of Lima* (Albuquerque, 1980), 109; and Nutini, *Wages of Conquest*, 255–56.

14. See Susan Socolow, *Bureaucrats of Buenos Aires: Amor al Real Servicio* (Durham, 1988), chap. 5; Linda Arnold, *Bureaucracy and Bureaucrats in Mexico City, 1742–1835* (Tucson, 1988), chap. 6; and Phelan, *Kingdom of Quito*, 147, 327.

15. Weber, "Class, Status, and Party." On occupation as a source of deference see also Edward A. Shils, "Deference," in *The Logic of Social Hierarchies*, ed. Edward O. Laumann et al. (Chicago, 1970), 421–48, esp. 423–24.

16. Juan A. Villamarín and Judith E. Villamarín, "The Concept of Nobility in Colonial Santa Fe de Bogotá," in *Essays in the Political, Economic and Social History of Colonial Latin America*, ed. Karen Spalding (Newark, DE, 1982), 125–53, esp. 128; Powis, *Aristocracy*, 21; Phelan, *Kingdom of Quito*, 127, 324.

17. Phelan, *Kingdom of Quito*, 334; Nutini, *Wages of Conquest*, 255–56.

18. Hipólito Villaroel, *Emfermedades políticas que padece la capital de esta Nueva España en casi todos los cuerpos de que se compone y remedios que se le*

deben aplicar para su curación si se quiere que sea útil al Rey y al público (Mexico, 1982), 198.

19. See Bartolomé Arzans de Orsúa, *Tales of Potosí* (Providence, RI, 1975), 176–82; Germán Pérez Sarmiento, ed., *Causas célebres a los precursores* (Seville, 1939), vol. 1; Pitt-Rivers, "Honor and Social Status," 54–55; and John L. Phelan, "The Ceremonial and Political Roles of Cities in Colonial Spanish America," University of Wisconsin-Milwaukee Center for Latin American Studies, Discussion Paper No. 41, March 1972.

20. See *relaciones de méritos y servicios* of numerous colonial Latin Americans in Fondo Pineda, No. 1066, Biblioteca Nacional de Colombia, Bogotá. See also Mark Burkholder, "Relaciones de Méritos y Servicios: A Source for Spanish-American Group Biography in the Eighteenth Century," *Manuscripta* 21 (1977): 97–104.

21. See Weber, "Class, Status, and Party"; and Arthur Marwick, ed., *Class in the Twentieth Century* (New York, 1986), 3.

22. For interpretations of colonial social stratification mostly in terms of social class see Brooke Larson, *Colonialism and Agrarian Transformation in Bolivia: Cochabamba, 1550–1900* (Princeton, 1988); and Alida C. Metcalf, *Family and Frontier in Colonial Brazil: Santana de Parnaíba, 1580–1822* (Berkeley, 1992). On the difficulties of applying the concept of "social class" to the colonial context see Nutini, *Wages of Conquest*, 269–72.

23. Arzans de Orsúa, *Tales of Potosí*, 178, 188, 191.

24. Pérez Sarmiento, ed., *Causas célebres a los precursores*, vol. 1; Pitt-Rivers, "Honor and Social Status," 54–55; Phelan, "The Ceremonial and Political Roles of Cities"; Juan Pedro Viqueira Alban, *Propriety and Permissiveness in Bourbon Mexico* (Wilmington, DE, 1999), 10–15.

25. Felipe de Vergara Azcárate, *Relación genealógica de Felipe de Vergara Azcárate de Avila, Caycedo y Velez, Ladrón de Guevara.—Contiene una serie ordenada de los matrimonios que sus Ascendientes paternos y maternos han celebrado en Indias, desde el tiempo en que vinieron a este Nuevo Reino de Granada sus primeros conquistadores hasta el presente. La escribo para el uso y noticia de mis sobrinos* [1810?], in Julio C. Vergara y Vergara, *Relación genealógica* (Bogotá, 1962), 85–236, esp. 81, 88, 133–34.

26. Socolow, *Bureaucrats of Buenos Aires*, chap. 7, esp. 202–3.

27. See Richard Konetzke, *Colección de documentos para la historia de la formación social de Hispanoamérica, 1493–1810*, 3 vols. (Madrid, 1953); Dewitt S. Chandler, *Social Assistance and Bureaucratic Politics: The Montepíos of Colonial Mexico, 1767–1821* (Albuquerque, 1991), chap. 3, esp. 34, 38; and Socolow, *Bureaucrats of Buenos Aires*, chap. 7.

28. Socolow, *Bureaucrats of Buenos Aires*, 74, 79, 86, 89, 92–93.

29. Jacques Barbier, *Reform and Politics in Bourbon Chile* (Ottawa, 1980); Uribe, "The Lawyers and New Granada's Late Colonial State."

30. Some refer to this as the convertibility of the "power of rank" into the "power of cash." See Peristany and Pitt-Rivers, *Honour and Grace in Anthropology*, 5.

31. See, for instance, Jay Kinsbruner, *Spanish American Independence: Civil War, Revolution, and Underdevelopment* (Albuquerque, 1994); and Françoise-Xavier Guerra, *Modernidad e independencias* (Madrid, 1992).

32. Victor M. Uribe, "Kill All the Lawyers! Lawyers and the Independence Movement in New Granada, 1809–1820," *The Americas* 52, no. 2 (October 1995): 175–210.

33. This period is known in Colombian historiography as the "Patria Boba." In-depth studies of these years are still lacking. See Eduardo Posada, *La Patria Boba* (Bogotá, 1902); Gabriel Jiménez Molinares, *Los mártires de Cartagena de 1816 ante el Consejo de Guerra y ante la historia* (Cartagena, 1947); Julio C. Vergara y Vergara, 2 vols., *Don Antonio de Vergara y Azcárate y sus descendientes* (Madrid, 1952); Manuel Antonio Pombo and José Joaquín Guerra, *Constituciones de Colombia recopiladas y precedidas de una breve reseña histórica*, 3 vols., 3d ed. (Bogotá, 1951 [1892]); and José María Caballero, *Diario de la independencia* (Bogotá, 1974).

34. Other more complex regional disputes, such as those that pitted the Ciudades Confederadas del Valle del Cauca against Popayán and Cartagena and its neighboring cities against Santamarta, are mentioned in Alfonso Zawadzky, *Las Ciudades Confederadas del Valle del Cauca en 1811. Historia, actas, documentos* (n.p., 1943); Jiménez Molinares, *Los mártires de Cartagena*; Hermes Tovar Pinzón, "Guerras de opinión y represión social en Colombia durante la independencia (1810–1820)," *Anuario Colombiano de Historia Social y de la Cultura* 11 (1983): 187–232; and Gustavo Bell Lemus, "Conflictos regionales y centralismo. Una hipótesis sobre las relaciones políticas de la costa caribe con el gobierno central en los primeros años de la república, 1821–1840," in *El caribe colombiano*, ed. Gustavo Bell Lemus (Barranquilla, 1988), 39–48.

35. From as early as September 19, 1810, there had been disputes about the much-feared weight that Bogotá might have in the future government. See Eduardo Posada, *El 20 de Julio. Capítulos sobre la revolución de 1810* (Bogotá, 1914), 243–50. The subsequent conflict between Cundinamarca and the rest of the provinces gave rise to the earliest clusters of political factions. Most of the provincial lawyers lined up with the Provincias Unidas, whereas the lawyers of Cundinamarca (many of them with long bureaucratic careers in the colonial state) were supportive of the Cundinamarca government headed by Antonio Nariño Alvarez and his relatives, particularly his uncle, the lawyer and experienced colonial bureaucrat Manuel Bernardo Alvarez y Casal. See Pombo and Guerra, *Constituciones de Colombia*, 1:193–94 and 2:243.

36. On control by the Prieto Ricaurtes, Sanz de Santamaría Prietos, Vergara Santamarías, and Gutiérrez Vergaras of the mint's treasury office from the mideighteenth century until as late as 1861 see "Sanz de Santamaría," *Boletín de Historia y Antigüedades* (1970): 276–77; A. M. Barriga V., *Historia de la casa de la moneda* (Bogotá, 1969); Julio C. Vergara y V., *Don Antonio de Vergara Azcárate* (Madrid, 1952), 2:17–20, 37–38; José Caicedo y Rojas, *Memorias y apuntamientos* (Bogotá, 1950), 125–26; and Guillermo Hernández de Alba, *Estampas Santafereñas* (Bogotá, 1938), 41–43. For a similar situation in Popayán under the Valencias and Pérez de Arroyos see Gustavo Arboleda, *Diccionario biográfico y genealógico del antiguo Departamento del Cauca* (Bogotá, 1962), 449–50.

37. Uribe, "The Lawyers and New Granada's Late Colonial State"; Jaime Jaramillo Uribe, "Entre bambalinas burocráticas de la revolución Comunera de 1781," *Historia Crítica* 6 (January–June 1992): 99–105. See the career trajectories of Francisco Robledo and Luis Robledo y Alvarez, Nariño's uncle and first cousin, in Mark Burkholder and D. S. Chandler, *From Impotence to Authority: The Spanish Crown and the American Audiencias, 1687–1808* (London, 1977), 201, 226 passim.

38. For the "aristocratic" nature of numerous officers in those armies see José M. Baraya, *Biografías militares o historia militar del país en medio siglo* (Bogotá, 1874).

39. On the late bureaucratic network of the Vergaras see Uribe, "The Lawyers and New Granada's Late Colonial State."

40. For the general's fear of democracy and popular participation see Julio C. Vergara y Vergara, *Don Antonio de Vergara Azcárate y sus descendientes* (Madrid, 1952), 1:274. For a similar situation in postcolonial Mexico see Richard Warren, "Vagrants and Citizens: Politics and the Poor in Mexico City, 1808–1836" (Ph.D. diss., University of Chicago, 1994).

41. Vergara y Vergara, *Don Antonio de Vergara Azcárate*, 1:206–11; 2:53–58 passim.

42. Ibid., 2:52–53. Cartagena native José M. Castillo y Rada, who came from a traditional aristocratic family, accompanied him in the cabinet. Bogotá native Alejandro Osorio, a protégé of the aristocratic Caicedo clan, was another minister. See Eduardo Rodríguez P., *La vida de Castillo y Rada* (Bogotá, 1949); and Venancio Ortíz, "Alejandro Osorio," *Colombia Ilustrada* 4–5 (June 1889): 58–66.

43. Julio C. Vergara y Vergara, *Vida de Estanislao Vergara, 1790–1855* (Bogotá, 1951).

44. Rodríguez P., *Vida de Castillo y Rada*; Vergara y Vergara, *Vida de Estanislao Vergara*, passim.

45. José M. Rivas, *Biografía del ilustre Procer General Rafael Urdaneta* (Maracaibo, 1888).

46. Frank R. Safford, "Aspectos sociales de la política en la Nueva Granada, 1825–1850," in *Aspectos del siglo XIX en Colombia*, ed. Frank R. Safford (Medellín, 1977), 153–99, esp. 171; Fondo Cultural Cafetero, *Aspectos polémicos de la historia colombiana del siglo XIX. Memoria de un seminario* (Bogotá, 1983). The Peruvian case seems somewhat different and political alliances appear to have obeyed conflicting economic interests over free trade. See Paul Gootemberg, *Between Silver and Guano: Commercial Policy and the State in Post-Independence Peru* (Princeton, 1989).

47. Ignacio Gutiérrez Ponce, *Vida de don Ignacio Gutiérrez Vergara y episodios históricos de su tiempo (1806–1877)* (London, 1900), vol. 1, passim; Vergara y Vergara, *Don Antonio de Vergara Azcárate*, 1:227, 237.

48. Frank Safford, well versed in this period and one of the most prominent critics of the "economic interpretations" of Latin American political history, has reiterated that "landowners, merchants and professionals are to be found prominently figuring in almost all political groups." Frank Safford, "Politics, Ideology and Society in Post-Independence Spanish-America," in *Cambridge History of Latin America*, ed. Leslie Bethell (Cambridge, UK, 1985), 3:347–421, esp. 355; and idem, "Acerca de las interpretaciones socioeconómicas de la política en la Colombia del siglo XIX: Variaciones sobre un tema," *Anuario Colombiano de Historia Social y de la Cultura* 13–14 (1985–86): 91–150.

49. Safford, "Acerca de las interpretaciones socioeconómicas de la política."

50. See William M. Reddy, *Money and Liberty in Modern Europe: A Critique of Historical Understanding* (Cambridge, 1987); and Jesús Cruz, "Notability and Revolution: Social Origins of the Political Elite in Liberal Spain, 1800–1853," *Comparative Studies in Society and History* 36, no. 1 (January 1994): 97–121.

51. Benjamin Keen and Mark Wassermann, *A Short History of Latin America* (Boston, 1988), 176.

52. Tulio Halperin Donghi, *The Aftermath of Revolution in Latin America* (New York, 1973), 1–43; idem, *The Contemporary History of Latin America* (Durham, 1993), chaps. 3 and 4.

53. Safford, "Politics, Ideology and Society," esp. 349, 371.

54. Safford, "Aspectos sociales de la política," esp. 189–92; idem, "Bases of Political Alignment in Early Republican Spanish America," in *New Approaches to Latin American History*, ed. Richard Graham and Peter Smith (Austin, TX, 1971), 71–111, esp. 102–11.

55. Safford, "Aspectos sociales de la política," 177, 199.

56. Bendix and Lipset, *Status, Class, and Power* (New York, 1966), 21.

57. Uribe, "The Lawyers and New Granada's Late Colonial State."

58. See José M. Restrepo and Raimundo Rivas, *Genealogías de Santafé de Bogotá* (Bogotá, 1928), passim.

59. Warren, "Vagrants and Citizens." That popular participation in politics was indeed challenging and threatening, not precisely due to the masses' ignorance or lack of sense, is well documented in the pioneering work of Florencia Mallon, *Peasant and Nation: The Making of Postcolonial Mexico and Peru* (Berkeley, 1995).

60. See Hernando Valencia Villa, *Cartas de batalla. Una crítica del constitucionalismo colombiano* (Bogotá, 1987).

61. On the Socorranos' political activism during the late 1820s see David Bushnell, *The Santander Regime in Gran Colombia* (Westport, 1954), passim.

62. See *Congreso de Cúcuta. Libro de Actas* (Bogotá, 1923); and Antonio Nariño, "Defensa del General Antonio Nariño ante el Senado. April 24, 1823," in *El Precursor*, ed. Eduardo Posada (Bogotá, 1903), 551–91.

63. He was ultimately rehabilitated in 1837 and served in judicial positions afterward. Vergara y Vergara, *Vida de Estanislao Vergara*, 325, 328.

64. This phenomenon has been discussed at length in the case of the Mexican and Brazilian aristocracies. See Nutini, *The Wages of Conquest*, esp. 264–67; and Eul-Soo Pang, *In Pursuit of Honor and Glory: Noblemen of the Southern Cross in Nineteenth-Century Brazil* (Tuscaloosa, 1988).

65. García de la Guardia [1806], *Kalendario manual o guía de forasteros* (Bogotá, 1988), passim.

66. On Neiva's colonial economy see Joaquín García Borrero, *Neiva en el siglo XVII* (Bogotá, 1939), 67–72, 137–39, 145–46, 182–83; and Jaramillo Uribe, "La economía del Virreinato (1740–1810)," in *Historia económica de Colombia*, ed. José A. Ocampo (Bogotá, 1987), 49–85, esp. 74.

67. The director cynically argued that the *colegio* included "aun los Pardos y los Lombanas," a pun on the word *pardo* (that is, mestizo)—also a common last name. See Archivo Histórico Nacional de Colombia (henceforth AHN), Anexo, Inst. Pub. vol. 3: 566.

68. See Estanislao Gómez Barrientos, *Don Mariano Ospina y su época* (Medellín, 1913), 1:48; and Emiro Kastos, *Artículos escogidos* (Bogotá, 1972), 154 [1855].

69. His wife, María Antonia Buendía Ortíz, was the daughter of a provincial middling colonial bureaucrat. María Antonia's sister, María Josefa, was married to the equally influential and politically active lawyer José María Céspedes. See Francisco de P. Plazas, *Genealogías de la Provincia de Neiva* (Bogotá, 1985), 113–18; and Restrepo Sáenz, *Gobernadores y próceres de Neiva* (Bogotá, 1941), 182, 301.

70. See Victor M. Uribe, "Educación legal y formación del Estado colombiano durante la transición de la colonia a la República, 1780–1850," in *Etnias, educación y archivos en la historia de Colombia*, ed. Javier Guerro Barón (Tunja, 1997), 179–203.

71. See Ignacio Gutiérrez Vergara to Rufino Cuervo, September 29, 1841, in *Epistolario de Doctor Rufino Cuervo*, ed. Luis A. Cuervo (Bogotá, 1918), 2:120–

23; *Almanaque Nacional 1837* (Bogotá, 1837), 83; Carlos Cuervo Márquez, *Vida de José Ignacio de Márquez* (Bogotá, 1917), 2:82–83; AHN, Inst. Pub., vol. 127, 279, 434; and David Sowell, *The Early Colombian Labor Movement: Artisans and Politics in Bogotá, 1832–1919* (Philadelphia, 1991), chap. 2.

72. *El Día*, January 30, 1842; José A. Plaza, "Memorias Intimas del Historiador Plaza" [1847], *Boletín de Historia y Antigüedades* 23, no. 259–260 (May 1909): 625–56, esp. 649.

73. On Andrés de Iriarte and his nephew, see Guillermo and Alfonso Hernández de Alba, "Galería de hijos insignes del Colegio de San Bartolomé," in *El Colegio de San Bartolomé*, ed. Daniel Restrepo (Bogotá, 1928), 295–96; Burkholder and Chandler, *From Impotence to Authority*, 182; and Plazas, *Genealogías de Neiva*, 326–27.

74. See Gustavo Arboleda, *Historia contemporánea de Colombia desde la disolución de la república de ese nombre hasta la época presente*, 3 vols., 2d ed. (Bogotá, 1933), vol. 1.

75. See the position of lawyers Eladio Manrique and Gaspar Díaz in *El Observador*, April 15, 1840; and Arboleda, *Historia contemporánea*, 1:291–92, 364–65. Along with plebeians Azuero and Romualdo Liévano, Gaspar Díaz had also supported the impeachment of President Márquez in 1837. See Cuervo Márquez, *Vida de José Ignacio de Márquez*, 2:82–83.

76. See Restrepo and Rivas, *Genealogías de Santafé*, 378; Arboleda, *Historia contemporánea*, 1:25, 279; and *La noticia como historia* (Bogotá, 1988), 1:35.

77. Plazas, *Genealogías de Neiva*, 321–22; Próspero Pereira Gamba, "Los conflictos de Bogotá en 1840 y 1841," *Revista Literaria* 48 (April 1894): 530–31; José M. Samper, *Historia de un alma*, 2 vols. (Bogotá, 1946), 1:170.

78. *La Bandera Negra* (October 29, 1837): 23–24; Salvador Camacho Roldán, *Mis memorias* (Bogotá, 1946), 68.

79. Plazas, *Genealogías de Neiva*, 291, 358–60, 580; Restrepo Sáenz, *Gobernadores de Neiva*, 323, 354–55, 496–97.

80. Lombana was removed from the *colegio* and sold his properties to tycoon Judas T. Landínez in 1841. See Ignacio Gutiérrez Vergara to Rufino Cuervo, September 29, 1841, in Cuervo, *Epistolario de Doctor Cuervo*, 2:120–23; *Almanaque Nacional 1837*, 83; Cuervo Márquez, *Vida de José Ignacio de Márquez*, 2:82–83; AHN, Inst. Pub., vol. 127, 279, 434; and Sowell, *Early Colombian Labor Movement*, chap. 2.

81. See May 23, 1837, decree creating the *cantón* of Chaparral in *Codificación nacional de todas las leyes de Colombia desde el año de 1821*, 15 vols. (Bogotá, 1926–1929), 6:325.

82. Restrepo Sáenz, *Gobernadores de Neiva*, 356–57; Plazas, *Genealogías de Neiva*, 175–77.

83. Murillo graduated in 1836, Castilla in 1837. Their contemporary, Patrocinio Cuellar, a modest law student from Chaparral, was initially pro-aristocrat but during the 1840s joined the provincial ranks. See José M. Samper, *Galería nacional de hombres ilustres o notables* (Bogotá, n.d.), 118; Gustavo Otero Muñóz, *Boceto biográfico de cien cancilleres colombianos* (Bogotá, 1942), 185; and Gutiérrez Ponce, *Vida de don Ignacio Gutiérrez Vergara*, 1:492.

84. Samper, *Galería nacional*. See AHN Indexes Notaria 1a, vol. 16, 1842–1848, fol. 42: 15–21; Samper, *Historia de un alma*, 1:165. Natives of other regions, such as student Santos Gutiérrez from Cocuy in the region of Tunja, "pobrísimo y nacido de familia modesta," or José de Obaldía, from a merchant Panamanian family whose modest origins were ridiculed by aristocratic newspa-

pers, were also part of this group. See Samper, *Galería nacional*, 197; and *La Bandera Negra* 26 (April 8, 1838): 310–11.

85. Rafael María Vásquez, "Exposición documentada que R.M.V. hace de su conducta" (1832), Documentos Biblioteca Nacional de Colombia, F. Pineda, 734, 11; Celiano Monge, "El Doctor Rafael María Vásquez," *Boletín de Historia y Antigüedades* 9, no. 108 (April 1915): 718–28, esp. 720; Pereira Gamba, "Los conflictos de Bogotá," *Revista Literaria* 47 (March 1894): esp. 480–81.

86. See *Recopilación de Leyes de la Nueva Granada* (Bogotá, 1845).

87. On the struggles surrounding, for instance, the enfranchisement of the military see Victor M. Uribe, *"Honorable Lives": Lawyers, Family, and Politics in Colombia, 1780–1850* (Pittsburgh, 2000): chaps. 7 and 8. Similar struggles around the so-called political rights of citizenship in nineteenth-century England were long ago pointed out by T. H. Marshall in *Citizenship and Social Class* (Cambridge, UK, 1950) and *Class Citizenship and Social Development* (Garden City, NY, 1965).

88. On the transformation of legal education see Robert Means, *Underdevelopment and the Development of Law. Corporations and Corporation Law in Nineteenth-Century Colombia* (Chapel Hill, 1980); and Uribe, *"Honorable Lives,"* chap. 9.

89. Uribe, *"Honorable Lives,"* chaps. 2 and 4.

90. Cerbeleón Pinzón, *Filosofía moral* (Bogotá, 1840); Juan F. Ortíz, *Reminiscencias* (Bogotá, 1907).

91. José A. Ocampo, "Librecambio y proteccionismo en el siglo XIX," in *Crisis mundial, proteccionismo e industrialización. Ensayos de historia económica de Colombia*, ed. José Ocampo and Santiago Montenegro (Bogotá, 1984).

92. Uribe, *"Honorable Lives,"* chap. 11.

93. Richard Graham, *Patronage and Politics in Nineteenth-Century Brazil* (Stanford, 1990), 6–7.

4

Doing Business in the Age of Revolution
The Major Import-Export Merchants of Chile

Marti Lamar

Marti Lamar, a professor of history at Saint Norbert College in De Pere, Wisconsin, has done extensive research on the merchant community of late colonial Chile. Her findings reveal more continuities than changes in these merchants' lives and economic practices after independence. Lamar focuses on the thirty-three top import-export merchants of the 1795–1823 period, noting their unwavering efforts to diversify trade and other economic endeavors. Their strategies to accomplish this objective including selling a wide range of goods and investing in rural and urban land, agriculture and ranching, and mining. Chile's merchants had behaved this way as early as the 1790s and persisted long after independence. Postcolonial merchants also continued to build networks of agents, assistants, and business partnerships and retained patterns of familial participation in business that were characteristic of the colonial period. Yet, Lamar also finds some major transformations in the merchants' economic behavior. In particular, she notices that some merchants in the postindependence era integrated family and business much less than their counterparts before independence. She also explains that by the early 1820s the colonial generation of top import-export merchants had changed dramatically as its members died, left commerce, or fell into disgrace with the new ruling elite because of their royalist sympathies. Nonetheless, Lamar's essay emphasizes the continuities downplayed in previous academic works, and she concludes that Chilean merchants continued to do business much as they had done before Chile gained its independence from Spain.

Historians conventionally divide Spanish American history since 1492 into colonial and national periods. Until recently, the independence years were often treated as an afterthought to the colonial era, a prelude to the national period, or studied separately. This periodization by political events is convenient for political history, but it obscures historical continuities—not only economic, social, and cultural but also political ones. Moreover, specificity in periodization requires operating at the level of "events" and always implies discontinuity.

This volume on the "Age of Revolution" asks historians to re-examine the conventional periodization of Spanish American history and to identify changes and, especially, continuities during the period 1780–1850. This chapter approaches the subject by looking at one social group in Chile, the elite import-export merchants, and attempts to identify the continuities and changes in their economic lives, particularly their ways of doing business. The principal themes are the economic diversification of the merchants, the opportunities and limitations of Chilean commerce, and the organization and strategies of commercial enterprises. The emphasis is on continuities, not because the changes were not significant but rather because the continuities have been neglected and deserve exploration. From the point of view of the historical actors, change in this era was often dramatic and even personally devastating. But beneath the political drama of independence, economic and social continuities characterized the "middle period" in Chilean history.

This chapter is in large part a study of the major import-export merchants of Chile during the late colonial and independence eras (roughly 1795–1823), and as such is based largely on original research.[1] This study tries, however, to move beyond the chronological framework, which means reliance on a secondary literature rich in political topics but somewhat thin in economic, and especially social, history. More specifically, we lack prosopographical studies of merchants with which to compare the men of 1795–1823. The broader comparisons and conclusions of this chapter are therefore speculative in nature.

Characterization of the Group: The Overseas Merchants of Chile

The core group under study, Chile's top import-export merchants, consists of thirty-three individuals who lived in Santiago (see table). Like elite merchants elsewhere in Spanish America,[2] they came mostly from Spain; twenty-one of the thirty-three were *peninsulares* from northern Spain, nine of them from the Basque provinces.[3] While some immigrant merchants had resided in cities and had been raised in noble families, most had left small towns and belonged to families of modest means. All Chilean-born top merchants were members of families who had already entered the ranks of the elite; therefore, the Chilean-born did not experience the great upward social mobility that the immigrant merchants did. In general, however, the major merchants began their careers with few or modest resources and worked their way to the top of Chilean society.

Chile's Top Merchants, 1795–1819
(In Approximate Order of Their Commercial Activity)

Name	Birthplace
Chopitea, Pedro Nicolás	Vizcaya
Sol, Antonio del	Catalonia
Lazo, Francisco	(Chile)
Undurraga, Manuel María	Vizcaya
Alzérreca, Agustín Antonio	Vizcaya
Bernales, Francisco	Vizcaya
Cruz, Juan Manuel de la	Chile
Izquierdo, Santos	Old Castile
Urmeneta, Tomás Ignacio	Guipúzcoa
Beltrán, Rafael	Old Castile
Valdés, Francisco de Borja	Chile
Riesco, Manuel	León
Fresno, Juan Antonio	Old Castile
Trucios, José de	Chile
Laviña, Juan	France
Cea, Esteban	Old Castile
Andia y Varela, Francisco	Chile
Barrena, José Manuel	Guipúzcoa
Urmeneta, Julian	Guipúzcoa
Landa, Ignacio	Chile
Izquierdo Codes, Francisco	Old Castile
Villota, Celedonio	Old Castile
Castillo Albo, Felipe de	Old Castile
Vicuña, Francisco Ramón	Chile
Arriaran, Lucas	Navarra
Ríos, Francisco Javier	Chile
Ortúzar, Manuel	Chile
Zavalla, José Ramón	Vizcaya
Barros, Diego Antonio	Chile
Reynals, Olaguer	Catalonia
Ortiz, Tomás	unknown
Urmeneta, Juan Bautista	Guipúzcoa
Terán, Miguel	Old Castile

Source: Archivo Nacional, Tribunal del Consulado, vols. 10–21. Parentheses indicate some lack of certainty as to the merchant's birthplace.

Like successful merchants elsewhere in Spanish America, they secured their fortunes with the aid of advantageous marriages, networks of family and associates, and their personal abilities and business savvy. When the political independence of Chile became an issue, the *peninsular* merchants sympathized with the royalist cause, and most Chilean-born merchants with the patriot cause.[4] While all elite merchants suffered the upheavals of war, the royalists paid a particularly high price for being on the losing side when independence was finally achieved. Despite their decline as a group, however, the merchants of postindependence Chile, who were now largely British and Chilean, continued in many ways to do business as merchants had in the late colonial era.

The Merchants and Economic Diversification

At the end of the colonial period, Chile remained a remote outpost of the Spanish empire, isolated by natural boundaries and the Araucanian frontier. In spite of this isolation, external markets exerted the greatest influence on the structure of the colonial economy. After a brief gold-mining cycle, ranching developed in response to Peruvian demands for livestock products; and at the end of the seventeeth century, again in response to Peruvian demands, agricultural production shifted to wheat. Chile experienced substantial growth in the last century of the colony; its population rose significantly, the cultivation and exportation of wheat developed, mining production revived, and, with the opening of the trans-Andean and Cape Horn trade routes, commercial activity increased dramatically.[5] This general economic growth was reflected in higher tax revenues, which were used by the reform-minded governors of the Bourbon era to develop the colony's infrastructure and institutions. Chile received its own general accounting office, mining court, merchants' guild, mint, and university, and road construction significantly improved commercial transportation to Mendoza and Valparaíso. These and other developments increased Chile's self-sufficiency and independence from Peru, adding to a sense of rivalry with its richer, more powerful northern neighbor and a growing sense of Chilean patriotism.[6]

This general growth did not eliminate economic limitations. Historians usually agree that colonial Chile's economic growth was hindered primarily by a lack of markets. Although Chile experienced significant population growth, the internal market was still limited by a relatively small population,[7] much of which lived outside of the money economy; an abundance of natural resources, which facilitated subsistence; and a lack of specie in circulation. At the same time, the external market was extremely limited for the products of faraway Chile.[8] This situation would begin to change around the middle of the nineteenth century, when technological change (steam navigation and the railroad) and foreign demand for its products (nitrates, copper, and, briefly, wheat) brought Chile more fully into the global economy.[9]

In spite of improving economic conditions and opportunities for the elite, no single sector of the eighteenth- and early nineteenth-century economy was dynamic enough or secure enough to support a high degree of individual economic specialization. In any sector, risks and marginal profits encouraged Chilean elites, and merchants specifically, to diversify their economic interests.[10] In their efforts to secure their fortunes and their place in society while minimizing the risks that might be necessary to achieve their goals, the merchants invested not only in commerce but also in real estate, mining, and shipping.

Peruvian demand for Chilean wheat spurred the eighteenth-century reorientation of Chile's economy toward wheat production and export. Internal demand for wheat also grew as the population increased and consumption of wheat spread to all social classes.[11] While livestock products, primarily hides and tallow, fell to a secondary position behind wheat as an export in the eighteenth century and later, ranching was also an expanding sector. The decreased volume of livestock exports may have been offset by population growth and the increased consumption of mutton and beef together with rising prices for mutton, beef, and tallow. Jerked beef also gained some importance as an export.[12] While the eighteenth-century reorientation to wheat is significant in Chilean economic history, the significance of agricultural exports, particularly the wheat trade, should not be exaggerated when examining the country's commerce as a whole and the merchants' participation in it. As will be discussed further, total Chilean exports seldom amounted to even one-half of imports. The wheat trade alone represented about 7 to 12 percent of the total import-export trade.[13]

For the late colonial estate owner, opportunities in agriculture were limited by small markets and transportation costs.[14] Moreover, the agriculturalist faced the usual vagaries of nature as well as the uncertainty stemming from lack of control over the wheat trade itself. With an abundance of wheat and with Peru as the only market, Chilean growers found themselves at the mercy of Lima merchants and shipowners who, with the collusion of the Valparaíso *bodegueros* (warehouse owners), were able to drive down wheat prices in Chile and raise them in Peru.[15] In the last decades of the colony, direct participation of the major merchants as *bodegueros* appears to have been minimal; these men appear to have had closer ties to the established landed families.[16] It is possible that so few merchants invested directly in *bodegas* because there were simply few openings in a relatively small enterprise[17] and because of the host of uncertainties related to the wheat trade and manipulation of the *bodega* system.

Although wheat exports expanded, before the midnineteenth century only the rare individual made his fortune in agriculture.[18] In their efforts to diversify their investments, elites bought rural real estate for both status and profit. In addition to agricultural earnings, the expansion of wheat cultivation meant that land values rose, resulting in capital gains for the owners.[19] Land could be used as collateral for loans, and abundant cheap labor kept costs down for agricultural estates. The emergence of a labor force more closely tied to the estate also meant that landowners could enjoy a leadership role since the services of laborers enhanced the owners' social status.[20]

While the top merchants of 1795–1823 bought land for all of these reasons, some particular characteristics emerge in their pattern of rural landownership.[21] In spite of the shift to wheat cultivation, most large estates, including those belonging to merchants, remained agriculturally diversified. The principal activity of most merchant estates, however, was ranching, which produced meat, hides, tallow, and lesser products for both domestic and overseas markets.[22] Many top merchants owned or rented rural property in the central valley south of the wheat-growing region around Santiago.[23] They may have chosen to invest in livestock ranching in this area for several reasons. With an expanding internal market and rising prices for livestock products, ranching may have seemed a more profitable and secure venture than cereal production. It required less capital investment from merchants eager to expand their economic horizons beyond commerce, and cheaper prices for land in the south may have encouraged investment there.

The Wars of Independence and Chile's war against the Peru-Bolivia confederation in the 1830s disrupted trade, but Peru continued to be the principal market for Chilean agricultural products until midcentury, when the California and Australian gold rushes created a demand for Chilean wheat and fostered, as Arnold Bauer describes it, "the first major development in the export market since the beginning of the Peruvian wheat trade."[24] This boom was followed by Argentine and English demand for grain; foreign competition squelched this overseas demand by about 1880, but the Chilean mining boom then generated increased internal demand for grain.[25] Based on limited evidence, merchants seem to have continued to invest in agricultural properties in the period between independence and midcentury, probably for the reasons outlined above and not because their fortunes were to be made there.[26] For example, José Tomás Ramos Font, one of the most successful and wealthiest postindependence merchants, used the capital accumulated through trade to acquire several small agricultural properties and flour mills in the 1840s.[27]

In addition to investing in agricultural properties, the top merchants of Santiago also put their money into urban real estate. Most of the major merchants owned a residence within a few blocks of the Plaza de Armas, the central square of Santiago, and acquired urban properties that could be rented out or used as collateral. Merchants rented out entire homes as residences, but, even more commonly, they rented out shops or rooms within their residences and other properties to artisans, lodgers, and other merchants.[28] In short, the merchant used his urban real estate, including his residence (which was usually his place of business), to generate rental income. Postindependence merchants apparently continued to invest in urban real estate for similar reasons, although with the rapid growth of the port city of Valparaíso, many more merchants lived and owned property there. However, the wealthiest continued to own homes and other property in Santiago for reasons of prestige and political contacts as well as income.[29]

The revival of mining in eighteenth-century Chile offered another avenue for elites to diversify their economic interests. As in other sectors, in mining the Bourbon reforms gave Chileans institutions that reduced their dependence on Peru and increased their opportunities. The mint was completed, the Tribunal de Minería established, a better supply of mercury assured, and, along with population growth, relocation programs improved the labor situation for the northern mines. After revivals of gold and silver production, copper production increased. Copper exports rose throughout the eighteenth century, reaching 13,000 quintales per year at the end of the 1780s and rising above 20,000 quintales per year in the 1790s and beyond.[30] By the end of the colonial period, Spain had probably displaced Peru as the primary market for Chilean copper, although the Spanish market remained small. Copper, however, was the only export of any value that the Chileans had to offer in the trade with Spain.[31]

Over one-half of major merchants participated in the mining sector in some capacity. Some held mining grants, sat on the Tribunal de Minería, or acted as guarantors for loans to miners.[32] They also financed miners in *compañías*.[33] Manuel Riesco, for example, acted as *habilitador* for Pedro Huidobro's mining ventures from 1809 to 1822. The top merchants frequently engaged in the copper trade and advanced money or commercial goods to the miners, who repaid them with metals. Payment was usually in the form of copper, which the merchants then sold in Peru or Spain.[34] After independence, copper remained one of Chile's principal exports and found new markets in Europe and Asia. Copper production and prices rose steadily from a minimum of 20,000 quintales per year (at 6–8 pesos per quintal) in 1810 to 140,000 quintales at 13–14 pesos in 1840. Merchants, both foreign- and Chilean-born, continued to invest directly and indirectly in copper mining. As in preindependence days, however, their greatest role was as financiers for miners.[35]

When Pedro Nicolás Chopitea, probably the most successful of the merchants of 1795–1823, advanced money and goods to miners, the contracts usually stipulated that he be paid in copper that must be shipped on his frigate, *Dos Amigos*.[36] Chopitea thus avoided shipping charges on his own goods and increased his income on the charges to others. He also was able to stipulate that if the copper was not delivered when *Dos Amigos* arrived in port, he could buy copper at current prices and demand cash repayment from the miner who had failed to deliver as contracted.[37] Under Chopitea's ownership, *Dos Amigos* regularly plied the Pacific coast for at least ten years until it was wrecked during a winter storm in 1816. Chopitea also owned the frigate *Resolución*, which engaged in the Pacific and Atlantic trades.[38] Only a few other top merchants are known to have been shipowners in the period 1795–1823, although other Chileans owned ships that participated in the overseas trade.[39] From the end of the eighteenth century through independence, Chileans expanded their participation in overseas shipping and, as Sergio Villalobos has suggested for the end of the colonial period, demonstrated that the Peruvian shipping monopoly could be broken.[40]

Ship ownership presumably offered the possibility of profits, although it is difficult to show quantitative evidence to that effect. Like Chopitea, talented merchants whose ships sailed without incident for many years probably earned solid profits from their investments. In the case of one frigate, contemporaries estimated that the vessel could earn about 8,000 pesos per year.[41] Shipowners, however, faced the very real possibility that their vessels or cargoes could be lost at sea for a variety of reasons, including natural causes, lack of maintainence and repairs, and seizure during times of war.[42] Merchants probably did not conceive of shipowning as an independent enterprise in and of itself; rather, it was an attractive investment because it increased their chances of profiting on overseas trade.[43] The merchant who owned a ship could enhance the order and security of his business and influence prices and markets. As in Chopitea's case, he could schedule the departure and arrival dates of his ship, thus increasing the independence and efficiency of his trade. Arrival in port at an opportune time could mean the sale of the cargo at higher prices and/or purchase of desired goods at lower prices. Also, the shipowning merchant had the advantage of placing his cargo in the direct care of his own agent, the ship's captain; as with all commercial agents, the captain's ability to carry out his instructions and at the same time to adapt to changing circumstances was crucial to the success of the venture.[44]

With the increase in size and carrying capacity, seagoing vessels could haul more cargo and travel safely year-round.[45] Improvements in land transportation also benefited Chilean commerce. The trail between Santiago and its port, Valparaíso, became accessible to wheeled vehicles in 1797, and the road from Santiago to Mendoza was improved with the building of shelters and its widening and grading (completed in 1791). Overland transportation to Buenos Aires remained a difficult and dangerous enterprise, but with the improvement of the Santiago-Buenos Aires route, commercial goods could arrive more quickly overland than by ship around Cape Horn. Spain's inability to protect its maritime shipping enhanced the popularity of the overland route, which became the preferred means of sending merchandise destined for Buenos Aires and Spain.[46]

The Reconquest forced the closing of the trans-Andean route.[47] The overland trade never recovered after independence, in large part because the opening up of maritime commerce provided cheaper, faster transportation. With Peruvian shipping destroyed during the war and the Chileans faced with stiff foreign competition, the United States and Britain dominated Chilean overseas shipping in the first years of independence.[48] However, merchants such as José Tomás Ramos Font, Felipe Santiago del Solar, Diego Portales, and Francisco Alvarez invested in ships. Although no systematic studies exist to date, it is likely that merchants increased their participation in shipping compared to the colonial era.[49] Ultimately, Chilean merchants may have abandoned shipping, as Ramos Font did in the 1860s, after failing to compete with international firms that could offer cheaper and more efficient service.[50]

The Merchants and Commerce

In spite of the limitations of the colonial Chilean economy, the political, economic, and demographic developments of the eighteenth and early nineteenth centuries stimulated commerce. The significant rise in commercial activity obviously did not mean an end to the problems of markets, the flight of specie, and the difficulties of transportation nor to complaints about various aspects of trade. However, the improving commercial situation offered the intelligent and enterprising merchant opportunities to expand his business and build his fortune.

The best-known Chilean example of a merchant's dramatic rise to economic success may be that of José Ramírez de Saldaña, an immigrant who did not come from the lowest reaches of society but who did begin his commercial career with limited financial resources. He started by exporting agricultural products to Peru and importing sugar to Chile. This "industrious man with a knack for business" expanded his trade within Chile, entered the Platine trade (the provinces of Río de la Plata), and eventually dealt with major Cádiz merchants. Ramírez acquired two valuable haciendas and a house near the Plaza de Armas in Santiago. In addition to obtaining seats on the cabildo, he was appointed first prior of the Consulado. His marriage into the prestigious Velasco Cañas family produced five children, who married into leading families in commerce and government. Ramírez became one of the richest men in Chile; he left an estate of nearly 500,000 pesos at a time when a Chilean worth 100,000 pesos was regarded as truly wealthy.[51]

Although Ramírez attained greater wealth than most men, the trajectory of his career was not unlike that of most successful merchants in the late eighteenth and early nineteenth centuries. Many were young immigrants with little capital or experience who had served on board ships or had come to join relatives already living in Chile. They usually built their businesses on the growing trade in American products, which were less prone to problems of market saturation, while also investing in riskier, but profitable, European manufactures and generally diversifying their economic activities beyond commerce, as described above. With economic success came the opportunity to marry into a prominent family, which in turn could enhance a merchant's business through financial gain and familial ties. In an age of slow, uncertain communication, the merchant needed a network of trusted agents, partners, and other associates to make wise business decisions and have them executed with profitable results.

This eighteenth-century economic expansion put money into the hands of Chilean consumers, particularly the wealthier classes, thus generating a demand for European goods. Demographic growth and a spreading taste for sugar and yerba maté also increased the domestic demand for imports of colonial products. The loosening of commercial restrictions and the addition of new trade routes as well as increased foreign contraband diversified the sources and nature of imports. As trade increased, a wider variety of goods was available to Chilean consumers, often at lower prices. Although the small Chilean market was easily satisfied, merchants in the overseas trade were able to increase the scale of their operations and the scope of their commercial networks, thus profiting from the economic expansion.[52] Spain's wars with England and then the Wars of Independence generated increased uncertainty and dislocations in commerce, but overall the major import-export merchants weathered the storm of disruption and political antagonism with minimal damage to their businesses or wealth. In fact, a fair number of royalists continued their commercial expansion with few setbacks and reached the peak of their activity during the Reconquest. Only with the decisive political moment of independence were these major merchants ruined.

By the end of the eighteenth century, the value of Chile's external trade had risen to about 2 million pesos per year. Of that figure, about 30 percent were in exports. By the 1780s and 1790s, colonial imports surpassed European imports, which now constituted about one-third of the import trade. The erosion of Peruvian dominance in the Chilean trade and the rise of the Platine trade are also reflected in the area of imports. In the 1770s the value of Peruvian imports was nearly double that of imports from the Platine area; in the 1780s and 1790s, however, Peruvian imports declined to slightly over one-half of colonial imports, while products from the Platine area rose to a little under one-half of this figure.[53]

Consulado records suggest that in the first decade of the nineteenth century, exports continued to constitute about one-third of Chile's external trade. Some 15 percent (almost entirely in copper) of the exports went to Spain and the rest to the colonies. Of the

latter, about two-thirds were Chilean products and the rest were re-
exports of American, Spanish, and foreign goods. Colonial products constituted 60 percent of imports, with imports from Spain at
40 percent. The single most valuable category of trade in these years
was the imported agricultural products of the colonies.[54]

The major merchants generally dealt in imported colonial products at one time or another in their careers. Yerba maté from the
Río de la Plata and Peruvian sugar were the preferred American
products for top merchants;[55] in the eighteenth century, Chilean
population growth and changing dietary habits created a growing
market for these goods. Over the course of the century, sugar imports rose from nearly nothing to almost 60,000 *arrobas* per year,[56]
and in the trade with Peru, textile imports fell to second place as
sugar took the lead as the most valuable import commodity.[57] Rising demand and prices in Chile provided merchants with an opportunity to make a steady profit in the sugar trade. It appears that the
opportunities were similar in the case of yerba maté, although the
statistical data for this product are less abundant and reliable. Nevertheless, yerba maté experienced a growing and widespread demand and constituted the most valuable item of the Platine trade.[58]
As seen in the case of José Ramírez de Saldaña, merchants frequently began building their businesses by dealing in American
products. For example, Agustín Antonio Alzérreca, a Basque merchant, began his commercial career in Chile by trading heavily in
yerba maté and sugar. While these and other colonial products never
disappeared from his warehouse, Alzérreca turned increasingly to
the trade in Asian and especially European goods.[59]

Although most merchants dealt in imported colonial products,
the most active and wealthier ones devoted a larger share of their
business to the European trade than did lesser merchants. European goods experienced a growing demand and promised a higher
profit margin, but since the number of Chilean consumers demanding European imports was still relatively limited, merchants had to
guard against specialization within this area of commerce. They
offered a wide variety of European goods to ensure a certain volume of sales. While Pedro Nicolás Chopitea took advantage of opportunities in yerba maté, sugar, and other colonial products,
European goods, also in wide variety, dominated his import business.[60] When Chopitea's business was inventoried in 1817, it included non-European goods, but the majority of items—textiles,
Spanish wine, and iron and steel bars—came from Europe.[61]

In their efforts to secure and build their businesses and pay for their imports, the major wholesale merchants developed their export trade as best they could in a colony with few valuable export commodities. As indicated above, few of the top merchants participated in a significant way in the export of wheat, but they not uncommonly exported livestock products—hides, sheepskins, tallow, and jerked beef—which brought relatively good prices in this era and probably included goods produced on their own haciendas.[62] Chile's top merchants exported substantial amounts of copper, the most valuable export in the trade with Spain. Re-exports of foreign and colonial goods also constituted a part of the top merchants' export business.[63] And although the evidence is slight, these men engaged in occasional transactions in goods that never passed through Chile.[64]

In short, the major import-export merchants of late colonial and independence Chile diversified their interests within the field of commerce, as they had in other types of economic activity. They all bought and sold a wide variety of goods as the opportunities for profit presented themselves. While seeking high profit margins, the merchant at the same time sought the assured sale; since few single trade items fulfilled both aims, the merchant had to diversify in order to guard against the possibility of ruinous transactions and take the risks necessary to build his fortune.

Juan Eduardo Vargas C.'s study of José Tomás Ramos Font, one of nineteenth-century Chile's wealthiest merchants, indicates this continued diversity. In the internal trade, Ramos Font seems to have dealt in everything then imaginable. Overseas, like earlier merchants, he traded heavily in South American products such as yerba maté, rice, cacao, and especially sugar; his reach extended to Peru, Ecuador, Uruguay, Brazil, and later California. Ramos Font's career, however, indicates a certain commercial specialization as compared to earlier Chilean-born merchants. It appears that he had little or no involvement in exporting metals or livestock products; instead, he preferred to export primarily wheat and flour, and he vertically integrated his commerce with investments in milling operations. Moreover, and perhaps more obviously, Ramos Font, although he dealt in the manufactured goods of the industrialized nations, bought these goods through the foreign, especially British, merchants who now dominated the trade with the North Atlantic nations. With independence and the end of Spain's commercial monopoly, the *peninsular* merchants were in effect replaced by the

British (and to a lesser extent, the North Americans, French, and Germans), who had the knowledge, connections, capital, and ships to monopolize the Atlantic trade. Merchants such as Ramos Font, the Chilean-born son of an immigrant, used their experience and networks to build their fortunes in the markets they knew best and which thus offered a better chance of success.[65]

Building the Commercial Business

In an era of uncertain and slow transportation and communications, the merchants of the late colonial and independence period sought out contacts wherever possible and attempted to build a network of reliable business associates and employees. In a commercial world in which each transaction was a discrete deal and the potential for conflict of interest enormous, trusted loyal agents and partners were all the more crucial to success. As indicated, the major merchants diversified their interests, and their businesses were composed of a multitude of separate deals; they sought to buy and sell any item that offered the potential for profit.

One common form of making a business deal was the *compañía*.[66] Sometimes, merchants entered into *compañías* with one another on an equal basis, but more commonly, the senior partner, or *habilitador*, contributed the capital in cash, commercial goods, or a combination of the two. The junior partner, or *habilitado*, contributed a lesser amount (sometimes only his personal efforts) and was usually the administrator of the association. *Compañías* in which the *habilitado* contributed little or no cash or goods usually had a smaller capital investment, and the two partners divided the profits equally. When larger amounts of capital were involved, the profits were more often divided in proportion to the capital invested.

The major import-export merchants sometimes created *compañías* with a small capital investment, often for the sale of goods in Santiago or elsewhere in Chile. For example, Agustín Antonio Alzérreca created a *compañía* primarily for the sale of his yerba maté in the south. He contributed 4,000 pesos in yerba maté and 2,000 pesos in cash, while his junior partner contributed an unspecified amount of commercial goods and went to Concepción to sell the *compañía*'s products. When this successful venture ended in 1808, Alzérreca got back his investment plus one-half of the profits.[67]

Many of the top merchants' *compañías* were constituted with the external trade in mind and often involved larger amounts of capital, the largest usually in the range of 20,000 to 50,000 pesos.[68] Because the stakes were higher, because the Santiago merchants could not know the other markets as well as their own, and because the merchant could not maintain close contact with the partner abroad, the partners in *compañías* for external trade were often relatives who could be trusted to serve the interests of the *compañía* first.

The Solo de Saldívar family provides an example. In 1798, Felipe Solo de Saldívar, a wealthy Castilian-born merchant, formed a *compañía* with his son, José Santiago, who contributed 20,000 pesos, and his new son-in-law, José Ramón Zavalla, a Basque immigrant, who invested 30,000 pesos. Zavalla, who later became prior of the Consulado, administered the *compañía* in Santiago while José Santiago journeyed to Cádiz to handle the European end of the business. This enduring *compañía* was liquidated only after the death of Zavalla in 1810. Felipe Solo de Saldívar, Hijo y Compañía apparently never formalized its association in a public document; it was based instead on the "good faith between fathers and sons."[69] The Solo de Saldívars illustrate the importance of faith and trust, since the partners were not bound to do business exclusively for the *compañía*—which was not always the case in *compañía* contracts. As the agent in Cádiz, José Santiago sought the best possible deals for himself and his partners, but he also served as a commission agent for other Chilean merchants who expected him to serve their interests.[70] Presumably, José Santiago sometimes found himself in circumstances that required him to make choices as to whose interests he would serve. This delicate balancing required him to act judiciously and honorably if he was to maintain the high reputation for honesty and competency that was necessary in the commercial world of the major overseas merchants.

Not all merchants used the *compañía* as a means to conduct business. Indeed, such major merchants as Antonio del Sol, Juan Laviña, and Manuel Riesco seldom formed *compañías*.[71] To build his trade in Spain, Riesco sent his son Miguel there as his agent and *apoderado*, or proxy. In his instructions to his son, Riesco acknowledged that *compañías* had their advantages but that he nevertheless avoided them. He described them as labyrinths that commonly resulted in ill will and litigation, and he preferred the independence and certainty of managing his own funds and taking commissions.[72]

The *compañía* endured as a principal way of doing business throughout the "middle period" in Chile. In the 1830s and 1840s, his years of greatest commercial activity, Ramos Font used numerous *compañías* with various associates to advance his career and build his fortune. His early *compañías* were formed to produce beer and flour, to sell agricultural products, and, most important for his accumulation of capital, to trade abroad in partnership with Francisco Alvarez, then one of Chile's wealthiest merchants. Once established, Ramos Font formed *compañías* largely with junior partners, some of which were used to send the junior partner out to new markets. Ramos Font and his partners began trading in California, as well as financing miners there, in this manner.[73] Although the evidence is limited, it appears that this practice of using *compañías* to enter new markets contrasts with the behavior of the late colonial merchants, who tended to send out goods on consignment.

For the top merchants of Santiago, the most common business association was the relationship with their commission agents. In an era when consignment was still the main way of doing business, the success of a merchant's enterprise depended on his agents. In addition to simply buying and selling, the agent had to seek out new possibilities, know the current fashions, wisely assess the state and direction of the market, and generally keep the merchant well informed about all aspects of trade in the agent's marketplace. Moreover, due to the slowness of transportation and communications, instructions from merchant to agent could seldom be more than guidelines suggesting the ideal transaction while acknowledging the variety of contingencies and limitations. Ultimately, the agent himself often made crucial decisions regarding the nature and conditions of purchases and sales in his marketplace.

The relationship between merchant and agent varied greatly. On the one hand, the agent might be an established businessman in Lima, Buenos Aires, or Cádiz who served the Santiago merchant year after year and became a crucial link in his commercial network. Such an agent would buy requested goods for the Santiago merchant and also send his own wares to be sold in the capital. The agent abroad would also order goods from the Santiago merchant and receive shipments to sell in his marketplace or perhaps to send on to some other destination. The Santiago merchant might occasionally send goods to, or receive them from, a merchant with whom he had no established relationship. These agents were sometimes recommended by a third person and were often located in areas where the merchant had few agents or minor business interests and perhaps intended to expand his trade. At times the merchant appears to have remitted small commissions to untried agents to test their ability to serve him well in the future.[74]

A crucial link in the commercial network of the merchants of the period 1795–1823 was their agents in Mendoza and Valparaíso, the intermediate points in the import-export trade. While sometimes buying and selling for the merchants, the primary responsibility of these agents was to receive, store, and transship the merchants' goods. If they did this job well, the agents maintained the merchandise in good condition, paid the relevant fees and taxes, communicated expeditiously with the merchants, arranged for ships and/or muleteers, and, above all, conveyed the merchandise in the most timely and cheapest way possible. In one example from Mendoza, Juan Miguel García and his son Juan Francisco appear to have been reliable agents for numerous Santiago businessmen, including Juan Manuel de la Cruz, José de Trucios, and Francisco Bernales.[75]

From independence to midcentury, trade continued to be based on consignment and commission agents. The center of Chilean trade shifted to Valparaíso, the trans-Andean route declined in importance, maritime communications improved somewhat, and overseas markets changed. Until the commercial changes of the late nineteenth century, however, merchants in Chile continued to rely on networks of agents and the consignment of goods much as described for the late colonial period. As seen in the career of Ramos Font, merchants' success still had everything to do with their agents' performance.[76]

In addition to the associates mentioned above, the major merchants of the "middle period" needed trustworthy, competent men to work in their trading houses. These employees performed such tasks as keeping the books and handling money, expediting the passage of goods through the customshouse, and supervising the warehouse. At least in the period 1795–1823, it appears that the hierarchy of commercial employees was never very extensive or elaborately developed, presumably due to the relatively small size of the trading houses. Many assistants appear to have accomplished a wide variety of tasks for their employers while developing their own trade. Employees in commercial houses were often young men who wanted to learn the business and hoped to rise in the firm while earning the capital to trade on their own.[77]

While the commercial house served the purpose of teaching young men the business, the merchant needed the best possible employees. From the late colonial merchant's point of view, the best employees-cum-students were members of his own kin network. Merchants felt both that they should assist the young men in their families and that relatives would be particularly loyal and careful in serving their interests. Some of these trainees would go on, of course, to become agents or partners in far-flung commercial networks and perhaps even major merchants themselves.

The networks of the top merchants of 1795–1823 conform in many ways to the patterns of familial participation in business as described in the literature for the period.[78] While the merchants of Santiago allied their businesses with every type of relative, kinship ties through marriage were the most prevalent among the major import-export merchants of Santiago,[79] with the tie between father and son-in-law the most common and especially characteristic of the notable commercial families. Perhaps the most successful such association was that of Celedonio Villota and Pedro Nicolás Chopitea, both wealthy merchants. Chopitea, a Basque immigrant, had already made a substantial fortune when he married one of Villota's daughters in 1800, and the two men prospered as partners until Villota's death in 1816. Villota also married two other daughters to José Mariano Astaburuaga, a Chilean merchant of moderate commercial success, and to Agustín Antonio Alzérreca. While Villota's commercial ties to Alzérreca and especially Astaburuaga were minimal, these sons-in-law surely kept a watchful eye on the prosperity of their wives' families.[80]

Most categories of consanguineous relationships show much weaker links in the commercial setting. Father-son ties in commerce were not common,[81] and, as demonstrated for other areas of colonial Latin America, the sons of major import-export merchants tended to pursue careers in more prestigious occupations such as the law, the military, and the Church. This generalization holds true in late eighteenth- and early nineteenth-century Chile. Brother-brother relationships were also fairly uncommon.[82] Uncle-nephew ties were the exception to the general rule that consanguineous links were weak, but such relationships often overlapped with father-son-in-law relationships. Studies of other Latin American colonies have shown that merchants commonly employed young male relatives, particularly nephews, from Spain and brought them up in the firm with the expectation that the immigrant relative would marry the boss's daughter and thus continue the business.[83] The leading merchants of Santiago frequently relied on uncle-nephew relationships and the participation of Spanish relatives, but the particular case of the immigrant nephew marrying the merchant's daughter pertained to only a few cases.

According to John Rector and Juan Eduardo Vargas C., after independence family members played a diminishing role. While acknowledging that immigrant merchants continued to use marriage and family networks for business purposes, Rector suggests that many foreign-born merchants used friendship and written contracts as the basis for doing business. As compared to previous Spanish immigrants, the new immigrants had superior overseas connections and could escape the limitations of the family as a pool of potential associates.[84] More cautiously, Vargas C. points to a lessening role for family members in business, at least in the enterprises of the Ramos family. José Tomás Ramos Font had various business relationships with family members, but Vargas C. suggests that these relationships were more individualistic and "professional." He argues that the more "bourgeois" Ramos Font occasionally worked with relatives because they could do the job, not because they needed help in entering commerce or advancing their careers.

At the same time, in describing the minimal use of family in the enterprises of Antonio Ramos (José Tomás's father, who emigrated to Chile in the 1790s), Vargas C. implies that this change in attitude toward family in business had already begun in the late colonial era.[85] Antonio Ramos might have been less successful because he failed to utilize family effectively—at least compared to Rafael Beltrán, a wealthy late-colonial merchant with an elaborate kin network whom Rector uses as the contrast to postindependence merchants. Not all of the wealthier men of the earlier group, however, used family in business or believed that bringing *peninsular* relatives to America was a wise move. Manuel Riesco, for example, did not incorporate immigrant relatives into his business or immediate family. He expressed concern that should he bring a *peninsular* to Chile, that person could turn out to be a liability and thus a regrettable expense. When Riesco's son traveled to his father's birthplace in Spain, Riesco advised him to excuse himself from any commitments to relatives who wanted to emigrate and suggested that the best course was to give them alms in compensation.[86]

The major merchants of 1795–1823 built extensive networks of *compañeros*, agents, and assistants whose guiding principle was to buy low and sell high so as to ensure the merchants' financial security. These men could be parsimonious and even stingy in their accounting and finances; they could be cautious and mistrustful with distant and unknown vendors and agents, and they might even engage in deceptive or fraudulent business practices.[87] At the same time, colonial merchants operated according to ethical guidelines that imparted a sense of honor and mannerly constraint to their dealings. One was obliged to adhere to these guidelines to enhance the prospects of success. In other words, sheer acquisitiveness for its own sake and unbridled self-interest not only challenged ethical boundaries but were also bad for business. In a commercial system based on personal relationships, the merchant had to cultivate good-will and develop a sense of mutual trust among his associates, as seen above in the case of the Solo de Saldívars. The use of relatives in business facilitated the development of networks of trustworthy, faithful associates and at the same time satisfied merchants' more altruistic impulses to care for family and friends. While some merchants undoubtedly engaged in unethical business practices, most thought that they needed a reputation as honest, sober, and competent businessmen if they were to develop the networks necessary to rise to the top of the commercial world.[88]

Sergio Villalobos argues that a new "bourgeois" mentality emerged in the first half of the nineteenth century, as economic activity accelerated and foreigners introduced a new dynamism to business. The old colonial ethic valuing honor, sobriety, and prudence did not suddenly disappear, but merchants more intensely sought wealth for its own sake and were willing to subordinate moral considerations to the drive for profits. The nineteenth-century entrepreneur was more audacious and innovative in the pursuit of wealth, and he used that wealth to indulge in a new taste for luxury and a more ostentatious life-style.[89] Vargas C.'s portrait of Ramos Font supports the idea of the development of a new entrepreneurial spirit that encouraged such men to seek profits unrelentingly and to accumulate endless wealth.[90]

Conclusion

During the "middle period," Chile fought a war to shed its colonial status and become an independent state. The significance of this political revolution for the people of the times or for their descendants should not be underestimated, but it might be argued that even in the political arena, Chile experienced less change, or at least less instability, than most other Spanish American colonies. As Jacques Barbier has argued, no "revolution in government" occurred in Bourbon Chile; as its bureaucracy and other institutions were elaborated, political behavior did not change, and the local elite continued to co-opt officials and to exert significant political influence.[91] After the Wars of Independence, the political experiments and instability of the 1820s came to a quick end relative to other Spanish

American nations with the establishment of Diego Portales's government and the authoritarian Constitution of 1833.

Nevertheless, Chile had thrown off Spanish rule, and the fight to achieve that end produced winners and losers. By the early 1820s, the generation of top merchants whose dominance of the import-export trade dated back to before the turn of the century had largely disappeared from the commercial scene. In some cases, death or retreat from commerce in their advanced years explains this disappearance. In the case of many of the royalist merchants, however, their allegiance to Spain contributed heavily to their fall from the top of the business hierarchy. Throughout its colonial history, the Chilean elite successfully co-opted and incorporated upwardly mobile newcomers, such as *peninsular* merchants and bureaucrats, and until 1808 relative harmony characterized the relationship between Creoles and *peninsulares* in Chile. With Napoleon's invasion of Spain and the successive political crises, relations worsened as political lines were drawn and then hardened with each ensuing battle. As Spanish natives with close ties to the homeland and as the beneficiaries of Spain's commercial system, the majority of the top merchants resisted the changes promoted by the revolutionaries. Although suffering some setbacks during the Patria Vieja, the *peninsular* merchants survived fairly well, even enhancing their economic and political status during the Reconquest, until the final achievement of Chilean independence. Contrary to the conventional view, most top merchants did not leave Chile permanently after 1817; nevertheless, sequesters and forced loans took their toll on the fortunes of the royalists. This economic hardship, combined with their political disgrace, generally removed the colonial generation of merchants from the summit of the social order.

With the disappearance of the *peninsular* merchants from the center stage of commerce, Chileans often filled the vacuum in the internal and South American trade. With the demise of the Spanish commercial system, however, they were limited by a lack of knowledge and resources with which to organize the new trade with the North Atlantic powers. John Mayo suggests that following independence, Chileans may have been satisfied with controlling their land and mines and exploring new opportunities in government and internal trade.[92] In essence then, it was the British who replaced the colonial *peninsulares* in the Atlantic trading system. In the wake of the Industrial Revolution, the British needed new sources of raw materials and new markets for their manufactured goods. Although

Chile was never an important factor in British commerce, the country needed the British and their commercial expertise and resources. Besides the addition of new foreign markets and merchants, commerce also changed with improved maritime shipping, the decreased importance of the trans-Andean trade route, and the rapid growth of Valparaíso as a commercial center. After independence, merchants seem to have integrated family and business less and to have developed a more profit-oriented, acquisitive outlook.

In spite of these political and commercial changes, however, in many ways merchants of all nationalities continued to do business much as they had in previous decades. Like immigrants before them, the first British merchants in Chile often came as individuals and hoped to earn their fortunes as agents; those who stayed and were successful joined the ranks of the Chilean elite. All merchants continued to work with the consignment system. Further continuity in commerce may be seen in the organization of commercial houses, in the use of the *compañía* and elaborate networks of agents, and in the diversity of trade. Successful merchants continued to diversify their economic interests and invest in the various sectors of the economy.

Nineteenth-century Chile experienced export-oriented economic growth and integration into the world economy. This process accelerated sharply around midcentury, as demand in the developed nations for Chilean products (wheat, silver, copper, and, later, nitrates) increased and technological changes (steam navigation and the railroad) facilitated export growth. Beginning in 1850, in contrast to the "middle period," Chile maintained a favorable balance of trade. As commerce became more specialized, incorporated companies appeared on the scene, and specialized firms handled shipping, insurance, banking, and so on. British merchants now operated on a much larger scale, and most of them went to Chile as agents for major British trading houses. After 1850, the British increasingly dominated the import-export trade, while Chilean merchants, like Ramos Font, turned their attention to other enterprises.[93]

Notes

1. The principal sources were the records of the Chilean Consulado (established in 1795), the notaries of Santiago (and to a lesser extent, Valparaíso and Talca), merchant correspondence found largely in Fondo Varios and Fondo Salvador de Trucios, and the judicial archives of Santiago; all of these are housed in the Archivo Nacional in Santiago.

2. See, for example, D. A. Brading, *Miners and Merchants in Bourbon Mexico, 1763–1810* (Cambridge: Cambridge University Press, 1971), 104–6; Susan Migden Socolow, *The Merchants of Buenos Aires, 1778–1810: Family and Commerce* (New York: Cambridge University Press, 1978), 17–19; and Catherine Lugar, "Merchants," in *Cities and Society in Colonial Latin America*, eds. Louisa Schell Hoberman and Susan Migden Socolow (Albuquerque: University of New Mexico Press, 1986), 47. Other studies of colonial merchants include Louisa Schell Hoberman, *Mexico's Merchant Elite, 1590–1660: Silver, State, and Society* (Durham: Duke University Press, 1991); Sergio Villalobos R., *El comercio y la crisis colonial: Un mito de la independencia* (Santiago: Universidad de Chile, 1968); John E. Kicza, *Colonial Entrepreneurs: Families and Business in Bourbon Mexico* (Albuquerque: University of New Mexico Press, 1983); Ann Twinam, *Miners, Merchants, and Farmers in Colonial Colombia* (Austin: University of Texas Press, 1982); Jackie R. Booker, *Veracruz Merchants, 1770–1829: A Mercantile Elite in Late Bourbon and Early Independent Mexico* (Boulder: Westview Press, 1993); and Richmond F. Brown, "Profits, Prestige, and Persistence: Juan Fermín de Aycinena and the Spirit of Enterprise in the Kingdom of Guatemala," *Hispanic American Historical Review* (hereafter *HAHR*) 75, no. 3 (August 1995): 405–40.

3. These thirty-three merchants were identified by using reputational and quantitative methods and a wide variety of sources, most importantly the Consulado and notarial archives. Also very useful in identifying merchant origins were Chile's extensive genealogical literature and parish registers. For further details on sources and methods, see Marti Lamar, "The Merchants of Chile, 1795–1823: Family and Business in the Transition from Colony to Nation" (Ph.D. diss., University of Texas at Austin, 1993), esp. 19–36. For a list of the top merchants (in approximate order of their commercial activity) and their geographical origins, see this chapter's table.

4. While the sympathies of some merchants are unclear, this generalization conforms to the pattern of merchant allegiance seen elsewhere in Spanish America. See, for example, Brading, *Miners and Merchants*, 341–47; and Socolow, *The Merchants of Buenos Aires*, 134–35, 176. Sources on the political allegiance of the merchants in Chile include: 1) records of government sequesters of property, including the Contaduría Mayor, 1st series (hereafter CM1st), v. 1149–1157, and the Real Audiencia (hereafter RA), v. 2498, pza. 14; 2) notarial records that show sales of sequestered property, powers-of-attorney granted by merchants going into exile, and *fianzas* for the release of political prisoners; and 3) the secondary literature, which more commonly treats patriot sympathizers. Helpful works include Jaime Eyzaguirre, "La conducta política del grupo dirigente chileno durante la Guerra de Independencia," *Estudios de Historia de las Instituciones Políticas y Sociales* 2 (1967): 227–69; and Raúl Silva Castro, *Asistentes al Cabildo Abierto de 18 de septiembre de 1810*, 2d ed. (Santiago: Academia Chilena de Historia, 1960).

5. Jacques Barbier, *Reform and Politics in Bourbon Chile, 1755–1796* (Ottawa: University of Ottawa Press, 1980), 19–24; Sergio Villalobos R., *Breve historia de Chile* (Santiago: Editorial Universitaria, 1983), 67–70; Hernán Ramírez Necochea, *Antecedentes económicas de la independencia de Chile*, 2d ed. (Santiago: Universidad de Chile, 1967), 51–54.

6. Ramírez Necochea, *Antecedentes*, 53–54; Barbier, *Reform and Politics*, 9–10; Simon Collier, *Ideas and Politics of Chilean Independence, 1808–1833* (Cambridge: Cambridge University Press, 1967), 21–31.

7. Estimates of the Chilean population at the turn of the nineteenth century are generally around 500,000 inhabitants. See, for example, Collier, *Ideas and Politics*, 4; and Marcello Carmagnani, "Colonial Latin American Demography: Growth of Chilean Population, 1700–1830," *Journal of Social History* 1 (1967): 179–91.

8. Villalobos, *El comercio y la crisis*, 182–83; David Hugh Edwards, "Economic Effects of the Intendancy System on Chile: Captain-General Ambrosio O'Higgins as Reformer" (Ph.D. diss., University of Virginia, 1973), 107; Arnold Bauer, *Chilean Rural Society from the Spanish Conquest to 1930* (Cambridge: Cambridge University Press, 1975), 11.

9. See Bauer, *Chilean Rural Society*, 27, 38, 62–74; Juan Eduardo Vargas Cariola, *José Tomás Ramos Font: Una fortuna chilena del siglo XIX* (Santiago: Ediciones Universidad Católica de Chile, 1988), 211–13, 261–62; and John Mayo, *British Merchants and Chilean Development, 1851–1886* (Boulder: Westview Press, 1987), 3, 9.

10. Barbier, *Reform and Politics*, 37, 40–41, 114, 189.

11. Annual exports of wheat to Peru first reached 100,000 fanegas in 1711 and rose to 200,000 fanegas by the end of the century. Armando de Ramón and José Manuel Larraín, *Orígenes de la vida económica chilena, 1659–1808* (Santiago: Centro Estudios Públicos, 1982), 97–99, 105, 111, 287–89; Bauer, *Chilean Rural Society*, 13–14.

12. Ramón and Larraín, *Orígenes de la vida económica*, 78–91, 127, 177, 224, 267; Barbier, *Reform and Politics*, 21–22; Jaime Eyzaguirre, *Historia de Chile* (Santiago: Zig-Zag, 1982), 266.

13. While the volume of the wheat trade increased, wheat prices fell in the eighteenth century to around one peso per fanega; from the 1780s prices rose somewhat but in an erratic fashion. Ramón and Larraín, *Orígenes de la vida económica*, 34, 115–16, 245–46, 287–88; Villalobos, *El comercio y la crisis*, 188, 280–81; Diego Barros Arana, *Páginas escogidas* (Santiago: Editorial Universitaria, 1982. Comp., Alfonso Calderón), 174–75; Brian Loveman, *Chile: The Legacy of Hispanic Capitalism* (New York: Oxford University Press, 1979), 102; Carlos Ugarte, "El cabildo de Santiago y el comercio exterior del reino de Chile durante el siglo XVIII," *Estudios de Historia de las Instituciones Políticas y Sociales* 1 (1966): 5–43.

14. This statement applies not only to Chile but also to many other areas of colonial Spanish America. See, for example, Magnus Morner, "Rural Economy and Society in Spanish South America," in *Colonial Spanish America*, ed. Leslie Bethell (Cambridge: Cambridge University Press, 1987), 286–314; Eric Van Young, *Hacienda and Market in Eighteenth-Century Mexico: The Rural Economy of the Guadalajara Region, 1675–1820* (Berkeley: University of California Press, 1981); and, for a useful historiographical essay on rural estates in Mexico, Eric Van Young, "Mexican Rural History since Chevalier: The Historiography of the Colonial Hacienda," *Latin American Research Review* (hereafter *LARR*) 18, no. 3 (1983): 5–61.

15. For details on this system, see Gabriel Salazar, *Labradores, peones y proletarios: Formación y crisis de la sociedad popular chilena del siglo XIX* (Santiago: Ediciones Sur, 1985), 97–100; Ugarte, "El cabildo de Santiago," 17–21; and Ramón and Larraín, *Orígenes de la vida económica*, 290–93.

16. Salazar, *Labradores, peones*, 98. Juan Manuel de la Cruz appears to have been the only top merchant with significant investment in the *bodegas*. See, for example, Archivo Nacional (hereafter AN), Escribanos de Santiago (hereafter

ES), vol. 948: 223; AN, Notarios de Santiago (hereafter NS), vol. 22: 47; and AN, NS, vol. 36: 334–35.

17. At the beginning of the nineteenth century, Valparaíso was still a tiny port with 4,000 to 5,000 inhabitants and perhaps a dozen *bodegas*. Vargas C., *José Tomás Ramos Font*, 28, 78; Barbier, *Reform and Politics*, 189.

18. Barbier, *Reform and Politics*, 21–22; Bauer, *Chilean Rural Society*, 19–20.

19. Barbier, *Reform and Politics*, 33–34, 40–41; Bauer, *Chilean Rural Society*, 14–16; Eyzaguirre, *Historia de Chile*, 265.

20. Barbier, *Reform and Politics*, 33–34, 114; Bauer, *Chilean Rural Society*, 16. See Bauer's excellent study for an analysis of the evolution of this force of rural workers, called *inquilinos*, from the late colonial period to 1930.

21. Evaluation of merchant land ownership is based mainly on the bills of sale, rental contracts for rural real estate, and estate settlements found in the notarial and judicial archives.

22. See, for example, AN, NS, vol. 14: 613; AN, NS, vol. 22: 16–18, 72–74; AN, NS, vol. 36: 89–92, 109–10, 265; AN, NS, vol. 37: 468; and AN, NS, vol. 52: 402.

23. Merchants in this group include Juan Manuel de la Cruz, Celedonio Villota, Santos Izquierdo, Francisco Bernales, Rafael Beltrán, and Manuel Ortúzar.

24. Bauer, *Chilean Rural Society*, 27, 64.

25. Ibid., 62–73.

26. See, for example, ibid., 29–30, 38, 49–50.

27. Vargas C., *José Tomás Ramos Font*, 86, 129–131. Ramos Font expanded his real estate holdings after 1850 when various agricultural products had better markets.

28. Regarding merchants and urban real estate, see, for example, AN, ES, vol. 906: 204; AN, NS, vol. 4: 384; AN, NS, vol. 10: 356; AN, NS, vol. 15: 120; AN, NS, vol. 2: 267; AN, NS, vol. 23: 705, 972; AN, NS, vol. 30: 141; AN, NS, vol. 32: 618; AN, NS, vol. 36: 371; AN, NS, vol. 42: 16; AN, NS, vol. 52: 275; AN, NS, vol. 53: 364; AN, Judiciales de Santiago (hereafter JS), leg. 947, no. 8; AN, Tribunal del Consulado (hereafter TC), vol. 14: 293; AN, Fondo Varios (hereafter FV), vol. 247, pza. 2; and AN, FV, vol. 697, pza. 39.

29. See, for example, AN, JS, leg. 1110, no. 1; AN, JS, leg. 794, no. 2; AN, Notarios de Valparaíso (hereafter NV), v. 27: 127, 152; Bauer, *Chilean Rural Society*, 29–30; Vargas C., *José Tomás Ramos Font*, 43, 215–16; and John Rector, "Merchants, Trade, and Commercial Policy in Chile, 1810–1840" (Ph.D. diss., Indiana University, 1976), 63–64, 140.

30. Barbier, *Reform and Politics*, 20–22, 36, 114, 158, 191; Edwards, "Economic Effects," 40; Barros Arana, *Páginas escogidas*, 171–72; Eyzaguirre, *Historia de Chile*, 268.

31. Ramírez Necochea, *Antecedentes*, 51–52, 71, 151n.41; AN, TC, vol. 33: 11, 19, 20. In the years 1805–1807, annual exports of copper bar to Spain exceeded 20,000 quintales and constituted 11 to 17 percent of Chilean exports.

32. AN, Tribunal de Minería (hereafter TM), vol. 12, pza. 8; AN, TM, vol. 9, pza. 2; AN, TM, vol. 11; and AN, TM, vol. 8, pza. 4. Top merchants involved included Juan Antonio Fresno, Esteban Cea, Francisco de Borja Valdés, Manuel María Undurraga, Lucas Arriaran, Juan Manuel de la Cruz, Ignacio Landa, Juan Laviña, and Celedonio Villota.

33. See the description below in the context of commerce.

34. AN, JS, leg. 811, nos. 4, 5; and see, for example, AN, TC, vol. 11: 262–66; AN, NS, vol. 30: 50, 356, 371, 387; and AN, NS, vol. 42: 69, 282. In addition to Riesco, top merchants most heavily involved were Antonio del Sol, Agustín Antonio Alzérreca, Juan Manuel de la Cruz, and Pedro Nicolás Chopitea.

35. TM, vol. 11, f. 190; Rector, "Merchants, Trade, and Commercial Policy," 37, 140–41, 153–55, 202–4; Mayo, *British Merchants*, 3, 86–88; and Eduardo Cavieres Figueroa, *Comercio chileno y comerciantes ingleses, 1820–1880: Un ciclo de historia económica* (Valparaíso: Instituto de Historia, Universidad Católica de Valparaíso, 1988), 17, 61–62. See also, especially for the relationship between miners and the state, Steven S. Volk, "Mine Owners, Moneylenders, and the State in Mid-Nineteenth-Century Chile: Transitions and Conflicts," *HAHR* 73, no. 1 (February 1993): 67–98. A quintal was a unit of weight equaling 100 pounds.

36. See, for example, AN, NS, vol. 30: 255; and AN, NS, vol. 42: 75.

37. AN, NS, vol. 30: 80, 255. Other merchants also stipulated that nondelivery would result in cash payment for compensatory purchases at current prices. See, for example, AN, NS, vol. 30: 50. For a typical voyage of *Dos Amigos* involving the northern miners, see AN, TC, vol. 20: 175.

38. AN, NV, vol. 9: 476v; AN, NS, vol. 46: 405v; AN, NS, vol. 52: 17–32.

39. At least thirty-three ships had at least one owner resident in Chile; forty such owners (including twenty-six merchants) had full or part ownership in these thirty-three ships. In addition to Chopitea, top merchants who owned ships included Francisco de Borja Andia y Varela, Rafael Beltrán, Celedonio Villota, and José de Trucios. See, for example, AN, NS, vol. 4: 53; AN, NS, vol. 22: 485; AN, NS, vol. 45: 9; AN, NV, vol. 9: 321–22v; and AN, Fondo José Ignacio Víctor Eyzaguirre (hereafter JIVE), vol. 20, pza. 118.

40. See Villalobos, *El comercio y la crisis*, 213–17. For the view asserting the absence of Chilean shipping, see Barros Arana, *Páginas escogidas*, 175.

41. AN, TC, vol. 8: 103.

42. See, for example, the case of the seizure of Francisco de Borja Andia y Varela's frigate, *Aurora*: AN, JIVE, vol. 20, pza. 118.

43. In the one instance found in which a merchant, Manuel Riesco, discussed his possible acquisition of a frigate, he did not explain exactly why he wanted to invest in a ship. At one point, however, he compared shipowning favorably with commerce in that shipping charges yielded high earnings, and cash earnings at that, whereas commercial goods could suffer from overabundance and have to be sold on credit or at a loss. Riesco later suggested, however, that shipping can suffer from oversupply and thus lack of profitability. (Manuel Riesco), "Instrucciones que da Manuel Riesco a su amado hijo Miguel, que con su bendición pasa a estos Reinos de España a negocios de comercio," *Revista Chilena de Historia y Geografía* (hereafter *RCHG*) 48 (1922): 456–57.

44. See, for example, the instructions given to the captain of the *Amianto* in 1804: AN, TC, vol. 14: 320. For a supporting comment on the general importance of ship captains to business, see (Riesco), "Instrucciones que da Manuel Riesco," 234.

45. Ramírez Necochea, *Antecedentes*, 53; Barros Arana, *Páginas escogidas*, 181. Ramón and Larraín indicate that the average carrying capacity of the ships in the Chile-Callao trade rose from 402 toneladas in 1732–1736 to 492 toneladas in 1797–1801. They also advise caution in using such figures because contemporary observers indicated that ships were often grossly overloaded. Ramón and Larraín, *Orígenes de la vida económica*, 251–52.

46. Ramón and Larraín, *Orígenes de la vida económica*, 303; Edwards, "Economic Effects," 78, 102; Barros Arana, *Páginas escogidas*, 175–80; Eyzaguirre,

Historia de Chile, 277–78; AN, Fondo Claudio Gay (hereafter CG), vol. 18 (27): 3.

47. In Chilean history the period between the *cabildo abierto* of September 18, 1810, and the defeat of the patriots by viceregal forces on October 2, 1814, is referred to as the Patria Vieja. The following period of repressive royalist government, called the Reconquest, ended with the victory of José de San Martín and Bernardo O'Higgins over the royalists at Chacabuco on February 12, 1817.

48. Rector, "Merchants, Trade, and Commercial Policy," 36. Foreigners were technically excluded from the coastal trade, but the law was not always enforced.

49. Ibid., 35–36, 45, 49–51, 69, 138, 140, 149–52; Vargas C., *José Tomás Ramos Font*, 50, 67, 93–94, 128, 135–36.

50. Vargas C., *José Tomás Ramos Font*, 140.

51. Juan Ricardo Couyomdjian, "Los magnates chilenos del siglo XVIII," *RCHG* 136 (1968): 317, 319; Juan Luis Espejo, *Nobiliario de la Capitanía General de Chile* (Santiago: Editorial Andés Bello, 1967), 678; Villalobos, *El comercio y la crisis*, 203–4; AN, RA, vol. 895, pza. 1.

52. Ramón and Larraín, *Orígenes de la vida económica*, 35, 158–62; Barbier, *Reform and Politics*, 23–24; Ramírez Necochea, *Antecedentes*, 53.

53. Barbier, *Reform and Politics*, 79 (according to the figures given, the subtotal for the 1770s and the value of trade for the 1780s are in error); for relatively similar estimates for miscellaneous years, see Loveman, *Chile*, 102, and Ugarte, "El cabildo de Santiago," 78. Apparently due to his inclusion of the last colonial decade, Barros Arana offers a higher general estimate of the value of import-export trade at the end of the colonial era: approximately four million pesos per year. Barros Arana, *Páginas escogidas*, 174.

54. AN, TC, vol. 33: 56, 66, 73, 87. These numbers pertain to legal trade only and should be regarded as no more than indicators of trends. For the entire "middle period," reliable trade statistics are lacking, and quantitative studies vary in their findings. See Mayo, *British Merchants*, 4, 89–90; and Rector, "Merchants, Trade, and Commercial Policy," 170.

55. Conclusions regarding the nature of the major merchants' trade are based largely on inventories, debt records (*obligaciones*) for the sale of goods, and merchant correspondence.

56. One arroba equaled 25 pounds. In *Orígenes de la vida económica*, Ramón and Larraín provide a very useful chapter (pp. 358–78) that discusses weights and measures in colonial Chile.

57. Ramón and Larraín, *Orígenes de la vida económica*, 158–62, 189–91; see also Barros Arana, *Páginas escogidas*, 175.

58. Barros Arana, *Páginas escogidas*, 176. According to Vicuña Mackenna, yerba maté was especially popular with women. Benjamín Vicuña Mackenna, *Historia de Santiago*, vol. 2 (Santiago: Universidad de Chile, 1938), 161–62.

59. See, for example, AN, NS, vol. 4: 18, 98, 218; AN, NS, vol. 15: 95, 267, 371; AN, NS, vol. 30: 55, 229; AN, NS, vol. 46: 213.

60. See, for example, AN, NS, vol. 15: 92, 150, 343; AN, NS, vol. 22: 13, 328; AN, NS, vol. 36: 115, 118; AN, NS, vol. 46: 293. Other examples include Celedonio Villota, Santos Izquierdo, Francisco Izquierdo Codes, Antonio del Sol, José de Trucios, and Juan Manuel de la Cruz.

61. AN, JS, leg. 1550, no. 21.

62. See, for example, AN, Fondo Salvador de Trucios (hereafter FST), vol. 15: 51, 71, 89, 120; AN, FST, vol. 18: 77, 87, 131; AN, NS, vol. 36: 190; AN, JS, leg. 136, no. 8; AN, FV, vol. 660: 98, 104.

63. The correspondence of José de Trucios, for example, shows that sugar, rice, indigo, Castilian and English goods, yerba maté and other non-Chilean products were periodically shipped out of Chile to the surrounding colonies. See, for example, AN, FST, vol. 15: 68, 70, 73, 113; AN, FST, vol. 18: 86. The merchants were also involved in the external slave trade; see Lamar, "The Merchants of Chile," 101–2.

64. See, for example, AN, FST, vol. 18: 70.

65. Vargas C., *José Tomás Ramos Font*, 31, 50–51, 111–31.

66. This was a formal association that after 1795 had to be publicly recorded with a notary. AN, TC, vol. 28: 3v; Vargas C., *José Tomás Ramos Font*, 25.

67. AN, NS, vol. 4: 211–13.

68. Since the merchants of Santiago occasionally formed *compañías* with residents of more important commercial centers such as Buenos Aires, Lima, and Cádiz, it is possible that contracts for more heavily capitalized *compañías* would have been recorded there. Unfortunately, I have not yet been able to do the necessary research in such locations.

69. AN, NS, vol. 35: 26v–27v, 262–65v; Espejo, *Nobiliario*, 881; Church of Jesus Christ of Latter-day Saints Family History Library (hereafter FamHisLib), Archivo de la Parroquia de el Sagrario (hereafter el Sagrario), Santiago de Chile, Matrimonios, 1781–1802, microfilm no. 0774541.

70. See, for example, AN, NS, vol. 22: 31–32; AN, FST, vol. 18: 14, 70, 185, 210.

71. While not all volumes of the notarial records for the period were consulted, the majority were, including all of those of Ignacio Torres, the notary of the Consulado who was used by almost all of the merchants for their commercial transactions. So while some of these top merchants may have had *compañías*, I believe that they could not have been numerous.

72. Villalobos, *El comercio y la crisis*, documento 15: 357; (Riesco), "Instrucciones que da Manuel Riesco," 233.

73. Vargas C., *José Tomás Ramos Font*, 41–52, 85–92, 100, 125–28; see also Mayo, *British Merchants*, 92–97. As regards mining, see Rector, "Merchants, Trade, and Commercial Policy," 202–3; and Cavieres, *Comercio chileno*, 69, 137, 142.

74. See, for example, AN, FST, vol. 15: 73, 96, 113; AN, FV, vol. 660: 17, 26v, 31v, 47v, 50v, 69, 70v, 74v.

75. AN, NS, vol. 15: 129; AN, NS, vol. 22: 64; AN, RA, vol. 895, pza. 1; AN, FV, vol. 671: 16; AN, FV, vol. 244, pza. 13; AN, FST, vol. 15: 59, 64, 68; AN, FST, vol. 18: 113–19, 179, 189, 191.

76. See Vargas C., *José Tomás Ramos Font*, 77, 94–101; see also Mayo, *British Merchants*, 85–126, and Rector, "Merchants, Trade, and Commercial Policy," 193–95.

77. Vargas C., *José Tomás Ramos Font*, 81–96; see, for example, AN, RA, vol. 2834, pza. 11: 173; AN, TC, vols. 12, 17; AN, NS, vol. 36: 84–85; AN, JS, leg. 1550, no. 21; and Virgilio Figueroa, *Diccionario histórico y biográfico de Chile*, vol. 5 (Santiago: Establecimientos Gráficos "Balcells & Co.," 1925–1931), 904.

78. See Socolow, *The Merchants of Buenos Aires*, 21–53; Brading, *Miners and Merchants*, 103–12; and other works cited in note 2 above. On the social, and especially family, history of the merchants of Chile, see Lamar, "The Merchants of Chile," especially chapters 4 and 5; and Marti Lamar, " 'Choosing' Partible Inheritance: Chilean Merchant Families, 1795–1825," *Journal of Social History* 28, no. 1 (Fall 1994): 125–45.

79. This generalization conforms to the pattern found in Socolow's analysis of the merchants of late colonial Buenos Aires. Socolow, *The Merchants of Buenos Aires*, 21–53.

80. AN, JS, leg. 296, no. 3; FamHisLib, el Sagrario, Santiago, Matrimonios, 1781–1802, microfilm no. 0774541; Couyomdjian, "Los magnates chilenos," 318. Brothers-in-law often worked together in the commercial world; this affinal relationship probably ranked third in frequency after father–son-in-law and uncle-nephew ties.

81. Among the top merchants, exceptions to this pattern were Manuel Riesco, Esteban Cea, the Solo de Saldívars mentioned above, and Salvador de Trucios and his son José.

82. A notable exception was the partnership of Chilean-born Nicolás and Juan Manuel de la Cruz. Nicolás emigrated to Spain in 1783 and earned a place among the richest merchants of Cádiz and a title of nobility. He emigrated as the equal partner in a *compañía* with his brother Juan Manuel, and their prosperous commercial relationship lasted until Juan Manuel's death in 1822. AN, NS, vol. 15: 304–6; AN, NS, vol. 49: 377–81; Ricardo Donoso, *El Marqués de Osorno, don Ambrosio Higgins, 1720–1801* (Santiago: Universidad de Chile, 1941), 144–54; Stephen Clissold, *Bernardo O'Higgins and the Independence of Chile* (New York: Frederick A. Praeger, 1968), 55, 67; Villalobos, *El comercio y la crisis*, 205.

83. See, for example, Brading, *Miners and Merchants*, 103–4, 109, 112; and Socolow, *The Merchants of Buenos Aires*, 21, 39.

84. Rector, "Merchants, Trade, and Commercial Policy," 190–92.

85. Vargas C., *José Tomás Ramos Font*, 61–69

86. (Riesco), "Instrucciones que da Manuel Riesco," 451.

87. On questionable business practices, see, for example, AN, FV, vol. 660: 28–28v, 37; AN, FST, vol. 15: 116; Rector, "Merchants, Trade, and Commercial Policy," 182; and Vargas C., *José Tomás Ramos Font*, 169.

88. See Sergio Villalobos, *Origen y ascenso de la burguesía chilena* (Santiago: Editorial Universitaria, 1987). Regarding the colonial ethic, Villalobos's analysis highlights the revealing letter of the merchant Manuel Riesco to his son. This letter expressed Riesco's ethical assumptions about the roles of trust, honesty, and personalism in business as well as his religiosity and concerns as a father and family patron. The letter was published in its entirety in *RCHG* 48 (1922): 434–65, and 49 (1923): 232–41. Although more formulaic and prosaic and less explicit than Riesco's letter, most commercial correspondence suggests the same underlying ethic cum strategy.

89. Villalobos, *Origen y ascenso*, esp. 18–19, 59–63, 105–10.

90. Vargas C., *José Tomás Ramos Font*, esp. 147–48.

91. Jacques Barbier, "Elite and Cadres in Bourbon Chile," *HAHR* 52, no. 3 (August 1972): 417.

92. Mayo, *British Merchants*, 4.

93. Ibid., 1–6; Vargas C., *José Tomás Ramos Font*, 211–13, 261–63; Bauer, *Chilean Rural Society*, 213.

III
Gender and Family Relations

5

Marriage and Family Relations in Mexico during the Transition from Colony to Nation*

Sonya Lipsett-Rivera†

The ideas and expectations held by Mexican men and women of the "marriage bargain" are the central focus of Sonya Lipsett-Rivera's essay. Relying on documents indicative of the Church's official policy toward a proper married life as well as on sixteenth- and seventeenth-century manuals by moralists, late colonial clerical sources, and judicial and administrative records of marital disputes, she notices slow and subtle changes in Mexicans' attitudes toward marriage and family. For instance, the inclusion of children in divorce petitions, which became disputes over the conduct of wives or husbands as spouses as much as parents, was a new phenomenon, as was an emphasis on the education and upbringing of children. This shift corresponded to the increasing focus on female education in the late eighteenth century. The rights of fathers and husbands diminished in importance at the same time that those of wives and children were gaining more prominence. For example, women who filed for divorce or alleged mistreatment ceased to be consigned to ("deposited in") institutions such as convents and hospices. However, changes in the marriage bargain were slow at best. Like Elizabeth Anne Kuznesof in chapter 6, Lipsett-Rivera here finds that women gained some autonomy, but she notes that marriage continued to be less equitable for wives than for husbands.

Lipsett-Rivera is the author of several essays on the gender history of late colonial Mexico and is co-editor of a recent anthology on the meaning of honor in colonial Latin America. She

*Research for this essay was made possible by a generous grant from the Social Sciences and Humanities Research Council of Canada.

†I would like to thank Richard Boyer, Jeffrey Pilcher, and Sergio Rivera Ayala for their comments.

teaches Latin American history at Carleton University in Ottawa, Canada.

When nineteenth-century Mexicans married, they entered into a union governed by centuries of tradition. The expectations brought by couples to their wedding influenced the way they behaved and their complaints about their subsequent married life. These ideas were deeply rooted within Mexican culture and were the product of centuries of social construction. The Spanish tradition, as expressed by clerics and commentators in guides to proper conduct, provided a model for marriage that was reciprocal but hierarchical. In reality, of course, many couples did not correspond to the ideal. Tensions arose when a husband could not fulfill the duties assigned to him as the head of the family. When wives earned more than their spouses or when fathers-in-law rather than husbands supported the couple, the balance of reciprocal duties and obligations was upset as well as the hierarchy of marriage. In such situations both husbands and wives struggled to reassert this balance.

During the period under study, transformations within Mexican society as a result of the Bourbon reforms and then independence meant a slow change in the model for marriages. These modifications were subtle, but it is clear that by the middle of the nineteenth century Mexican elites, at least, had begun to reshape their model for marriage and family relations. Political events such as the Wars of Independence did not alter the problems that afflicted the majority of couples who appear in the documentation, nor did the governing elites try to change the legal codes that governed marriage and family in the early nineteenth century.[1] By looking at documents that touch upon marital problems from 1750 to 1856, however, it is possible to discern not only continuities but also some slow changes in the beliefs that governed Mexican marriages and the social practices of the day.[2] This essay examines the ways in which Mexican men and women understood the "marriage bargain"—that is, how a couple was supposed to behave in the ideal—and the reality that emerges in their complaints.

Two main sets of sources form the basis of this study. First, ecclesiastical documents provide the basis for official pronouncements on the proper modalities of married life. These documents include manuals written by Spanish moralists in the sixteenth and seventeenth centuries as well as Mexican clerical sources for the later part of the colonial period. These writings provide a starting point for this discussion of the "marriage bargain," since they were the foundation for the societal expectations that were implanted in Mexico through the Conquest and lasted into the coming centuries. Much of the language and the ideas expressed by the moralists were still very much present in eighteenth- and nineteenth-century petitions, and some scholars might argue that faint echoes of their ideas still pervade present-day Mexican society. A second source for this study are 89 complaints of spousal abuse (*malos tratos*) and 125 suits for ecclesiastical divorce. The latter documents provide a counterpoint of the ideal presented in cases of *malos tratos*.[3] In these complaints, women or men requested official intervention to correct offensive behavior on the part of their spouse, whereas in the divorce papers, men and women asked for separation. Although ecclesiastical divorce did not dissolve the marriage, the couple could live apart, usually with the woman in seclusion but supported by a pension from her husband.[4]

Both types of documents deal with troubled marriages, but their usefulness as sources goes beyond the information that they provide about the patterns of conflicts. In these documents, men and women explained why they were disappointed with their partner and, in effect, revealed their expectations. These two sources also reflect class differences, since women of modest means were more likely to have recourse to *malos tratos* than to sue for divorce. One disadvantage is that the documents are skewed temporally; although an effort was made to locate any and all relevant documents from 1750 to 1856, the actual cases are clumped in certain periods and even years. The sample of *malos tratos* is more complete for the first half of the time frame, whereas more divorce cases are available for the latter half. These concentrations of cases are unfortunate, but since both sets of sources deal with marital problems, they complement each other and cover the period in question.

Models for Marriage

The moralists represented the act of marriage as a fusion of bodies; it was literally the joining of two fleshes.[5] Much as the Church and political structures were portrayed as bodies, so too were couples.[6] The model for marriage was expressed as a bodily metaphor: the husband was the head and the wife a limb. The man was clearly the spouse with greater authority, moral stature, and preeminence. Yet the moralists reminded husbands that the head depended upon the limbs just as the husband needed his wife. As such, the head and limbs were interdependent even while greater authority was vested in the head/husband. Men and women had reciprocal rights and obligations within marriage, but husbands had greater authority.

The Spanish legal doctrine of *patria potestad* confirmed the father's dominant position within the family. It apportioned authority over children to the father and only allowed the mother limited powers. Mothers were expected to provide nourishment for their babies until weaning but had few rights commensurate with their obligations beyond that stage.[7] The actual authority that a husband had over a wife is less clear in some areas. Although a father or a master had the prerogative to correct and discipline his children, servants, or slaves, he could not legally correct and discipline his wife. Nonetheless, husbands held certain legal rights over their wives.[8] As Silvia Arrom states, in compensation for his "support, protection, and guidance" a husband held authority over nearly all aspects of his wife's life. A married woman needed her spouse's consent for "legal transactions, property, and earnings, and even her domestic activities."[9]

Although civil law gave husbands specific rights and society conferred even more prerogatives to the husband, canon law as well as Church teachings emphasized the reciprocal and equal nature of the bond of marriage.[10] In his *Manual de administrar los santos sacramentos*, Fray Angel Serra emphasized that a woman did not enter into marriage to become her husband's unpaid servant: the wife became only a "spiritual wife and companion" and not a "slave, nor servant."[11] The nineteenth-century wedding ceremony warned the bridegroom that "we are not giving you a slave, rather a woman."[12] This standard was reiterated and evoked by women and their representatives, although the idea of marriage expressed in wedding vows often contrasted with the treatment that many women could expect. An attorney representing a woman seeking divorce restated this principle to emphasize the divergence between the ideal and reality: on the day of the wedding, "he [her husband] hit her just after swearing to treat her as a sweet companion and not as a slave."[13]

These vows, although part of a rite, were used as a very real standard from which to judge the marriage. When wives complained that they were treated like servants or slaves, they used language that evoked the marriage sacrament and that was designed to gain a hearing. Josefa Mayorga, a *molendera* (domestic servant/cook) from Huayacocotla, stated that "during the period that I have been married, I have lived like a captive or the most wretched slave." María Rosa Ximénes described life with her husband as worse than life in prison or slavery.[14] In most plebeian marriages, the new bride came to live in the house of her in-laws and worked under the supervision of her mother-in-law.[15] Some women, such as Luisa Ayala, complained that this period of service was really one of servitude: "he made me his servant and that of his family."[16] Instead of being part of a new family, these wives were treated like servants, contrary to the ideal of marriage.

The moralists' model was an ideal, but one that influenced Mexicans' marriage. It provided women and their lawyers with a language that they could employ to indicate exactly why their conditions were unacceptable. As such, the model—while a mostly unattainable ideal—provided a framework and a measuring rod for real marriages. Many of these ideas as well as the language of reciprocity did not change after independence.

The Marriage Bargain I: Duties of the Husband

Commentators went further in elaborating what men and women could and should expect after their wedding. Marriage was a type of bargain in which both partners had reciprocal obligations. Men, first of all, were expected to maintain their wife and children according to their rank and possibilities. Spanish moralist Pedro Galindo noted that it was a mortal sin to deny wives food and the necessary clothing.[17] This responsibility, according to the moralists, came naturally to husbands. By virtue of the wedding ceremony, they argued, "now you are not two: but rather one flesh." Because of this union, the moralists added, "just as you are obligated to maintain your own body, you must maintain your wife, you are obligated to work for her . . . you must give her food and drink and clothing, and all that is necessary to maintain her person"; otherwise, they implied, the deprived wife might be forced into sin or betrayal.[18]

Mexican husbands, by and large, accepted the fact that material provisions were their obligation. If they fulfilled this part of the bargain, then they believed that they had acquitted themselves quite well. Defending himself against charges of adultery, Leonardo Rafael, an Indian of Calimaya, countered, "I give her all that is expected in food and clothing without failing my obligation." Juan Antonio de Zepeda, a *castizo*, said much the same, explaining that his wife had no reason to complain: "As a decent man I sought to provide and assist her with all that I have been able to acquire from my own work."[19] Women of all classes also stated that the "laws of

Holy Matrimony" obligated their husbands to support them. The general understanding of the fundamental role of husbands to provide for their families crossed race, culture, and class and to some extent excused husbands from other peccadillos as long as this central function was respected.[20]

The financial support provided by husbands was called the *diario*, *los alimentos*, or *lo preciso*—a sum of money considered by wives to be the minimum with which to run the household. The amount varied according to the number of persons in the household, how many meals were served, and the relative luxury of these meals, as well as other factors. The actual sum mentioned most often in the documents was two *reales* daily, although in one case one peso per day supplied food for a household.[21] One wife complained that her husband "had the cheeky pretension to expect me to provide good and abundant food for seven persons and a horse on nine pesos weekly."[22] Either as a part of this *diario* or in addition to it, wives expected their husbands to pay for clothes and sometimes shoes for them and their children. Many wives complained that their husbands did not give them clothes or, even worse, took away their clothes to pawn them.[23] It was understood that the husband would have some source of income, but a sizeable group of husbands had no profession or means of support. Indeed, many bridegrooms gambled and drank away their wives' dowries.[24]

The most common grievance of Mexican women who lodged complaints was that their husbands did not give them enough money to feed themselves and their children or provide them with clothes. Lack of *lo preciso* was mentioned in 47 of the 100 divorce petitions, and in 37 of the 78 complaints of *malos tratos* presented by women. Arrom found lack of financial support in 39 percent of her sample.[25] During work-related absences, many husbands—muleteers and soldiers, for example—left no money at home and expected their wives to subsist.[26] No doubt, some husbands did not maintain their families simply because they lacked the funds, but a corollary to wives' laments about support was that their husbands spent all their cash on gambling, drink, and, at times, their mistresses. This financial burden caused considerable tension within couples, as wives were forced to depend on their extended family or sometimes even on their neighbors.[27] Men sometimes dissipated what little was available in the household by pawning clothes and taking their wives' meagre earnings from charity.[28] Some men also expected a greater female contribution to the family income. In three cases, husbands suggested that their wives prostitute themselves.[29]

Antonio Estrada actually left his wife as a *prenda*, or guarantee, against a loan at the *pulquería*.[30]

Although Mexicans believed that the man was primarily responsible for earning money outside the home, many women were involved in work beyond the household. Many had to leave their homes to perform tasks necessary to the domestic economy, but work outside the home was not limited to these duties. In divorce and *malos tratos* petitions, twenty-five women declared that they either had work or wanted employment to distance themselves from their abusive husbands. They supported themselves and their families independent of male or extended family backing, or they wished to do so. The occupations mentioned vary: weaving *paños* (cloth), making cheese, running errands, cleaning, working in the cigar factory, laundering, employment as a *molendera*, *atolera* (maker of the drink *atole*), servant, or *portera* (supervisor of a building), selling various foodstuffs and supplies, darning stockings, and running a school for girls.[31] Over the course of the period, the number of working women represented in the sample grew.

This change was related to alterations in the prevailing ideas about women and work. As Arrom notes, starting in the late eighteenth century, intellectual currents and even royal policy encouraged changes in guild laws and other employments so that women could become active members of new professions.[32] Writers such as José Joaquín Fernández de Lizardi bolstered the idea of female professionals in his novel *La Quijotita y su prima*,[33] and the topic was debated in newspapers.

Women who could not support themselves and their children independently of their husbands counted on their parents and extended family to survive. In 22 out of 78 female-initiated cases of *malos tratos*, women stated that they and their children would have starved without the support of their extended family. The abrogation of the principal duty of husbands at times meant tension within these families. In particular, husbands resented those who stepped in as providers, since in a sense this was proof of their own incapacity. Many husbands considered their in-laws' assistance as interference and reacted with hostility to what they considered a nefarious attempt to subvert their authority. Wives often wondered at the lack of gratitude displayed by their husbands when their parents provided needed food for the household. Juana Aguirre, for example, complained that her husband had not supported her or their four children during the eleven years since she had married him. Instead, her father provided clothes and food for the family.

Rather than thanking his father-in-law, José, Juana's husband, was disrespectful and threatened to kill him.[34] Husbands seem to have interpreted outside assistance as interference and as a plot to undermine their power within the household.

Colonial officials often upheld the requirement that husbands support their families materially, but they could not or did not enforce it. After independence, legal grounds to compel delinquent husbands to turn over their salaries were considered—at least in the army. Soldiers who were separated from their wives could not avoid supporting their families; the army took one-third of their pay and gave it to their wives.[35] This practice differs from the colonial period, when many husbands ignored the requirement that they pay a stipend to their wives when separated. Although this procedure only benefited the wives of military men, it signaled a change in Mexican attitudes toward the family. No longer were husbands depended upon to do the proper thing; the rights of wives and their children began to be recognized in legal doctrines.

The ideal man went out to work, gave his wife an adequate *diario*, and bought clothes and shoes for his family. Real life was not so simple, and many men could not earn enough to carry out these functions adequately. Others were addicted to drink and gambling, and still others simply chose not to support their families. In such cases, husbands did not fulfill their duties within the marriage bargain. By not doing so, they also lost some of their claim to authority and hierarchy. Such problems were not new to this period. What changed after independence was a recognition by military authorities of the need to respond to the problems caused by family deprivation.

The Marriage Bargain II: Duties of the Wife

While men were ideally responsible for work outside the home and for the financial support of the household, women were accountable for the domestic economy. Managing the members of the family and extended family, including servants, was the realm of wives. They were to supervise food preparation, the education of children, and the orderly functioning of all other aspects of the household.[36] Even wealthy women who had servants to do most domestic tasks were supposed to keep busy; in free moments, the moralists advised that they should either weave and spin or occupy themselves in prayer.[37] Husbands could expect their wives to "take much care of the cleanliness of their house, children and family; and serve their husband in his clothes and food."[38] Francisco de la Cruz, an *alcalde* of the *barrio de naturales*, used this language of reciprocity to describe what he considered a good marriage between two *indios*: "They showed respect to one another, and they got along very well; as their neighbor I never saw them fight or mistreat each other; and he gave his wife whatever he earned for their food, and she kept a good house and clean clothes for him within the possibilities of their class."[39] In rural households, wives usually carried the midday meal to the fields where their husbands were working.[40] Yet some husbands expected their wives to accomplish all these tasks without fulfilling their own role as provider. Some refused to give money to their wives despite their own relative wealth;[41] and they complained violently when they did not come home to a complete meal, even though they gave their wives no money.[42] Francisco Javier, for example, complained that his wife refused to cook for him, although he gave her neither money nor ingredients.[43]

In the twenty-five cases in which men petitioned for divorce, six husbands referred to the abandonment of feminine duties by wives. The dereliction of domestic tasks was often mentioned as a justification for violence against women. These men protested the absence of their wives, complaining that they were then forced to eat with strangers and have outsiders wash and mend their clothes.[44] One husband criticized his wife for her lack of solicitude toward his household and her refusal to render "those courtesies and services which correspond to a consort"; another described these as "the obligations which are imposed by the laws of Matrimony."[45] When Juan Antonio de Zepeda returned home from his job as a cook, his wife would not even prepare him a cup of chocolate.[46] The most obvious route for a wife to signal her rebellion against the duties imposed upon her by marriage was to leave, but many women simply refused to do their household tasks. María Josefa Martínez actually demanded money from her husband before she would cook meals or wash clothes.[47] Husbands and wives had reciprocal duties, and when one-half of the couple did not discharge them, the household was strained. The role of women in food preparation was particularly vital in the countryside, where the grinding of corn for tortillas was time consuming and onerous.[48] If a man did not have someone to do this work, he would be seriously prejudiced. In Mexico City, the poor who lived in tenements often did not have cooking facilities and ate prepared food, so this shirking of feminine duties might not have been as serious.

Husbands who provided for their wives expected submission and obedience in return. In reality, the hierarchy was not so clear. Men derived their authority from the fulfillment of their side of the marriage bargain. When women lodged complaints of *malos tratos*, men often defended their public reputation as husbands by stating that they took care of their wives. But women believed that the bargain could also work the other way; by letting down their side of it, husbands lost authority—they were no longer the head of the family. Doña Luisa Ayala expressed the correlation between support and authority when she complained that her husband did not give her any money: "What is the authority of a husband who does not maintain his wife? Where there is no food there is no obedience."[49]

When Mexican women had a separate income, the potential independence that their earnings gave them upset the balance. As mentioned earlier, in the analogy so often applied to marriage, the husband was the head and the wife a limb. What happened when the limb became independent of the head, thus subverting the normal order of things and inverting the ideal prototype? Husbands frequently reacted by disrupting their wives' workplaces, demanding their wages, and generally making it difficult for them to continue on the job. Such men continually interfered with women's employment; they stormed into the houses where their wives were servants, took the raw materials or the profits of their businesses, or stole from the buildings where they worked as *porteras*.

Some women who applied for divorce did not ask for a pension, but only for the liberty to earn a living without the interference of their husbands.[50] Josefa Mayorga stated that she did not want her husband to support her or their son; instead, she asked "only that he would set me free because I am confident that I can maintain myself honestly and with decorum."[51] Other women eventually abandoned their businesses or jobs because of this continual sabotage and then asked for a pension from the very spouse who had made their independence impossible. Women's jobs or businesses were a direct threat to the identity of husbands as providers and heads of households. These men could only regain their role by undermining their wives' earning capacity.

Solutions for Marital Breakdown

In an ideal marriage, both men and women understood their duties and obligations and performed them without acrimony or difficulty.

In reality, however, many partners were less than ideal and did not live up to the model presented in guides and sermons and accepted by Mexican society. Clerics proposed several methods to correct such spouses. Although the common assumption was that wives were more in need of correction, both spouses had the right to correct each other. The moralists instructed wives to advise their husbands to cease drinking, gambling, blaspheming, or overspending, but to do it gently, with patience, "without showing arrogance, without raising their voices, in order not to call attention in public."[52] In turn, wives who reprimanded their husbands were expected to conform to a high standard of morality and proper conduct.[53] The same respect was to be accorded to wives by their husbands, who were also expected to avoid humiliating their spouses in front of servants and family members. The difference was that although the husband was exhorted to correct his wife with loving words, it was understood that these words would escalate to punishment if necessary.[54] In his guide to a proper confession, Pedro Galindo assured husbands that they were allowed to "correct and punish them [their wives] with moderation, but must not wound or insult them seriously, because this is not allowed even for serfs or slaves."[55] In contrast, moral authorities advised wives not to strike their husbands except in self-defense. However, when women tried to defend themselves, husbands regularly justified abuse and even murder.[56]

Although many wives may have chided their husbands in private or in public, the notion that this was their reciprocal right within marriage was far from universally accepted. The experience of doña María Sosa was typical. When she told her husband that he should fulfill the obligations that marriage imposed upon him, he beat her so severely that she returned to her father's house and petitioned for divorce.[57] More often than not, men found any attempts by wives to chasten their husbands gently or otherwise as aberrant and improper. When Francisco Gerónimo killed his wife, for example, his *curador* excoriated the dead woman as "a provocative woman who herself sought her fate by wishing to provoke and irritate her husband on purpose."[58] She had asked her husband to moderate his conduct and to stop scolding a servant. In another case, José Tomás Mendoza killed his wife for trying to prevent him from beating his children. His defender explained his actions in these words: "What more legitimate motive could there be for my client who, being beaten by his wife who by all rights should be subordinate to him, was aggravated to this extent?"[59]

Marital problems were not at all uncommon, particularly when the marriage bargain broke down. The onus for repairs was most often placed on the wife. Juan de la Cerda recommended a twofold strategy; first, in the case of discord among spouses, the wife should pray continuously and ask God to revive the love in her husband's heart. Second, if the wife had provoked a fight, she should wait until her husband had calmed down and then apologize "with humility."[60] Fray Francisco de Osuna recommended that when husbands became angry, wives should say to them, "Please, sir, do not continue for the love of the One God: I would not want to hurt you any more than I would my own eyes."[61] Wives were expected to tame their spouses with honeyed words but especially to reiterate their submission and docility. If they did so, then they could expect reciprocal respect from their partners.

Women who petitioned for divorce and *malos tratos* were particularly at pains to emphasize their submission and docility. Their words often seem to echo the moralists' prescriptions: doña Ana María Santillán spoke of her "affection and love . . . my silence despite his major offenses"; doña Rosa Vásquez testified that despite a long-term pattern of abuse she chose to "keep silent, and with prudence give him counsels"; doña Mariana Peñas stated that "my sufferings have been without effect; reluctantly I must admit that neither my counsels nor my supplications nor my tears have been sufficient to regulate the bad conduct of my husband."[62] Did these women simply use the language expected of them, or had they really tried to live according to the models presented to them in the canons of marriage literature?

If these tactics did not succeed, the good wife could avail herself of outside assistance, but only without publicizing the marital discord. The moralists enjoined wives to approach their in-laws and ask for intervention with their husbands. The judicial documents show the inverse of this tactic; wives overwhelmingly approached their own families. The next step was to request the help of the husband's confessor, who might solicit an admission of abuse and impose a suitable penance. Finally, the wife could appeal to a priest, who could subtly shame the abusive spouse by including a reprimand in the Sunday sermon.[63] These recommendations avoided the shame of a public airing of problems and thus, in practical terms, were only applicable to elite wives whose houses afforded some modicum of privacy. If these recommendations did not resolve the discord in a marriage, wives could—as a last resort—appeal for protection to a judge or civil official.[64] Poor Mexican women were more likely to use this strategy, but even before their problems had reached such an impasse they were more likely to involve their neighbors and family. In fact, neighbors and family were vital to abused women, for whom they represented the greatest hope for prompt intervention. Upper-class women sometimes sought a moral adviser for their husbands, but lower-class women regularly secured a *fiador*, or guarantor, to ensure the good behavior of their husbands when they emerged from imprisonment for abuse.

Husbands were also enjoined to correct their wives in a civil manner and in private, but clearly, it was legitimate for husbands to resort to violence. In fact, Osuna proposed (although principally to lower-class couples) "a pair of punches to straighten her out." In the privacy of the home, he continued, "give her half or a dozen lashes with your belt until you dominate her."[65] Societal norms generally approved of male violence against wives, within certain limits. In his study of seventeenth-century marriages, Richard Boyer finds that women themselves tolerated considerable violence.[66] A much smaller number of women resorted to violence themselves. In seven of the twenty-five divorce petitions launched by men, husbands accused their wives of violence; the women scratched, hit, and even threatened to kill their husbands. Josef de Roxas, in his petition, reported that his wife became angry when he tried to discipline his daughter. She insulted him and chased him out of their residence; in the street, she and her friend pulled down his pants and grabbed his *partes*.[67] Despite these exceptions, most Mexicans of all classes and ethnicities seem to have accepted the fact that, within the marriage bargain, husbands had a monopoly on violence. Although many wives and their relatives complained about excesses of violence, the inherent right of men to correct their wives was not challenged.

Although the marital complaints of Mexican women fell into broadly the same categories, their timing varied. The majority lodged a complaint of *malos tratos* or ecclesiastical divorce within the first five years of marriage, but variations according to class are evident in the strategies adopted by these women. Those with the honorific *doña* were more likely to present their case for an ecclesiastical divorce than to protest *malos tratos*. This divergence was probably based on financial considerations, since lower-class rural women were less likely to be able to afford lengthy and expensive divorce proceedings. After 1808, judicial fees were waived and ecclesiastical courts appointed attorneys for women. As a result, Arrom finds a more balanced breakdown of class representation in the divorce petitions from 1808 to 1857.[68] But beyond the actual legal process, the final outcome of the divorce would not make sense for women whose husbands did not support them, unless they had an ally in their family. The actual purpose of the divorce was to deposit the wife in a convent or other suitable place to be supported by a pension paid by the husband.

In a few cases, women divorced only to find that their spouses were not willing to pay enough to place them in a decent situation; their only recourse was to agree to a reconciliation or to get their fathers to pay. This solution must surely have seemed ludicrous to the many women whose major complaint was that their husband did not support them when they actually lived together. The divorce petition of *molendera* Josefa Mayorga points to this distinction; she only wanted a divorce to be able to work without her husband's intervention. María Josefa Peralta also sought judicial relief because of her husband's interference with her selling tamales—work used to support herself.[69] Lower-class women attempted to gain some relief for their problems through petitions of *malos tratos*, but they ultimately depended on family and neighbors for protection unless they could live independently. Many simply left their spouses—they did not need the stamp of approval of an ecclesiastical divorce.

The ethos of the *depósito* also seemed to be changing. When women applied for an ecclesiastical divorce or lodged a petition of mistreatment, they were "deposited" in a respectable dwelling where they lived separately from their spouses. The actual places ranged from their parents' house to prison, if their husbands had accused them of adultery. In the late eighteenth century, the place of deposit was a common bone of contention between separated spouses. Wives often accused their husbands of trying to humiliate them by having them lodged in the *recogimiento*, an institution used to discipline prostitutes, adulteresses, and other women of ill repute. Toward the end of the colonial period, an alternate site of humiliation for rebellious wives was the *hospicio de pobres*, or poorhouse. In 1833, however, when Ignacio Murillo requested that his wife be deposited in a convent or *hospicio de pobres*, the official in charge told him that it was not the custom to send married women to such institutions and that he should find a suitable house for her.[70] This refusal may reflect the end of an important institution frequently mentioned in the documents, the Recogimiento de la Misericordia. According to Josefina Muriel, the Archbishop of Mexico transformed this building into a warehouse, while the other *recogimientos* became penitentiaries.[71] Still, the emphasis on deposit in "suitable" houses deprived husbands of a potent weapon with which to humiliate their wives and signaled the end of a centuries-old practice associated with the colonial regime.

The solutions to marital problems attempted by Mexican men and women varied according to their class. Wealthier women emphasized their submission and their quiet counsel—using the language of the moralists—but ultimately they petitioned for divorce. Plebeian women resorted to the help of family and neighbors before asking for official intervention. Poor husbands were frequently imprisoned for *malos tratos*, whereas wealthy wives were deposited when they asked for a divorce. The hierarchical nature of marriage was also reflected in the difference in acceptable behavior for men and women whose marriages broke down. Men were advised to use physical force, but any such efforts on the part of women was totally unacceptable. And yet, these patterns were not totally static. The 1808 decision to waive judicial fees for divorce signaled an understanding that women should be able to gain a legal separation from their spouse. The softening in deposit arrangements and the closure of the *recogimientos* also reflected new ideas about the purpose of women's enclosure. And finally, it is clear that in the early nineteenth century, women began to ask for divorce not so much to live on a pension from their husbands but to secure the independence to support themselves with their own work.

Sexual Relations

Intercourse and procreation were integral parts of the institution of marriage. Neither spouse was supposed to deny his or her partner sexual relations; this obligation was referred to as the *débito*, or marital debt.[72] Osuna argued that women too should ask for sex, and that men should make it easier for a timid wife to do so by responding to subtle signs such as hugging and kissing. Sexual satisfaction was equally important, and Osuna stated that attentive husbands "should wait for their wives in the business of marriage" so that wives would not "remain discontented."[73] In the divorce petitions, four women refused their husbands sex, although in only one instance did this lead to the initiation of divorce proceedings.[74] There were eight cases of male refusals of the *débito* in both divorce and *malos tratos* cases. The explanations offered by men were less than clear-cut; some denied their wives' allegations, others apparently asked for intercourse only when drunk, and others wanted to engage in sexual relations by using illegal positions and practices (sodomy, for instance).[75] These cases represent only a very small portion of the sample, but they indicate that women as well as men could use problems within sexual relationships as a reason for judicial intervention in their marriages. Wives, like husbands, were aware of their rights in this situation and could, if needed, recur to this prerogative to demand a divorce.

Fidelity, an accepted and integral part of the marriage bargain, was a much greater concern. Wives commonly protested that their spouses were adulterous; and husbands, not quite so frequently but with some regularity, complained that they had been cuckolded.[76] Arrom finds that many women endured their spouses' adulteries as long as the men continued to support them and behaved in an affectionate manner.[77] On the other hand, Steve Stern argues that plebeian woman objected to marital infidelity mostly because such relationships diverted much-needed income away from the domestic unit.[78] This economic factor is important, but it ignores the mechanics of adultery, which could be embarrassing as well. Without denying the financial impact on plebeian families, at another level, wives were trying to reassert the proper ordering of their marriages.

A number of husbands not only were unfaithful but also manifested their extramarital sexual interests in ways that must have been supremely humiliating for their wives. Their actions went beyond hidden dalliances; several husbands had open affairs with household servants, which could not fail to come to their wives' attention.[79] Others demanded that their wives provide money to entertain their mistresses or refused to support their legal family, saying that their *amasia* (lover) was more important.[80] These arrangements were an inverted form of the ideal marriage and were designed to mortify the wife. Two husbands in the sample insisted that their wives raise the children whom they had fathered outside the marriage.[81] Another ten men brought their mistresses to live in their own homes and, in some instances, demanded that their wives adopt a servile attitude toward their rivals.[82] Doña Ylaria Hernández described this treatment: "He had the audacity to bring his mistress to live with him in my residence obliging me to serve her, and when I did not do so punctually enough, together they would beat me furiously."[83]

The reasons why these husbands chose to humiliate their wives in a public manner are not always clear. In some cases, the wives showed a desire for autonomy by supporting themselves through independent employment. It is therefore possible that their husband's behavior was an attempt to redress lost status within the marriage.

The practice corresponds to a type of symbolic inversion; the respectable wife takes the place of humble servant, and the normally marginalized mistress becomes the center of the genteel household. This inverted situation embarrassed wives sexually, but perhaps rectified other perceived humiliations. These were not simply breaches of the marital vows of sexual fidelity but part of an attempt to remedy—through sexual and social humiliation—the balance of power, thus ensuring that the husband once more was at the head.

Most of the documentation does not provide enough information to determine the dynamic within the couple that led to such behavior, but one case does offer some clues. In 1816, doña María Josefa Mijares petitioned for divorce on the grounds of adultery. Her husband had a long history of extramarital relationships that he did not hide from his wife; he also often consorted with servants at times and in places where his wife was likely to discover him. According to doña María, his latest mistress, doña Regina Sauna, cooperated with her husband to humiliate her further by leaving letters in the hall of her house. These letters insulted doña María, "exulting that to my disadvantage she partakes of my husband and insults me by offering that if I wanted to have intercourse with my husband I should go to the foot of her bed and collect from her what is left over."[84]

What made a husband advertise his infidelity so publicly and seek so clearly to mortify his wife? In this instance the husband, don José Mariano García, gave reasons. He stated that his wife had never loved him. She believed herself to be from a distinguished family and implied that his status was inferior to hers. She compounded this offense by parading her learning, which he described as "her intellectual pretensions, taken out of four books which she read without any comprehension."[85] Moreover, his wife and her family insulted him publicly and constantly tried to shame him regarding his origins. Evidently, he found his revenge through his very public sexual dalliances. Don José did not degrade his wife by putting her in the position of servant, but rather pushed her out of her designated role as sexual companion and flaunted his extramarital relationships. Through this pattern of behavior, he made it clear that her education and family background did not protect her from public embarrassment.

Sexual relations within marriage were supposed to be reciprocal, as defined by the *débito*. The complaints of men and women in *malos tratos* and divorce petitions make clear that marital intercourse was not a big issue. But adultery, whether male or female, was an important concern. Such betrayals upset the balance within the marriage model but could also be used—primarily by men—to restore the hierarchy disturbed in other areas.

Children and Mothers

One of the purposes of marriage was, of course, procreation, yet children were not central to *malos tratos* and ecclesiastical divorce petitions. In the early part of the period under study, wives tended to mention the suffering of their children as an extension of their own. If their husbands did not provide the *diario*, then children, along with their mothers, suffered hunger and deprivation. Some women went further and claimed that they supported themselves and their children through their own work.[86] In essence, they asserted that they had taken over the father's role as head of the family. Such arguments became more frequent in the second half of this period, particularly after independence.

Children figured in the documents in other ways. Some couples fought over custody, and many others charged that one spouse was a bad parent. The appearance of children in these documents was related to a fundamental change in the way that Mexicans perceived the family, but most especially in their conception of the social utility of mothers. By and large, the fight over parenting represented an assertion on the part of wives that they had moral authority within the family, to the effect that they were its true head.

Such a radical transformation from the traditional model of the family did not occur overnight. It can be traced to the reassessment of women's social role in the eighteenth century, when Spanish and Mexican intellectuals began to connect a greater social good with female education.[87] The political reformers of the Bourbon period stressed female education so that women would become responsible mothers: they linked the well-being of the state to the welfare of families.[88] As a result, female education expanded in the late eighteenth century. Through the Colegio de Vizcaínas, for example, female students became teachers, and even poor girls had a chance to spend some time in the classroom.[89] The enrollment of girls in schools continued to grow after independence.[90]

The connection between parenting and the formation of future citizens increased the social importance of mothers, but it also allowed them to begin to displace fathers as the moral head of the family. By the middle of the nineteenth century, magazines portrayed mothers with cloying sentimentality, but they made it clear

that mothers were responsible for both religious and civic education and for inculcating patriotism in their offspring.[91] Also by the
middle of the nineteenth century, Mexican lawmakers began to debate legal changes that would reform the doctrine of *patria potestad*,
acknowledging the importance of mothers and giving widows more
control over their children.[92] These changes are reflected in the early
nineteenth-century ecclesiastical divorce petitions, in which women
accused their husbands of crimes ranging from neglect to setting a
bad example for their own children.

When wives indicted their husbands as bad parents, they also
attacked the traditional family model in which the father was the
head and the moral guardian. In presenting themselves as the party
primarily responsible for the moral education of their children,
women were placing themselves in the father's role. Josefa Leiva,
for example, stated that her husband set a bad example for her son
and treated him cruelly,[93] a theme that was echoed in many other
complaints.[94] The next step in the portrayal of bad fathers was to
show their excessive cruelty toward their children. Such accusations were quite rare, probably because the right of a father to discipline his children was sanctioned by law and socially accepted.
Yet mothers began to assert their right to determine whether their
husbands were excessively cruel toward their children, again effectively presenting themselves as the moral center of the family.
Doña Victoriana de Espíritu Santo, for example, accused her husband of demonstrating a profound hatred of his offspring by beating them continuously. She went on to describe many other instances
of cruelty.[95]

Another series of complaints focused upon the father's refusal
to provide an education for his children. The term *educación* was
used in both its meanings: schooling and proper upbringing. Women
in these cases argued—along the lines of Bourbon philosophy—
that they, and not fathers, could ensure properly socialized future
citizens, because they would take care to instill the right values and
conduct in their offspring. Dolores Gil de Arévalo stated that her
husband showed an "absolute disregard for the proper formation
(*educación*) of his children; far from inspiring them with the wisdom of proper morality, he induces them to join into his vices by
beating, insulting, and mistreating them." Later she stated that he
taught them to speak like sailors.[96] In doña Micaela Posada's
complaint of *malos tratos*, her lawyer contrasted her with her husband by describing her as "honorable and of good disposition." He
went on to portray her as a good mother whose "children behave

properly and know their religious doctrine; they are dutiful and obe-
dient to their stepfather who gives them nothing."[97]

Luisa López described her husband as a *padre desnaturalizado*
(unnatural father) because he objected to sending his children to
school. Her petition asserted that she took charge of both upbringing and schooling over her husband's objections.[98] Doña María Vargas protested that her husband took the money from her son's
capellanía (chaplaincy or endowed chantry fund) so that she had
nothing to pay for his schooling.[99] These complaints are particularly interesting because of their relation to the emphasis on female
education that began in the late eighteenth century. The link between female education and motherhood socially sanctioned
women's primary responsibility for the schooling and proper upbringing of their children.

The evolution of the concept of motherhood can be traced in a
few of these cases. In the eighteenth century, mothers emphasized
their *amor de madre* (maternal love) and *obligación de la madre*
(motherly duties).[100] But by the midnineteenth century, motherhood
had become not only a sacred duty but also a state that conveyed
rights. In 1853, when María Soledad Cabrales petitioned the court
for an ecclesiastical divorce, one of her main concerns was custody
of her young daughter. Her husband had some type of mental breakdown; and as a result, his mother and sister moved in and began to
nurse him. María Soledad found her in-laws intolerable, and she
left the household. She stated that she wanted to "exert over my
daughter my rights and authority which I have over her as a mother;
nobody in the world can deprive me of the sacred execution of them."
She also insisted that she had not committed any crime, and therefore there was no reason to doubt that she was respected in society.[101] María Soledad Cabrales was making these statements at a
time when Mexican lawmakers were debating the reform of family
law to recognize the importance of mothers. Her arguments were
slightly in advance of the law but in keeping with a growing sense
that mothers were the moral center of Mexican families. She did
not hesitate to describe motherhood as a type of sacred duty, but
she was also influenced by the knowledge that some mothers—notably widows—could lose their rights over their children when they
violated social norms of decency.

Mexican wives and husbands tried to reassert the reciprocal and
hierarchical natures of the marriage bargain in many ways, but
women went further than their husbands in portraying their spouses
as bad parents. By doing so, wives challenged the fundamental

model of marriage and the family—that husbands were the head and had exclusive moral authority over children. Although they did not dispute the husband's primacy as pater familias in all matters, they began to assert an equal footing as moral guardian. They began to argue that they could decide when fathers went too far in their efforts to discipline their children; when fathers were remiss in the example set for their offspring; and, most important, when fathers did not fulfill their civic obligation to educate their children. As such, the metaphorical body that represented marriage was sprouting a new head.

Conclusion

The changes in Mexican mentalities regarding women affected the marriage bargain, but did so only slowly and subtly. By the early nineteenth century, however, some old patterns within marriage were beginning to be viewed with less approval. Lizardi, who expressed the cutting edge of Mexican thought in this period, used his novel *La Quijotita y su prima* to comment on women and their education, morals, and place in society. Although Lizardi believed women to be physically inferior to men, he saw no reason for any spiritual or intellectual inferiority. He advocated female education and argued that the soul has no gender, declaring that "in the spiritual portion you are all [women] equal to us." He also praised women as being more naturally compassionate and kinder than men.[102] He deprecated men who beat their wives as barbarians, using the character Ramiro as an example of a scoundrel who gave all his money to his *dama*, beat his wife, and left his family in poverty.[103]

Contrast Lizardi's attitude to that of Fanny Calderón de la Barca, who lived in Mexico as the wife of the Spanish ambassador. She recounted a meeting with an Indian in a Michoacán village in which the man praised "beyond measure his own exemplary conduct to his wife, from which I infer that he beats her, as indeed all Indians consider it their particular privilege to do." She went on to relate that "an Indian woman who complained to a padre of her husband's neglect, mentioned, as the crowning proof, that he had not given her a beating in a whole fortnight."[104] Calderón de la Barca described a static situation, and her views are those of an outsider influenced by the elite society in which she circulated. Moreover, Lizardi does not deny marital abuse, but he rejects it as an accepted and acceptable value. Like doña Josefa Amar y Borbón, a Spanish woman who wrote at the end of the eighteenth century, he asserted that a well-ordered family is the basis of a healthy state.[105] Neither Lizardi nor Amar y Borbón could change prevailing patterns of abuse, but their ideas reflected a gradual transformation in the value attributed to women and the rights of men in the marriage bargain. It would be a mistake to dwell on Calderón de la Barca's portrait of the stereotypical and stagnant Indian. Instead, Lizardi represents a changing mentality in Mexico, including new ideas regarding women, children, and education.

Notes

1. Françoise Carner, "Estereotipos femeninos en el siglo XIX," in *Presencia y transparencia: La mujer en la historia de México* (Mexico City: El Colegio de México, 1987), argues for the continuity of family life and marriage in the early nineteenth century.

2. See the discussion by Roderick Phillips, *Putting Asunder: A History of Divorce in Western Society* (Cambridge: Cambridge University Press, 1988), on the use of divorce to gauge marital expectations.

3. Silvia Arrom, *La mujer mexicana ante el divorcio eclesiástico (1800–1857)* (Mexico City: SepSetentas, 1976), estimates that in the period from 1800 to 1857, fifteen ecclesiastical divorce cases were initiated.

4. Arrom, *La mujer mexicana.*

5. Juan de la Cerda, *Libro intitulado vida política de todos los estados de mugeres: En el qual dan muy provechosos y Christianos documentos y avisos, para criarse y conservarse debidamente las mugeres en sus estados* (Alcalá de Henares: Casa de Juan Gracian, 1599), 323v; Fray Francisco de Osuna, *Norte de los estados en que se da regla de bivir a los mancebos; y a los casados; y a los viudos; y a todos los continentes; y se tratan muy por extenso los remedios des desastrado casamiento; enseñando que tal a de ser la vida del cristiano casado* (Seville: n.p., 1531), 90v and 91; Fray Jayme de Corella as cited by Richard Boyer, "Women, *La Mala Vida*, and the Politics of Marriage," in *Sexuality and Marriage in Colonial Latin America*, ed. Asunción Lavrin (Lincoln: University of Nebraska Press, 1989), 257.

6. Colin MacLachlan, *Spain's Empire in the New World: The Role of Ideas in Institutional and Social Change* (Los Angeles: University of California Press, 1988), 9; Boyer, "Women," 254, represents the authority of kingship and the authority of the husband/father as being interconnected.

7. Silvia Marina Arrom, *The Women of Mexico City, 1790–1857* (Stanford: Stanford University Press, 1985), 56–57, 69–70.

8. Ibid., 72; Boyer, "Women," 268.

9. Arrom, *The Women*, 62–63, 65, provides an extensive discussion of the respective legal rights of husbands and wives.

10. Boyer, "Women," 257; Arrom, *The Women*, 65–66.

11. Fray Angel Serra, *Manual de administrar los santos sacramentos a los españoles y naturales de esta Provincia de los Gloriosos Apostoles S. Pedro y S. Pablo de Michoacán, conforme a la reforma de Paulo V y Urbano VIII* (Mexico City: Impreso por Joseph Bernardo de Hogal, 1731), fol. 63v; Cerda, *Libro intitulado*, 305v.

12. Arrom, *La mujer mexicana*, 46.

13. Archivo General de la Nación (Mexico City), Ramo Bienes Nacionales, legajo 76, expediente 16, folios 18–22v, 1855 [hereafter AGN, Bienes Nacionales, leg. 76, exp. 16, ff. 18–22v, 1855]; Boyer, "Women," 264, documents the complaints of wives about a "servantlike condition."

14. AGN, Civil, leg. 92, parte 2, no exp. num., 1848; AGN, Criminal, vol. 132, exp. 31, ff. 566–568, 1809.

15. Steve Stern, *The Secret History of Gender; Women, Men, and Power in Late Colonial Mexico* (Chapel Hill: University of North Carolina Press, 1995), 92.

16. AGN, Bienes Nacionales, leg. 874, exp. 7, 1833.

17. Pedro Galindo, *Parte segunda del directorio de Penitentes y practica de una buena y prudente confesión* (Madrid: Antonio de Zafra, 1680), 154–56, 160.

18. Osuna, *Norte de los estados*, 92v. See also Cerda, *Libro intitulado*, 338v.

19. AGN, Criminal, vol. 122, exp. 18, ff. 398–398v, 1783; AGN, Clero Regular y Secular, vol. 197, exp. 20, ff. 363–364, 1768.

20. See AGN, Criminal, vol. 624, exp. 2, ff. 39v–40, 1756; AGN, Criminal, vol. 597, exp. 13, ff. 422–423v, 1781; AGN, Bienes Nacionales, leg. 88, exp. 6, 1832; AGN, Bienes Nacionales, leg. 717, exp. 102, 1853.

21. AGN, Bienes Nacionales, leg. 76, exp. 42, 1856; AGN, Bienes Nacionales, leg. 292, exp. 30, 1790; AGN, Bienes Nacionales, leg. 470, exp. 15, 1836 (one and one-half reales daily is asked for, but the mother is provided with one peso daily). According to Arnold Bauer, "The Colonial Economy," in *The Countryside in Colonial Latin America*, ed. Louisa Schell Hoberman and Susan Migden Socolow (Albuquerque: University of New Mexico Press, 1996), 27, the statutory wage in New Spain was two reales per day.

22. AGN, Bienes Nacionales, leg. 717 exp. 80, 1853.

23. See, for example, AGN, Criminal, vol. 456, exp. 6, ff. 124–126, 1783.

24. Deborah Kanter, "¿Es mejor casarse que quemarse? Matrimonios indígenas, espetativas y realidades en la región de Toluca en los siglos XVII y XIX," Paper presented at the Coloquio Historia de la Familia y Vida Privada Iberoamérica, Mexico City, 1993. Kanter argues that in the region of Toluca, many native husbands were hampered in the fulfillment of their role as provider by poor or insufficient lands.

25. Arrom, *La mujer mexicana*, 29.

26. AGN, Civil, leg. 92, parte 2, no exp. num., 1848 [divorce of doña María Morales and don José Rodriguez—he left to fight with the Mexican forces during the war with the United States]; AGN, Civil, leg. 72, parte 2, no exp. num., 1848 [divorce of Juana Rodríguez and José Alvino Fiesco—he also went off to fight]; AGN, Bienes Nacionales, leg. 717, exp. 56, 1852; AGN, Bienes Nacionales, leg. 717, exp. 119, 1853; AGN, Bienes Nacionales, leg. 1128, exp. 1, 1788 [left to work in the *tierra caliente*]; AGN, Criminal, vol. 105, exp. 9, ff. 302–306, 1748; AGN, Criminal, vol. 716, exp. 11, ff. 141–150, 1762; AGN, Criminal, vol. 716, exp. 15 ff. 154–168, 1765; AGN, Civil, leg. 110, parte 2c, exp. 2, 1790.

27. AGN, Bienes Nacionales, leg. 1045, exp. 34, 1832; AGN, Bienes Nacionales, leg. 470, exp. 15, 1835; AGN, Criminal, vol. 611, exp. 6, ff. 125–380, 1752; Kanter, "¿Es mejor casarse que quemarse?"

28. AGN, Criminal, vol. 611, exp. 6, ff. 125–380, 1752; AGN, Bienes Nacionales, leg. 470, exp. 15, 1836; AGN, Bienes Nacionales, leg. 470, exp. 18, 1836; AGN, Bienes Nacionales, leg. 292, exp. 26, 1790; AGN, Criminal, vol. 456, exp. 6, ff. 124–126, 1783; AGN, Criminal, vol. 577, exp. 7b, ff. 192–202, 1782; AGN, Criminal, vol. 190, exp. 19, ff. 322–333, 1770; AGN, Criminal, vol. 275, exp. 1, ff. 1–101, 1766; AGN, Criminal, vol. 613, exp. 7, ff. 157–164, 1755;

AGN, Criminal, vol. 716, exp. 11, ff. 141–150, 1762; AGN, Criminal, vol. 716, exp. 15, ff. 154–168, 1765; AGN, Criminal, vol. 716, exp. 15, ff. 177–188, 1766; AGN, Clero Regular y Secular, vol. 192, exp. 2, ff. 18–27, 1760; AGN, Civil, vol. 113, no exp. num., ff. 1–2v, 1805; AGN, Civil, leg. 158, parte 7, exp. 13, 1791; AGN, Civil, vol. 1500, exp. 2, 1793; AGN, Criminal, vol. 118, exp. 13, ff. 473–481, 1807.

29. Doña María Vargas complained that her husband gambled and dissipated what little resources she had from honorable means and then "se balió Contreras para prostituir a su muger a que sea una Venus vaga constituyendose el su Lenon o Rufian . . . para vender por un vil interés el Cuerpo de su esposa y el abandono del Lecho nupcial." AGN, Bienes Nacionales, leg. 470, exp. 18, 1836. Doña Juana Santillán's husband threw her out of the house after refusing to give her money, saying that "lo Putee si quieres." AGN, Judicial, vol. 32, exp. 16, ff. 90–90v, 1796. See also AGN, Criminal, vol. 118, exp. 13, ff. 473–481, 1807.

30. AGN, Criminal, vol. 614, exp. 18, ff. 114v–115v, 1785.

31. AGN, Criminal, vol. 624, exp. 2, fol. 39v–40, 1756; AGN, Bienes Nacionales, leg. 76, exp. 11, 1856; AGN, Bienes Nacionales, leg. 76, exp. 45, 1856; AGN, Judicial, vol. 32, exp. 50, ff. 422–453v, 1809; AGN, Civil, leg. 92, parte 2, no exp. num. [divorce of Josefa Mayorga and Martín Lugo], 1848; AGN, Civil, leg. 92, parte 2 no exp. num. [divorce of doña Margarita Llata and Eusebio Bolaños], 1848; AGN, Bienes Nacionales, leg. 370, exp. 42, 1839; AGN, Bienes Nacionales, leg. 442, exp. 59, 1790; AGN, Bienes Nacionales, leg. 470, exp. 10, 1836; AGN, Bienes Nacionales, leg. 470, exp. 23, 1836; AGN, Bienes Nacionales, leg. 470, exp. 31, 1836; AGN, Bienes Nacionales, leg. 1045, exp. 35, 1832; AGN, Criminal, vol. 43, exp. 4, ff. 63–71, 1770; AGN, Criminal, vol. 556, exp. 10, ff. 119–122, 1798; AGN, Criminal, vol. 577, exp. 7b, ff. 192–202, 1782; AGN, Criminal, vol. 118, exp. 13, ff. 473–81, 1807; AGN, Criminal, vol. 614, exp. 18, ff. 112–122, 1785; AGN, Criminal, vol. 716, exp. 15, ff. 154–168, 1765; AGN, Clero Regular y Secular, vol. 192, exp. 2, ff. 18–27, 1760; AGN, Clero Regular y Secular, vol. 197, exp. 20, ff. 358–367, 1768; AGN, Civil, vol. 1469, exp. 19, 1794; AGN, Criminal, vol. 118, exp. 13, ff. 473–81, 1807.

32. Arrom, *The Women*, 26–32; Pilar Gonzalbo Aizpuru, *Las mujeres en la Nueva España. Educación y vida cotidiana* (Mexico City: El Colegio de México, 1987), 122–23.

33. José Joaquín Fernández de Lizardi, *La Quijotita y su prima* (Mexico City: Porrúa, 1967, first pub. 1818), 100–101.

34. Archivo Judicial de Puebla, 1776, number 4350, 10 folios [hereafter AJP, 1776, no. 4350, 10 ff.].

35. AGN, Civil, leg. 199, parte 2, exp. 4, 1846; AGN, Civil, leg. 118, exp. 7, 1827.

36. Doña Josefa Amar y Borbón, *Discurso sobre la educación física y moral de las mugeres* (Madrid: Imprenta de D. Benito Cano, 1790), xii; Osuna, *Norte de los estados*, 94v.

37. Cerda, *Libro intitulado*, 80v, 345; Padre Gaspar de Astete, *Tratado del buen govierno de la familia y estado de las viudas y doncellas* (Burgos: Juan Bautista Veredio, 1603), 60–61; Juan Luis Vives, *Instrucción de la mujer cristiana* (Buenos Aires: Espasa-Calpe, 1948, 4th ed.), 14.

38. Cerda, *Libro intitulado*, 345v.; Galindo, *Parte segunda*, 165.

39. AGN, Criminal, vol. 42, exp. 15, ff. 501–502, 1802. This portrait of harmony ended, according to the witness, when the wife began to drink pulque.

40. AGN, Criminal, vol. 42, exp. 15, ff. 467–469; AGN, Criminal, vol. 91, ff. 1–4v.

41. One husband beat his wife when she asked for the *diario*, saying that she would only give it to other men. See AGN, Bienes Nacionales, leg. 292, exp. 30, 1790. In another case, a wife complained that she was destitute despite her husband's wealth. See AGN, Bienes Nacionales, leg. 470, exp. 20, 1836.

42. AGN, Bienes Nacionales, leg. 1045, exp. 34, 1832; AGN, Bienes Nacionales, leg. 1128, exp. 1, 1788.

43. AJP, 1846, no. 21, f. 7v.

44. See in particular AGN, Judicial, vol. 32, exp. 51, ff. 454–464v, 1809, but also AGN, Civil leg. 92, parte 2, no exp. num. [divorce of José María Arce and Manuela Velásquez], 1848; AGN, Civil, leg. 92, parte 2, no exp. num. [divorce of don Francisco Coste and doña Guadalupe Manrreza], 1848; AGN, Bienes Nacionales, leg. 470, exp. 11, 1836; AGN, Bienes Nacionales, leg. 717, exp. 63, 1853; AGN, Bienes Nacionales, leg. 1128, exp. 1, 1788; AGN, Clero Regular y Secular, vol. 197, exp. 20, ff. 358–367, 1768. In cases initiated by women, husbands often responded by criticizing their wives' capacity to care for the household. This was also a common complaint in accusations of wife-murder.

45. AGN, Judicial, vol. 32, exp. 51, ff. 455–458v, 1809; AGN, Bienes Nacionales, leg. 470, exp. 11, ff. 2–4, 1836.

46. AGN, Clero Regular y Secular, vol. 197, exp. 20, ff. 358–367, 1768.

47. Ibid.

48. Eric Van Young, "Material Life," in *The Countryside in Colonial Latin America*, ed. Louisa Schell Hoberman and Susan Migden Socolow (Albuquerque: University of New Mexico Press, 1996), 54.

49. AGN, Bienes Nacionales, leg. 874, exp. 7, 1833.

50. AGN, Bienes Nacionales, leg. 370, exp. 42, 1836; AGN, Bienes Nacionales, leg. 470, exp. 10, 1836; AGN, Bienes Nacionales, leg. 470, exp. 23, 1836.

51. AGN, Civil, leg. 92, parte 2, no exp. num., 1848, ff. 3–4v. She worked as a *molendera*.

52. Cerda, *Libro intitulado*, 321v, 346; Osuna, *Norte de los estados*, 91v.

53. Osuna, *Norte de los estados*, 91v.

54. Cerda, *Libro intitulado*, 416v–417; Galindo, *Parte segunda*, 159.

55. Galindo, *Parte segunda*, 398–400.

56. Boyer, "Women," 269; Sonya Lipsett-Rivera, "La violencia en la familia formal e informal," in *Familia y vida privada en la historia de Iberoamérica*, ed. Pilar Gonzalbo Aizpuru and Cecilia Rabell (Mexico City: El Colegio de México and Universidad Nacional Autónoma de México, 1996); Galindo, *Parte segunda*, 162–63.

57. AGN, Bienes Nacionales, leg. 292, exp. 30, ff. 1–1v, 1790.

58. AGN, Criminal, vol. 262, exp. 11, ff. 190–193, 1801. Steve Stern, *The Secret History of Gender: Women, Men, and Power in Late Colonial Mexico* (Chapel Hill: University of North Carolina Press, 1995), provides a more detailed account of this case.

59. AGN, Criminal, vol. 712, exp. 1, ff. 18–19, 1805.

60. Cerda, *Libro intitulado*, 344v–345.

61. Osuna, *Norte de los estados*, 153–153v, also recommends asking husbands in a coquettish manner not to get mad.

62. AGN, Judicial, vol. 32, exp. 31, ff. 109–110, 1799; AGN, Civil, leg. 92, parte 2, no exp. num., ff. 2, 1848; AGN, Civil, leg. 92, exp. 30, ff. 3, 1848. For other examples see also AGN, Civil, leg 92, parte 2, no exp. num., ff. 2–7v [divorce of doña María Morales and don José Rodríguez]; AGN, Bienes Nacionales, vol. 705, exp. 6, ff. 54–55, 1763; AGN, Bienes Nacionales, vol. 292, exp. 1, ff. 2–4, 1790; AGN, Judicial, vol. 11, exp. 8, ff. 156–160v, 1816.

63. Osuna, *Norte de los estados*, 153.

64. Ibid., 153v.

65. Ibid., 154.

66. Boyer, "Women," 267.

67. AGN, Bienes Nacionales, leg. 292, exp. 26, 1790.

68. Arrom, *The Women*, 219.

69. AGN, Bienes Nacionales, leg. 292, exp. 28, 1790.

70. AGN, Civil, leg. 87, parte 1, no exp. num., 1833 [divorce of doña Francisca Cardiel and Ignacio Murillo].

71. Josefina Muriel, *Los Recogimientos de mujeres. Respuesta a una problemática social Novohispana* (Mexico City: UNAM, 1974), 223–24.

72. Galindo, *Parte segunda*, 165. See Asunción Lavrin, "Sexuality in Colonial Mexico: A Church Dilemma," in Lavrín, *Sexuality and Marriage*, 53–54.

73. Osuna, *Norte de los estados*, 70v–71v. Merry Wiesner, *Women and Gender in Early Modern Europe* (Cambridge: Cambridge University Press, 1993), states that early modern Catholic thought conceived of sexual relations as a mutual obligation.

74. AGN, Civil, leg. 92, parte 2, no exp. num. [divorce of José María Arce and Manuela Velásquez], 1848. The other three women offered medical reasons for their unwillingness. One complained that her husband had a disgusting skin disease, another that her spouse gave her venereal disease, and the other that she had just had a miscarriage. AGN, Civil, leg. 92, parte 2, no exp. num. [divorce of doña Margarita Llata and Eusebio Bolaños], 1848; AGN, Civil, leg. 92, parte 2, no exp. num. [divorce of doña María Morales and don José Rodríguez], 1848; AGN, Bienes Nacionales, leg. 874, exp. 7, 1833.

75. AGN, Bienes Nacionales, leg. 292, exp. 23, 1790; AGN, Bienes Nacionales, leg. 898, exp. 1, 1818; AGN, Criminal, vol. 43, exp. 4, ff. 63–71, 1770; AGN, Criminal, vol. 456, exp. 6, ff. 124–126, 1783; AGN, Criminal, vol. 206, exp. 20, ff. 236–251, 1802. Juan de Dios Muñoz only wanted to have sex in front of their daughter: AGN, Clero Regular y Secular, vol. 192, exp. 2, ff. 18–27, 1760. Another husband asked his wife to have sex with his friend as a stand-in: AGN, Criminal, vol. 577, exp. 7, ff. 140–191v, 1783; AJP, 1766, no. 3942, 34 ff.

76. In divorce and *malos tratos* cases, there were 41 female to 24 male complaints of adultery out of a total of 214 cases. It should be noted that a preponderance of the petitions were initiated by women.

77. Arrom, *La mujer mexicana*, 29–30.

78. Stern, *The Secret History*, 82.

79. AGN, Bienes Nacionales, leg. 470, exp. 12, 1836; AGN, Bienes Nacionales, vol. 88, exp. 6, 1832.

80. AGN, Criminal, vol. 118, exp. 13, ff. 473–81, 1807; AGN, Criminal, vol. 43, exp. 4, ff. 63–71, 1770; AGN, Criminal, vol. 131, exp. 37, ff. 421–423v, 1769; AGN, Civil, leg. 92, parte 2, no exp. num. [divorce of Josefa Mayorga and Martín Lugo], 1848.

81. AGN, Bienes Nacionales, leg. 1128, exp. 1, 1788; AGN, Bienes Nacionales, leg. 470, exp. 12, 1836.

82. AGN, Bienes Nacionales, leg. 76, exp. 16, 1855; AGN, Bienes Nacionales, leg. 292, exp. 19, 1790; AGN, Civil, leg. 92, parte 2, no exp. num. [divorce of Josefa Mayorga and Martín Lugo], 1848; AGN, Civil, leg. 92, parte 2, no exp. num. [divorce of doña Margarita Llata and Eusebio Bolaños], 1848; AGN, Bienes Nacionales, leg. 370, exp. 42, 1839; AGN, Bienes Nacionales, leg. 1045, exp. 34, 1832; AGN, Criminal, vol. 122, exp. 18, ff. 395–402v, 1783; AGN, Civil, leg. 110, parte 2c, exp. 2, 1790; AGN, Criminal, vol. 131, exp. 37, ff. 422–422v, 1769;

AGN, Criminal, vol. 206, exp. 20, ff. 236–251, 1802. In one case, the husband had an incestuous affair with a daughter from his first marriage, and father and daughter treated his new wife like a servant: AGN, Criminal, vol. 132, exp. 31, ff. 565, 1809. Virginia Gutiérrez de Pineda and Patricia Vila de Pineda, *Honor, familia y sociedad en la estructura patriarcal. El caso de Santander* (Bogotá: Universidad Nacional de Colombia, 1988), found many examples of Colombian husbands who brought their mistresses home and told their wives to accept the situation or leave.

83. AGN, Bienes Nacionales, leg. 370, exp. 42, ff. 2v, 1838.

84. AGN, Judicial, vol. 11, exp. 8, ff. 156–160v., 1816.

85. AGN, Judicial, vol. 11, exp. 8, ff. 169–213v., 1816.

86. Of the 214 *malos tratos* and ecclesiastical divorce petitions, 64 mention children in some manner. Of that group, 35 represented complaints that fathers did not provide materially for their children.

87. Johanna S. R. Mendelson, "The Feminine Press: The View of Women in the Colonial Journals of Spanish America, 1790–1810," in *Latin American Women; Historical Perspectives*, ed. Asunción Lavrin (Westport: Greenwood Press, 1978), discusses the ideas of Gerónimo Feijóo and the debates in favor of female education in late eighteenth-century Mexican periodicals.

88. Arrom, *The Women*, 15–19.

89. Dorothy Tanck de Estrada, "Tensión en la torre de marfil. La educación en la segunda mitad del siglo XVIII mexicano," in *Ensayos sobre historia de la educación en México* (Mexico City: El Colegio de México, 1981), 32, 65.

90. Anne Staples, "Panorama educativo al comienzo de la vida independiente," in *Ensayos sobre historia de la educación*, 102. According to Arrom, *The Women*, 21, enrollment in female schools dropped during the Wars of Independence but recovered by the 1840s. In her assessment, female education expanded after independence.

91. *La Semana de las Señoritas Mejicanas*, vol. IV (Mexico City: Imprenta de Juan Navarro, 1852), 109; *Presente Amistoso, Dedicado a las Señoritas Mexicanas* (1852): 1–7.

92. Arrom, *The Women*, 85–86.

93. AGN, Bienes Nacionales, leg. 76, exp. 21, 1854.

94. AGN, Criminal, vol. 76, exp. 43, 1856; AGN, Bienes Nacionales, leg. 76, exp. 47, 1856; AGN, Civil, leg. 92, parte 2, no exp. num., 1848 [divorce of doña Rosa Vásquez and don Juan Ruiz de la Mota]; AGN, Bienes Nacionales, leg. 470, exp. 32, 1836; AGN, Bienes Nacionales, leg. 717, exp. 119, 1853; AJP, 1773, exp. 28 (4242); AJP, 1773, exp. 28 (4242).

95. AGN, Bienes Nacionales, leg. 76, exp. 41, 1856. For other examples see AGN, Bienes Nacionales, leg. 76, exp. 47, 1856; AGN, Judicial, vol. 32, exp. 52, ff. 465–482v, 1809; AGN, Bienes Nacionales, leg. 717, exp. 119, 1853; AGN, Bienes Nacionales, leg. 854, exp. 4, 1807; AGN, Criminal, vol. 48, exp. 13, 1780; AGN, Clero Regular y Secular, vol. 192, exp. 2, ff. 18–27, 1766.

96. AGN, Bienes Nacionales, leg. 717, exp. 119, 1853. See also AJP, 1170, exp. 15 (4141), 13 July 1770.

97. AGN, Criminal, vol. 641, exp. 17, ff. 107–111v, 1785.

98. AGN, Bienes Nacionales, leg. 76, exp. 11, 1856. For another example see AGN, Civil, leg. 92, parte 2, no exp. num., 1848.

99. AGN, Criminal, vol. 641, exp. 16, 1785.

100. AGN, Clero Regular y Secular, vol. 192, exp. 2, 1766; AGN, Clero Regular y Secular, vol. 145, exp. 10, 1785.

101. AGN, Bienes Nacionales, leg. 717, exp. 81, 1853.

102. Lizardi, *La Quijotita*, 35. According to Carner, "Estereotipos femeninos," 102–3, this idealization of women's abnegation, silent suffering, and docility was common among Mexican writers of the nineteenth century.

103. Lizardi, *La Quijotita*, 36.

104. Fanny Calderón de la Barca, *Life in Mexico during a Residence of Two Years in that Country* (Boston: C. C. Little & J. Brown, 1843), 498. She goes on to recount another of this man's statements. When asked "if he allowed his wife to govern him," he replied, "Oh! no, that would be the mule leading the *arriero!*"

105. Amar y Borbón, *Discurso sobre la educación*, i–viii.

6

Gender Ideology, Race, and Female-Headed Households in Urban Mexico, 1750–1850

Elizabeth Anne Kuznesof

Elizabeth Anne Kuznesof teaches Latin American history at the University of Kansas in Lawrence. She has written extensively on the history of Brazil's urban families and provided historiographical insights into Latin American family history as a whole. Here she evaluates changes in the autonomy, equality, and quality of life of Mexican women, especially blacks and *castas* (mixed race), during the 1750–1850 period. Kuznesof looks at continuities and changes in marriage, household and family life, standard of living, and occupational structures and opportunities. Based on an in-depth discussion of abundant secondary sources, her essay establishes links with the ideologies of gender and race prevailing at the time. Her findings, including an improvement in women's education and legal rights for single women, generally agree with those of historian Silvia Arrom. Kuznesof also sees a considerable increase in female employment, although occupations for women of all races were limited to areas such as domestic service, production and sale of comestibles, and textile or tobacco production tasks. As Kuznesof argues, all of these activities were at the level of proletariat sectors undergoing change. Furthermore, the autonomy of married women, minor daughters, and subordinate males diminished—due in part to the decline in the use of the dowry and the requirement of parental permission for marriage, all of which brought about an increase in the power of the male head of household. Women's standard of living across social and racial boundaries was also negatively affected by rising levels of poverty and unemployment. In sum, although new ideologies and laws may have favored them, Kuznesof finds women's real economic circumstances to have been less than favorable.

Cynics sometimes characterize "periodization" as a kind of historians' parlor game, a trivial pursuit in which scholars expound the critical importance of their pet "transformation" to the essential nature of a time and place. Although such an egocentric focus may occasionally cloud the scholarly vision, periodization fulfills a basic function in the historical enterprise. It allows the necessary fitting together and synthesizing of different brushstrokes of a historical picture. This activity is important both for an understanding of society and history at the macro level, and for a more accurate and nuanced portrait of particular aspects and trends within social history. For a time to make sense, the dynamics of the complex forces that act in society must fit together coherently and be joined by connections and processes into what Eric Wolf called "processual and relational history."[1] Or, to paraphrase William Taylor, social historians must go beyond the "mainly descriptive" "recognition of people in categories previously neglected" to the "new kind of history" predicted by Lucien Febvre and Charles Tilly: the study of how ordinary people in different places and of different fortunes "lived the big changes" of the rise of capitalism and state formation.[2]

A focus on social change over time almost necessarily means that dramatic political events, such as the Wars of Independence or the dictatorship of Antonio López de Santa Anna in Mexico, will not receive much attention. Instead, the focus shifts to characteristics of the *longue durée*, including population movements, quality of life, and income. A reader of Mexican historiography might easily perceive a discontinuous leap in the themes and interpretations of social and economic history from the Bourbon period to the last third of the nineteenth century. Octavio Paz was one of the first to suggest that the traditional periodization does not reflect the actual historical experience of Mexico. According to Paz: "the reforms undertaken by the Bourbon dynasty, particularly Charles III, improved the economy and made business operations more efficient, but they accentuated the centralization of administrative functions and changed New Spain into a true colony, that is, into a territory subject to systematic exploitation and strictly controlled by the center of power."[3]

This idea that New Spain became a "true colony" under the Bourbons was taken up by Richard Morse, who argued that the so-called colonial period in Latin America actually occurred between 1760 and 1920. Morse based his argument on the vulnerability of Latin America in that period not so much to Spain and Portugal but to the Western world and, one would surmise, to industrial capitalism.[4] Woodrow Borah, another advocate of a colonial "break" in 1760, argued in somewhat different terms that this date saw the "change from God-centered reasoning to man-centered speculation and concerns that marked the Enlightenment."[5]

Even if modern scholars were to consider 1760 a "break," this in no way implies agreement concerning continuity between the Bourbon period and the period after Mexican independence. Few scholars have specifically looked for continuity or even for change between the late eighteenth and the early nineteenth centuries. There seems to be little agreement on the characteristics of the early nineteenth century beyond the idea of "the search for political stability." In particular, the early nineteenth century has been seen as a time of enormous confusion. William Taylor has labeled it the "orphan period" and argues, on the basis of micropolitical changes in privilege and especially the increase in individual and mass violence, for the return of the independence wars to a "prominent place in the chronology of Latin American social history."[6] Conversely, looking primarily from the perspective of continuity over time in elite ideology, Edmundo O'Gorman contended that there were no basic ideological differences between the liberal and conservative factions of nineteenth-century Mexico: all agreed on the need to preserve the Spanish/Mediterranean/Catholic heritage as well as on the need for economic development, and all were Mexican nationalists.[7]

Bradford Burns also saw substantial consistency in elite views, combined with a counter-discourse of resistance, in the ideological currents of nineteenth-century Latin America. The dominant discourse ranged across issues of civilization and barbarism, race, secularism and nationalism, and, of course, economic development. Nevertheless, according to Burns, "carefully constructed definitions were assigned (sometimes) to the illusive term *modernization*, but despite the search for deep meaning the drive to modernize in nineteenth-century Latin America usually and simply meant an eagerness on the part of the governing elites to ape Europe."[8] On the face of it, these ideologies suggest more continuity than change from the late eighteenth to the early nineteenth century.

Remarkably, thirty years after Morse's proposal for a new periodization, scholars have made little effort to focus on social and economic trends over the period from 1750 to 1850. As Eric Van Young observed in 1985, "most of us have been working for some time as though we thought that the late eighteenth century had no politics and the early nineteenth century no economics."[9]

Not only that, but beyond the larger area of political economy the histories of race and class, labor, the family, gender relations, and women's rights have been written all too frequently with little thought to change over time. These important subareas of social history need to be analyzed rigorously in terms of change and continuity, and the ways in which they fit together and make sense within the period. While important studies on gender relations in Mexico and Latin America have appeared in the last twenty years, many of these works suffer from a tendency to separate women's experience from that of society as a whole, rather than seeing women's legal position, employment, and life chances within the context of social life in general and class and race relations in particular in a given time period.[10]

In the areas of race, gender ideology, and the family, the danger among historians, as among sociologists, has been to take an essentially ahistorical view, seeing these ideologies or formations as timeless and static. In part, this is because of the real but misleading linkage of race, gender, and family to biological and somatic differences between people, which are also invoked as objective externalities independent of subjective historical change. It is not only that certain periods are left out of the analysis but also that the idea of periodization in and of itself is entirely neglected in some cases. For example, Joan Scott has criticized "patriarchy" as a theory of gender relations because the analysis provides no material explanation for its appearance, nor any understanding of how gender inequalities affect or relate to other inequalities.[11] Instead, the concept of patriarchy tends to be timelessly reified and itself applied as an explanation for structures and behavior. A similar charge can be made for racism.

As social categories, it is clear that gender and race are embedded in each other. Tessie Liu has observed that "racial categories are predicated upon control of women and sexuality." As a concept, race depends upon reproduction for "the transmission of an indelible common substance," which "unites the people who possess it in a special community."[12] According to medieval physiological theory, purity of blood meant descent from Christian women.[13] In colonial New Spain, the categories and ideologies of race and gender were specifically interconnected. Not only was the race of individuals in colonial Mexico a subjective and malleable category that could be influenced and changed during a person's lifetime, but gender and gender relations had a strong influence on the "stickiness" of race as a social category.[14] This interaction also had a history and was related to other factors, such as demography (that is, the absence of Spanish women in the Americas in the sixteenth century) and changes in the economy and the labor market in the eighteenth and nineteenth centuries. Table 1 suggests a possible periodization for gender/race relations in Mexico from 1520 to 1850.

This chapter attempts to analyze change and continuity from 1750 to 1850 in the areas of marriage, urban household and family life, standard of living, and occupational structures and opportunities, relating each to ideologies of gender and race. It takes the position that gender concerns the relations of women to men, not only individually as in marriage but also within the larger societal context. The legal rights of women and the effective limits to certain sectors on their employment also fall under the rubric of gender relations within the larger society.

Relevant questions for the period from 1750 to 1850 include: 1) Which aspects of gender/race relations led toward greater autonomy and a better quality of life? 2) Which aspects of gender/ race relations worked against gender and racial equality and female autonomy for the same period? 3) Did independence somehow affect gender/race relations and the position of women and castes? And if so, how? 4) How did trends in gender/race relations from 1750 to 1850 relate to larger issues of economic and political change and stability?

Gender, Race, and the Family in Mexican History

The family in Spanish American colonial society was regarded as the "pillar" of civilization and "central" to the social and political network of New Spain.[15] The nurturance and preservation of marriage and the family was one of the main concerns of the state and the Church. While the state provided a legal basis for the family and for intrafamily relations, the Church watched over the moral and social aspects of marriage, the family, and women. Ecclesiastical courts investigated all reported cases of marital abandonment by wife or husband, adultery, concubinage, bigamy, or incest. Asunción Lavrin affirms: that "any couple not living in proper marital union was not only a source of scandal for society, but was also endangering its standing before God."[16] Moral transgressions were punished with whipping, exile from one's town or neighborhood, or, for women, a sentence in a *casa de recogimiento* (a cloistered institution, usually meant for the rehabilitation or protection of women).[17]

Table 1. Periodization for Gender/Race Relations in Mexico, 1520–1850

Period	Demography	Legal Change	Social Change
1520–1670	Substantial informal miscegenation combined with focus on racial endogamy; offspring of formal unions usually given race of father.	"Freedom of Marriage" doctrine for all Catholics. 1588 Mestizos of legitimate birth allowed into priesthood.	Gender ideology most important in definition of honor. "Sistema de Castas" operating by 1630–1650.
1670–1750	Sex ratio stabilizes; increased formal marriages, both within and between races, with illegitimacy at 20% to 40%.		Race increasingly important as a standard for gender-related honor.
1750–1850	Decline in marriage rate at independence. Age at marriage for Spanish creole women rises. Illegitimacy continues to decline.	1778 Royal Pragmatic requires parental permission for marriage and makes "equality between partners" a standard. 1799 Guilds abolished providing more employment options for women. 1803 Marriage promises must be in writing and notarized. 1842 Law requires obligatory primary education for girls and boys.	Race and social equality primary requirements for marriage. Honor no longer the provenance of all women. Use of dowry begins to decline. Education for women seen as a social good.

The ideology of gender relations in colonial Mexico was enmeshed with the concept of free will, or *voluntad*, and the concept of honor.[18] *Voluntad* was an early version of the concept of love as a legitimate reason for marriage. It implied that the individual (inspired by the will of God) understood the value of the other person as a potential mate, believed that this person was intended for him or her, and freely chose to feel affection toward the other person. "Love" (*voluntad*) in this sense stands in contradiction to "love" (*amor*), defined since medieval times as an overpowering feeling beyond the control of the individual. *Amor* also included lust, considered not only an inappropriate basis for marriage but also dangerous to family and society.

Honor was the supreme social virtue and could be divided into honor-status (a male attribute that depended on conquest, victory, and dominion) and honor-virtue (the maintenance of status over time, contingent upon female purity).[19] The concept of honor included premarital chastity and postmarital fidelity for women. Mary Elizabeth Perry invoked the Spanish proverb, "Neither broken sword nor wandering women," to signify two potent symbols of disorder—the dishonored man and female shame. The imagery also emphasizes the importance of enclosure as the key defense against disorder.[20]

In colonial Mexico, one of the fundamental principles of the honor system was the protection of Spanish women from African or Indian men. According to Patricia Seed, "this control [of Spanish women] created a basic social and sexual privilege for Spanish men by simultaneously granting them access to women of other racial groups and reserving exclusive access to women of their own group for themselves."[21] Ramón Gutiérrez argued that virtue among Spanish women was only possible because of the sexual exploitability of Indian, African, and mixed-race females.[22]

At the time of the Conquest, Spaniards confronted with the large "plebeian" Indian population adopted a belief in the fundamental equality of all Spaniards in the New World—that is, that all Spaniards had "honor." In this period, "free choice" in marriage, as demonstrated by the "will" of the consenting couple and the "honor" of the woman and her family (cited in cases when there was a previous promise to marry between the couple and carnal relations had already taken place), were compelling arguments in conflicts, which usually resulted in the marriage of the couple in spite of parental opposition.[23] Although a woman's honor was said to be "lost" if she entered into premarital sexual relations, the available evidence suggests that such relations were frequent. Historical demographers affirm that from 20 percent to 40 percent of births in New Spain occurred outside of wedlock in the seventeenth and eighteenth centuries.[24]

Women were often willing to enter into a premarital sexual involvement because of the promise of marriage, which was legally binding. After deflowering a woman, a man who wished (or was forced) to marry her would request authorization from ecclesiastical authorities. As Lavrin notes, "The argument most often used to support his petition was that the woman would otherwise be left 'exposed' in society. The wording commonly used also implied that the man felt that he 'owed' the woman her virginity and was repaying her for its loss. After presumably 'debasing' the woman, the man would use accepted stereotyped arguments of a potentially worse fate for the woman and assume the role of her savior through marriage."[25]

The juxtaposition of a rigid moral and legal code governing the relationships and everyday activities of citizens, and particularly of women, with high levels of illegitimacy seems anomalous. This pattern suggests the hypothesis, as stated by Silvia Arrom (though not with respect to illegitimacy) that the disparate elements of colonial society were "reflected in the coexistence of different marriage patterns among the descendants of the conquering and conquered groups."[26] While this hypothesis is consistent with data indicating that Indians married very young and in almost universal proportions (as compared to older ages and lower marriage rates among Spaniards), it is difficult to sustain with regard to the question of illegitimacy, which seems to have permeated the various cultures and ethnic groups of New Spain. Although some early students of population and illegitimacy thought it likely that relatively late ages of marriage and high proportions of the nonmarrying population would naturally be coupled with high levels of illegitimacy, recent studies have shown that the opposite is usually true.

The idea that the races represented different "cultural patterns" by the eighteenth century to some degree also implies a continuity of culture with race in the two hundred years since the Conquest. This idea is clearly in error. The changes in population, the cultural experience of growing up as the child of parents of mixed racial and ethnic backgrounds, and the variety of racial and ethnic mixtures undoubtedly resulted in a considerable intermingling of cultural and social attitudes between groups over time. While the early colonial period is often seen as one of "uncontrolled polygamy," some authors point to the many legal unions between Spaniards and Indians. The children of these unions were usually incorporated into the ethnic group of one of their parents. The early seventeenth century was a period of more stable unions, including —according to Richard Konetzke—the stable consensual union, most often consisting of an interracial couple. The earliest published data are from the 1753 census for Mexico City and indicate a level of illegitimate births of between 20 percent and 40 percent for all ethnic groups.[27]

This gender ideology substantially framed gender and race relations in the period before 1670, at which time increased numbers of black and mixed-race, or *casta*, women began to participate in legitimate religious marriage ceremonies, both endogamously and exogamously, approximating the rates of Spanish women.[28] This change, which was demographic as well as ideological, had a crucial effect on the transition to the next period.

Gender, Race, Household, and the Economy in Mexico City, 1750–1850

An understanding of the patterns of Mexican urban life in the period from 1750 to 1850 demands an analysis of the economy. Perhaps somewhat surprisingly, in view of the economic success traditionally attributed to the Bourbon reforms, Richard Garner and Spiro Stefanou wrote unequivocally in 1993 that "[in the eighteenth century] real economic growth could only have been modest at best."[29] Challenging the previous "Bourbon prosperity" thesis, such scholarship reversed historians' views of this period by focusing on the domestic economy and on regional population patterns.[30] In 1978, David Brading summed up these studies as depicting "a desperate world living close to the margins of subsistence, still afflicted by the twin scourges of epidemic disease and famine."[31] Brading further observed that "these [demographic] computations suggest that the rapid economic increase of the last Bourbon decades in certain measure rested on the prior demographic growth of the years before 1760. Moreover, in grim fashion they indicate the underlying unity of the century 1760–1860."[32]

The period from 1800 to 1850 was, unsurprisingly, disastrous for the Mexican economy. John Coatsworth estimates per capita income at $73 in 1800 (1950 U.S. dollars), declining to $49 by 1860. Total GNP (in millions of U.S. dollars) also declined from $438 in 1800 to $392 in 1860. In comparative terms the 1860 figure represented 50 percent of Brazilian GNP and only 4 percent of U.S. GNP. Mexico's economy declined dramatically relative to both Brazil and the United States from 1800 to 1860.[33]

These calculations assume a Mexican population of 6 million in 1800 and 15.2 million in 1910. By comparison, Robert McCaa's recent population estimates, based on aggregation, compilation, and extrapolations of local, state, and regional figures, suggest a total of only 4.1 million Mexicans in 1790, increasing to 13.6 million in 1900—an annual compounded growth rate of nearly 1 percent.[34] McCaa calculated the 1850 population at 7.6 million, a figure that assumes substantially lower growth in the period before 1850 than in the latter half of the nineteenth century. Cholera, smallpox, the Wars of Independence, and the Mexican-American war took their tolls in terms of mortality and emigration. Nevertheless, McCaa argued for a slight improvement in life expectancy and birth rates of about 45 to 55 per thousand over the entire period.

Commenting on urban Mexico, *fiscal* José Antonio Areche observed in 1774 that "as people deserted the countryside for the city ... the cities filled up with people who were unemployed and worse yet unemployable." He sharply condemned the small in-home weaving operations of the period as an inadequate base from which to develop a manufacturing sector.[35] These conditions clearly had a negative impact on the standard of living of the urban working class. The median "shifting proletariat" segment of several urban populations in early nineteenth-century Mexico has been estimated at one-half to two-thirds of the population.[36] Crime and vagrancy statistics between 1795 and 1807, and between 1800 and 1821, reveal that two-thirds of males arrested in Mexico City were skilled and semi-skilled workers, underlining the gravity of the social crisis.[37] How were the opportunities available to women and nonwhites affected by these difficult circumstances?

While the miscegenation of the sixteenth century was predominantly illegitimate, in the period 1670–1730 the racially mixed population increasingly began to participate in legitimate marriage. Levels of interracial marriage in the Sagrario parish of Mexico City increased dramatically after 1720 and involved many Spaniards—both male and female. According to Seed, this trend "presented potentially catastrophic consequences for a social structure primarily organized on the basis of racial distinctions."[38]

In this new environment, the concept of "will" became suspect. The earlier notion of social structure, which ascribed "honor" to all Spaniards (or all free non-Indians or Africans) had also begun to erode. The social convictions that a man's promise to marry was an unbreakable "word of Honor" and that a woman's shame had to be exonerated through marriage were no longer borne out in the results of marriage conflicts. Increasingly, it was possible to "compensate" a women or her family for her loss of virginity with a payment or a dowry. Increasingly, the most important question concerning the appropriateness of marriage was that of equality—racial, social, and economic—a criterion emphatically underlined by the 1778 Royal Pragmatic on marriage. This focus on equality over will (or property/race over love) also implied a victory of the state over the Church, and a greater priority for the nuclear family in society.[39]

A major problem in dealing with race, or *calidad*, as a category is that it implied not only the idea of race but also "a social definition of one's color, occupation, and wealth."[40] The types of racial mixings, the mobility of the population, and the desirability of social whiteness inevitably led to a gradual "whitening" of the population. This trend has been described by scholars in the cases of eighteenth- and early nineteenth-century Mexico City, Oaxaca, and Guadalajara.[41]

A particularly revealing analysis of race, class, status, and marriage patterns is Rodney Anderson's study of Guadalajara. He analyzed census data for 1821 by race, age, and marital status, separating the Spanish group into those with and without the status of *don*. The results indicate that the non-*don* Spanish group followed marriage patterns more similar to those of the Indian and *casta* populations than to those of the Spanish *dons*. The implication is that the non-*don* Spaniards were in reality a population with substantial mixed blood in their background.

Anderson has suggested that this group of untitled Spaniards may have been partially composed of "whitened" *castas* with mixed ethnic roots. The relative similarity of the illegitimacy rates of the separate racial and ethnic groups may be a result of this "whitening" or homogenization process, which would imply that behavior was ultimately determined more by circumstances and economic conditions than by racial or ethnic background. Anderson's conclusions are reinforced by Dennis Valdés, whose 1753 evidence indicates that mean income and household size of untitled Spaniards were more similar to those of non-Spaniards as a group than to those of titled Spaniards.[42] The period nevertheless appears to be one of increased legitimate marriage for all races and classes of people as well as of increased legitimate marriages of interracial couples. Yet, a number of authors have emphasized that increased intermarriage was also matched by continued high levels of racial endogamy, suggesting that *calidad* continued to be a strong priority. For example, Silvia Arrom's 1985 book, *The Women of Mexico City, 1790–1857*, gave an optimistic view of the changing position of women from the Bourbon period into the early nineteenth century.[43] Bourbon officials encouraged women's education and promoted their incorporation into the workforce. Since the transformation in values was seen as essential to social and economic development, motherhood became a "civic function." Free schools were founded, enrollment and literacy were expanded, and an 1842 law made education obligatory for girls and boys ages seven to fifteen. Arrom is careful to point out, however, that "female education was not intended to facilitate social mobility; on the contrary, it was meant to reinforce the existing social system while serving national goals."[44]

At the same time, the expansion of education for women undoubtedly broadened the intellectual horizons of Mexican women and increased their effective life options. Efforts to promote women's workforce participation also proceeded apace. This alteration on the part of the Bourbons contradicted centuries of traditional attitudes and statutes that discouraged women from working or even appearing very often in public. Guild restrictions against women's work were abolished in Spain in 1784, and in New Spain in 1799. The decree stated both that women and girls could "engage in all labors and manufactures compatible with their strength and the decorum of their sex" and that "under no circumstances will the Guilds or any other persons prevent women and girls from being taught all those labors appropriate to their sex, nor shall they be kept from freely selling their manufactures in person or through others."[45] Vocational education for women was also incorporated into the curriculum.

The promotion of women's employment was pursued with more reluctance than was education, however, both for social reasons and because of high male unemployment. Paraphrasing the early nineteenth-century Mexican writer and social critic José Joaquín Fernández de Lizardi's analysis of the apparent contradiction with respect to social structure, Arrom explained that "no real contradiction exists; there were two ways that women could contribute to economic development and social change: through enlightened motherhood, the role of all women, or through participation in the work force, the role of the poor."[46] She later concluded that "the notion of women's social utility gradually supplanted the older ideal of female seclusion."[47] According to Asunción Lavrin, the change "implied a softening of the prejudice against women of the better classes involving themselves more openly in intellectual life and in work."[48]

The period from 1750 to 1850 was one of slow economic and demographic growth, high unemployment, and legal changes favoring women's education and employment. The period also was characterized by an increase in legitimate marriages and declining illegitimate births for all races and ethnicities.

Female-Headed Households, Gender Relations, and Women's Lives

One striking characteristic of late eighteenth- and early nineteenth-century urban Latin American populations is the high proportion of female-headed households, with levels from 24 percent to 45 percent recorded in Caracas, Santiago, São Paulo, Belo Horizonte, Iguape (Bahia), and Mexico City.[49] While the majority of adult single or widowed women in Mexico City probably lived in households headed by married couples or men, an analysis of female-headed households can provide insight into the concrete material conditions surrounding the lives of this somewhat autonomous group of women.[50]

Household composition analysis for Mexico City indicates that from 1753 to 1848 the proportion of households headed by women varied from about 24 percent to 36 percent (see Tables 2–8). The vast majority of these women were widows (about 85 percent in 1753 and 69 percent in 1848), with the percentage never married growing substantially over time from about 4 percent in 1753 to 20 percent in 1848 (see Tables 2 and 3). One-half to two-thirds of female household heads were reported to be of "Spanish" blood. However, as Valdés demonstrated, "Spanish" households included families from a broad spectrum of society in terms of average household rent, household size, number of servants, and occupations. They ranged from the very wealthy and clearly eminent to households displaying characteristics equivalent to those of *casta* families.[51] Children were an important feature of female-headed households in 1753: about 63 percent included at least one child 14 or under (see Table 4). Twenty-seven percent included three or more. Undoubtedly, these children represented a significant source of family labor and future security for single or widowed mothers.

Table 2. Mexico City Household Composition, 1753–1848

Year	Female-Headed (percent)	Single Male (percent)	Male with Wife (percent)
1753	23.8	24.2	52.0
1811	32.7	13.0	54.2
1848	35.6	12.8	51.6

Sources: 1753: *Boletín del Archivo General de la Nación*, vol. 8; *Planos y Censos de la Ciudad de México 1753*, segunda parte, núms. 3–4 (Mexico City: Arreglado Alfabéticamente por Eduardo Báez Macías, 1967).
1811 and 1848: Calculated from census data presented in Silvia M. Arrom, *The Women of Mexico City, 1790–1857* (Stanford: Stanford University Press, 1985), 132.

Table 3. Female-Headed Household Composition in Mexico, 1753–1848

Year	Widows (percent)	Married/Husband Absent (percent)	Single (percent)
1753	84.7	11.5	3.9
1811	64.8	14.1	21.1
1848	68.6	12.4	19.1

Sources: See Table 2.

Table 4. Children in Female-Headed Households, Mexico City, 1753

Number of Children	Households (percent)
0	37.3
1+	62.7
2+	58.5
3+	26.8
4+	12.4

Source: See Table 2.

While the predominance of so-called Spanish women as female household heads might seem to imply an upper-class explanation (see Table 5), the occupations recorded give little suggestion of even a moderate standard of living. True, occupations such as musician *(música)*, teacher *(escuela de niñas)*, or landlord *(renta casa; se mantiene de fincas)* may have afforded the possibility of relative gentility. However, women's occupations for all races from 1753 to 1848 fell within a narrow range of possibilities. These included domestic service of some kind, the production and sale of comestibles, and textile and tobacco production (see Tables 6 and 7).

Table 5. Race of Female Heads of Households, Mexico City, 1753, 1811

	1753 *(percent)*	*1811** *(percent)*
Spanish	75.0	63.0
Casta	23.4	12.8
Indian	1.8	23.6

Sources: See Table 2. 1811: Arrom, *Women*, 135.
*Includes female heads of households age 25 and over.

Table 6. Occupations of Female Heads of Households, Mexico City, 1753–1848

	1753 *(percent)*	*1811* *(percent)*	*1848* *(percent)*
Service	14.8	8.9	24.7
Food production and sale	28.9	46.8	42.0
Crafts	46.1	34.8	28.8
Miscellaneous	3.9	9.5	4.7

Sources: See Table 2. 1811 and 1848: Arrom, *Women*, 162.

Table 7. List of Occupations of Female Heads of Households, 1753

Atolera	Dueña de Panadería
Comerciante	Dueña de Velería
Costurera	Dueña de Viñatería
Devanadora de Seda	Escuela de Niñas
Dueña de Accesoria	Hiladora de Algodón
Dueña de Cacahuatería	Lavandera
Dueña de Carrocería	Limosnera
Dueña de Chocolatería	Maestra de Misa
Dueña de Cigarrería	Música
Dueña de Cohetería	Peinadora
Dueña de Confitería	Dueña de Librería
Dueña de Hacienda	Renta Casa
Dueña de Lechería	Se Mantiene de Fincas
Dueña de Música	Tejedora
Dueña de Pajarería	

Source: See Table 2.

In 1753, Spanish women who headed households worked predominantly in crafts such as woolen and cotton textile production, or in food production and sale. *Casta* women worked mostly in services and less in food production and sale and crafts, while Indian women worked more in crafts (see Table 8). In terms of income level, essentially all of these occupations were at the lowest level and would be categorized as part of the "shifting proletariat." The large number of women who worked as live-in domestics is not included in this analysis. A notable change over time in women's occupations was the decline in crafts (mostly woolen and cotton textiles), from 46 percent to 29 percent of workers from 1753 to 1848. This decline was accompanied by the expansion of service occupations from 15 percent to 25 percent, and the increase of food production and sale from 29 percent to 42 percent. Since Spanish women had previously demonstrated a preference for craft occupations, their decline most likely implies a decline in occupational opportunities for women in Mexico City in this period.

Table 8. Proportion of Occupations of Heads of Female-Headed Households by Race, 1753

	Spanish (percent)	Casta (percent)	Indian (percent)
Services	2.8	44.4	25.0
Food production and sale	34.8	22.2	25.0
Crafts	55.1	22.2	50.0
Miscellaneous	7.2	11.1	0

Source: See Table 2.

The importance of wool and cotton textile production among urban occupations for women in this period suggests that an analysis of labor conditions in textiles might elucidate women's opportunities. An analysis by Garner and Stefanou implies, however, that the textile sector may have been unusually open to women precisely because of the unwillingness of most laborers to work in that field. The owners of textile mills, or *obrajeros*, "had to resort to slave, apprentice, and peon labor for 40 percent of the labor force in order to supplement free or wage labor because some potential workers simply rejected *obraje* employment. . . . In Querétaro . . . *obrajeros* faced labor resistance and yet refused to raise wage compensation."[52]

Obrajeros also believed that offering higher wages would not solve their labor problem, "because [workers] could not really spend more." In Mexico City and other cities, except for weavers, *obraje* wages were lower than those for day labor, and working conditions were probably worse.[53] One consequence of population growth in the late eighteenth century was both an increased market and more labor for textiles, so that small family-based textile producers (*trapiches*) could feasibly expand their at-home workforces and output. These small producers were subject to fewer regulations and had more versatility in terms of product.[54] They also employed a larger proportion of women than even the *obrajes*.[55] The *trapiches* gradually took over the much-reduced remnants of the textile market after 1820; Mexico's *obrajes* were virtually destroyed by civil war and foreign trade between 1810 and 1830.[56]

Both the 1753 and the 1849 censuses distinguished households according to type of living space. These included houses, apartments, lower-level dirt floor rooms (*accesorias*), single rooms, and shacks. Valdés concluded that in 1753, 100 percent of households headed by unskilled laborers and 22.4 percent of those headed by skilled laborers were living either in single rooms or in shacks. In 1849 the most prosperous section of Mexico City (the *traza*) included 52 percent of households living in the least desirable three categories of living space, with 32 percent living in single rooms. The more plebeian barrio included 78 percent of households in these less desirable quarters, with 62 percent living in single rooms.[57] According to Valdés, the population of Mexico City in 1753 was highly mobile in the geographical sense, particularly among those who lived in single rooms. Using data for rented single rooms from 1745 to 1771, Valdés concluded that 50 percent of individuals renting rooms in the sample stayed in one place for four months or less.[58] Frederick Shaw's study of Mexico City in 1849 also strongly suggests that the poor were frequently without a stable residence and often changed living quarters.[59] Such data imply uncertain living conditions and unstable family life for the popular classes, characteristics that do not bode well for women and *casta* society.

Conclusion

The conjunction between promodernization/economic development ideology and a relatively depressed economy had somewhat ironic consequences for Mexican women between 1750 and 1850. Several early nineteenth-century legal changes underscoring the acceptability of women in the labor force had little economic impact due to political instability, high levels of male unemployment, and the decline of key industries such as textiles. While the range of female occupations varied little from 1753 to 1848, the number of those women employed in the precarious areas of services and food production and sale relative to crafts declined significantly. All female occupations remained at the level of the "shifting proletariat." Perhaps the absence of capital for business investment and the resulting inability of employers to offer reasonable wages served as partial justification for encouraging poor women to enter the labor force.

Between 1750 and 1850, trends in gender/race relations that might improve the position of women and be conducive to racial equity included the expansion of female employment and education and improved legal rights for single women. At the same time, the power of the nuclear family (as compared with the extended family) and the authority of the male head of household (*patrio poder*) over other household members were extended, reducing the autonomy of married women, minor daughters, and subordinate males. These trends were reinforced in the civil codes of 1870 and 1884. Other divergent trends leading away from female autonomy and toward female subordination or loss of previous rights included the decline in the use of the dowry in the late eighteenth century (it disappeared altogether by the middle of the nineteenth century), more rigid racial boundaries, and a focus on equality and parental permission for marriage.[60] A decline in the importance of "honor" as a justification for marriage and a royal edict of 1803 requiring that a promise to marry be in writing and notarized to be legally binding similarly reflect an apparent erosion in the regard for women and especially reduced rights for women of color.[61] Effective barriers to racial intermarriage were an obvious consequence of increasingly rigid racial boundaries for gender relations by the eighteenth century. Elite discourse focused on the moral weakness of women, and especially of colored women, who were often blamed for the level of social disorder.

The independence period cut off the migration of Spaniards to urban centers, resulting in an increase in age at marriage and a decline in the marriage rate for "Spanish" creole women. Independence also had a negative impact on textile production and women's employment. At the same time, the number of female heads of household in Mexico City increased, especially among *castas* and Indians. This increase may indicate greater economic or social autonomy for these women, or simply a lack of marital stability.[62]

Most of the positive changes for women from 1750 to 1850, including improved access to employment and education, had little impact in terms of quality of life in that period. Like the rest of Mexican society, women were affected by poverty, high levels of general unemployment, and the disarray that characterized early national governments. Social mechanisms that had previously protected women, including the dowry, inheritance rights, and the importance of female honor, were much diminished. High birth rates and the cult of motherhood in Mexican society retained their force in spite of the absence of acceptable husbands for many "Spanish" women. Although the positive changes between 1750 and 1850 in terms of gender, ideology, and law make this period appear to be a favorable time for women and for gender relations, the objective economic circumstances tell a different story. The "quality of life" benefits of the new attitudes toward women and the economy would only begin to be realized in the Porfiriato.

Notes

1. Eric R. Wolf, *Europe and the People without History* (Berkeley: University of California Press, 1982), 9, 17, 355.
2. William B. Taylor, "Between Global Process and Local Knowledge: An Inquiry into Early Latin American Social History, 1500–1900," in *Reliving the Past: The Worlds of Social History*, ed. Olivier Zunz (Chapel Hill: University of North Carolina Press, 1985), 119.
3. Octavio Paz, *The Labyrinth of Solitude; The Other Mexico, Return to the Labyrinth of Solitude, Mexico and the United States, The Philanthropic Ogre*, trans. Lysander Kemp, Yara Milos, and Rachel Phillips Belash (New York: Grove Press, 1985), 117.
4. Richard Morse, "The Heritage of Latin America," in *The Founding of New Societies: Studies in the History of the United States, Latin America, South Africa, Canada, and Australia*, ed. Louis Hartz (New York: Harcourt, Brace & World, 1964), 165–66.
5. Woodrow Borah, "Discontinuity and Continuity in Mexican History," *Pacific Historical Review* 48 (February 1979): 24.
6. Taylor, "Global Process," 123, 170.
7. Edmundo O'Gorman, *México, el trauma de su historia* (Mexico City, 1977), as cited by Borah, "Discontinuity," 19.
8. E. Bradford Burns, *The Poverty of Progress: Latin America in the Nineteenth Century* (Berkeley: University of California Press, 1980), 13.
9. Eric Van Young, "Recent Anglophone Scholarship on Mexico and Central America in the Age of Revolution, 1750–1850," *Hispanic American Historical Review* (hereafter *HAHR*) 65, no. 4 (1985): 730.
10. Some important works on women's history and gender relations in Mexico include Silvia M. Arrom, *The Women of Mexico City, 1790–1857* (Stanford: Stanford University Press, 1985); Asunción Lavrin, ed., *Latin American Women: Historical Perspectives* (Westport: Greenwood Press, 1978); Patricia Seed, *To Love, Honor, and Obey in Colonial Mexico: Conflicts over Marriage Choice, 1574–1821* (Stanford: Stanford University Press, 1988). Also see Asunción Lavrin, ed., *Sexuality and Marriage in Colonial Latin America* (Lincoln: University of Nebraska Press, 1989); Gabriela Bécerra E. (coordinacion), SEP 80/41, *Familia y sexualidad en Nueva España* (Mexico City: Fondo de Cultura Económica, 1982); and Pilar Gonzalbo Aizpuru, ed., *Familias novohispanas: Siglos XVI al XIX* (Mexico City: El Colegio de México, 1991).
11. Joan W. Scott, "Gender: A Useful Category of Historical Analysis," *American Historical Review* 91, no. 5 (1986): 1058–59.

12. Tessie Liu, "Teaching the Differences among Women from a Historical Perspective: Rethinking Race and Gender as Social Categories," *Women's Studies International Forum* 14, no. 4 (1991): 265, 271.

13. Carolyn Walker Bynum, "The Female Body and Religious Practice in the Later Middle Ages," in *Fragments for a History of the Human Body 1*, ed. M. Feher et al. (Cambridge, MA: MIT Press, 1989), 182; Henry Kamen, "Una crisis de conciencia en la Edad de Oro de España: Inquisición contra la 'Limpieza de Sangre,' " *Bulletin Hispanique* 88 (3–4): 321–56; Verena Stolcke, "Mujeres invadidas: Sexo, raza y clase en la formación de la sociedad colonial," unpublished paper.

14. I specifically argued this thesis in Kuznesof, "Ethnic and Gender Influences on 'Spanish' Creole Society in Colonial Spanish America," *Colonial Latin American Review* 4, no. 1 (1995): 153–76.

15. Asunción Lavrin, "Introduction," in Lavrin, ed., *Latin American Women*, 16. Also see Elizabeth Kuznesof and Robert Oppenheimer, "Family and Society in Nineteenth-Century Latin America: An Historiographical Introduction," *Journal of Family History* 10, no. 3 (Fall 1985): 217.

16. Lavrin, "The Colonial Woman in Mexico," in Lavrin, ed., *Latin American Women*, 36–37.

17. Josefina Muriel, *Los recogimientos de mujeres: Respuesta a una problemática social novohispana* (Mexico City: Instituto de Investigaciones Históricas, 1974), passim. An important recent analysis of the ideology behind the use of the *recogimiento* is Nancy Van Deusan, "Recogimiento for Women and Girls in Colonial Lima: An Instrumental and Cultural Practice" (Ph.D. diss., University of Illinois at Urbana-Champaign, 1995).

18. This discussion will be based largely on Seed, *To Love, Honor, and Obey*; and Ramón Gutiérrez, *When Jesus Came, the Corn Mothers Went Away: Marriage, Sexuality, and Power in New Mexico, 1500–1846* (Stanford: Stanford University Press, 1991).

19. Seed, *To Love, Honor, and Obey*, 61; Gutiérrez, *When Jesus Came*, 176, 214.

20. Mary Elizabeth Perry, *Gender and Disorder in Early Modern Seville* (Princeton: Princeton University Press, 1990), 7.

21. Seed, *To Love, Honor, and Obey*, 150.

22. Gutiérrez, *When Jesus Came*, 215.

23. R. Douglas Cope, *The Limits of Racial Domination: Plebeian Society in Colonial Mexico City, 1660–1720* (Madison: University of Wisconsin Press, 1994), 3–26; Patricia Seed, "The Church and the Patriarchal Family: Marriage Conflicts in Sixteenth- and Seventeenth-Century New Spain," *Journal of Family History* 10, no. 3 (Fall 1985): 285.

24. Elizabeth Kuznesof, "Raza, clase y matrimonio en la Nueva España: Estado actual del debate," in Gonzalbo Aizpuru, *Familias novohispanas*, 386.

25. Lavrin, "Colonial Woman," 38.

26. Silvia M. Arrom, "Marriage Patterns in Mexico City, 1811," *Journal of Family History* 3, no. 4 (Winter 1978): 376.

27. Richard Konetzke, "La legislación española y el mestizaje en América," *Revista de Historia de América* 53–54 (1962): 178; Dennis Nodin Valdés, "The Decline of the Sociedad de Castas in Mexico City" (Ph.D. diss.: University of Michigan, 1978), Table 1.3, 33.

28. Seed, *To Love, Honor, and Obey*, 96–98.

29. Richard L. Garner and Spiro E. Stefanou, *Economic Growth and Change in Bourbon Mexico* (Gainesville: University Press of Florida, 1993), 5.

30. Enrique Florescano, *Precios del maíz y crisis agrícola en México (1708–1810). Ensayos sobre el movimiento de los precios y sus consecuencias económicas y sociales* (Mexico City: El Colegio de México, 1969); Claude Morin, *Michoacán en la Nueva España del siglo XVIII: Crecimiento y desigualdad en una economía colonial* (Mexico City: Fondo de Cultura Económica, 1979); Thomas Calvo, "Demographie historique d'une paroisse mexicaine: Acatzingo, 1606–1810," in *Cahiers des Amériques Latines* 6 (1972): 1–73; David Brading, *Haciendas and Ranchos in the Mexican Bajío: León, 1700–1860* (London: Cambridge University Press, 1978), 176–77.

31. Brading, *Haciendas and Ranchos*, 177.

32. Ibid., 176.

33. John H. Coatsworth, "Características generales de la economía mexicana en el siglo XIX," in *Ensayos sobre el desarrollo económico de México y América Latina (1500–1975)*, ed. Enrique Florescano (Mexico City: Fondo de Cultura Económica, 1979), 173.

34. Robert McCaa, "The Peopling of Nineteenth-Century Mexico: Critical Scrutiny of a Censured Center," in *Statistical Abstract of Latin America* 30, no. 1, ed. James W. Wilkie et al. (Los Angeles: UCLA Latin American Center Publications, 1993), 605.

35. Report of José Antonio Areche, *fiscal*, to Viceroy Antonio María Bucareli y Ursúa, cited in Garner and Stefanou, *Economic Growth*, 1.

36. Torcuato S. Di Tella, "The Dangerous Classes in Early Nineteenth-Century Mexico," *Journal of Latin American Studies* 5, no. 1 (1973): 94–95, 103–4. Di Tella uses the term "shifting proletariat" for the somewhat unstable lower class in his analysis of occupations in Querétaro in 1844.

37. Michael Scardaville, "Crime and the Urban Poor: Mexico City in the Late Colonial Period" (Ph.D. diss., University of Florida, 1977), 20–24; Teresa Lozano Armendares, *La criminalidad en la Ciudad de México, 1800–1821* (Mexico City: UNAM, 1987), 121–25.

38. Seed, *To Love, Honor, and Obey*, 146; Valdés, "Sociedad de Castas," 42.

39. Kuznesof and Oppenheimer, "Family and Society," 227–28.

40. Robert McCaa, "Calidad, Clase, and Marriage in Colonial Mexico: The Case of Parral, 1788–90," *HAHR* 64, no. 3 (1984): 477.

41. Valdés, "Sociedad de Castas"; John K. Chance, *Race and Class in Colonial Oaxaca* (Stanford: Stanford University Press, 1978), 176; Rodney D. Anderson, "Race and Social Stratification: A Comparison of Working-Class Spaniards, Indians, and Castas in Guadalajara, Mexico, in 1821," *HAHR* 68, no. 2 (1988): 240.

42. Anderson, "Race and Social Stratification," 220–27; Valdés, "Sociedad de Castas," 127–29.

43. Arrom, *Women of Mexico City*, 14–97; Asunción Lavrin, "Women in Spanish American Colonial Society," in *Cambridge History of Latin America*, ed. Leslie Bethell (Cambridge: Cambridge University Press, 1984), 2:355. Also see Sonya Lipsett-Rivera, chapter 5, this volume, for corroborating evidence of early nineteenth-century changes in gender relations.

44. Arrom, *Women of Mexico City*, 17.

45. As cited in ibid., 27.

46. Ibid., 30. Also see John E. Kicza, "La mujer y la vida comercial en la ciudad de México a finales de la colonia," in *Revista de Ciencias Sociales y Humanidades* 2, no. 4 (September–December 1991): 39–59.

47. Arrom, *Women of Mexico City*, 47.

48. Lavrin, "Women in Spanish American Colonial Society," 355.

49. Kathleen Waldron, "A Social History of a Primate City: The Case of Caracas, 1756–1810" (Ph.D. diss., Indiana University, 1977); Ann Hagerman Johnson, "The Impact of Market Agriculture in Family and Household Structure in Nineteenth-Century Chile," *HAHR* 58, no. 4 (1978): 625–48; Arrom, *Women of Mexico City*; Donald Ramos, "Marriage and the Family in Colonial Vila Rica," *HAHR* 55, no. 2 (1975): 200–225; Elizabeth Kuznesof, "The Role of the Female-Headed Household in Brazilian Modernization," *Journal of Social History* 13, no. 4 (1980): 589–613; Arlene J. Díaz and Jeff Stewart, "Occupational Class and Female-Headed Households in Santiago Maior do Iguape, Brazil, 1935," *Journal of Family History* 16, no. 3 (1991): 299–314. For Mexico, see also Cecilia Andrea Rabell, "Estructuras de la población y características de los jefes de los grupos domésticos en la ciudad de Antequera (Oaxaca), 1777," in Gonzalbo Aizpuru, *Familias novohispanas*, 273–98.

50. Arrom, *Women of Mexico City*, 133.

51. Valdés, "Sociedad de Castas," 128.

52. Garner and Stefanou, *Economic Growth*, 151–54.

53. Ibid., 151–53.

54. Richard J. Salvucci, *Textiles and Capitalism in Mexico: An Economic History of the Obrajes, 1539–1840* (Princeton: Princeton University Press, 1987), 142–43.

55. Di Tella, "Dangerous Classes," 92.

56. Salvucci, *Textiles and Capitalism*, 166, 170–71.

57. Valdés, "Sociedad de Castas," 114–22.

58. Ibid., 132.

59. Frederick John Shaw, "Poverty and Politics in Mexico City, 1824–1854" (Ph.D. diss., University of Florida, 1975), Table H-2, 388, compiled by the author from the census of 1849, Archivo del Ayuntamiento de la Ciudad de México, tomo 3406.

60. Silvia M. Arrom, "Changes in Mexican Family Law in the Nineteenth Century: The Civil Codes of 1870 and 1884," *Journal of Family History* 10, no. 3 (1985): 305–17; Edith Couturier, "Women and the Family in Eighteenth-Century Mexico: Law and Practice," *Journal of Family History* 10, no. 3 (1985): 294–304.

61. McCaa, "The Peopling of Nineteenth-Century Mexico," 621. See also Robert McCaa, "Gustos de los padres, inclinaciones de los novios y reglas de una feria nupcial colonial: Parral, 1770–1810," *Historia Mexicana* 40, no. 4 (1991): 579–614.

62. See Lipsett-Rivera, Chapter 5, this volume, on increased numbers of divorce petitions and a new focus on children in petitions of this period.

IV
Ideologies, Values, and Cultural Practices

7

Patriotic Footwork
Social Dance and the Watershed of
Independence in Buenos Aires*

John Charles Chasteen

John Chasteen, a professor of history at the University of North
Carolina at Chapel Hill, focuses on dance as a way to evaluate
changes in the relationship between popular culture and the state
in late colonial and early postcolonial Buenos Aires. This work
reflects his early efforts to trace the history of cultural practices
in the Southern Cone of Latin America, about which he has published a major monograph and numerous articles. In his essay
for this volume, he examines the Church and state reactions to
fandangos and other "indecent" dances that gave blacks, Indians, mulattoes, and mestizos the opportunity to intermingle during the post-1740 period. Prohibitions in place during the colonial
era continued after independence, becoming even stricter over
time. However, by the midnineteenth century a series of legal
and illegal dance hall-like establishments, or *academias*, spread
through Buenos Aires. Chasteen points out that during the independence period, dance became a manifestation of patriotic
nativism, exalted as an expression of collective identity. The best
example of this trend was a popular dance that came to express
the essential national spirit: the "*montonero*/National/Federal
minuet." As populist pride increased during the postcolonial period, other dances also gained acceptance. These changes are
the basis for Chasteen's conclusion that the relationship between

*Research for this chapter was conducted with funds from the University
Research Council and the Institute of Latin American Studies of the University
of North Carolina at Chapel Hill.

Adapted from John Charles Chasteen, "Patriotic Footwork: Social Dance,
Popular Culture, and the Watershed of Independence in Buenos Aires," *Journal
of Latin American Culture Studies* 5, no. 1 (June 1996): 11–24. Reprinted by
permission of Taylor & Francis, Philadelphia, Pennsylvania. All rights reserved.

popular culture and the state experienced significant long-term
transformations during the Age of Revolution.

From the perspective of the history of social dance, formal independence from the colonizing powers of Iberia marked an important watershed in the history of Latin American popular culture.
The reason is simple: independence fundamentally altered certain
aspects of the relationship between popular culture and the state.
After independence, popular dance was still officially restricted and
monitored, with varying intensity from year to year and from place
to place, just as it had been under Spanish rule. What changed in
the new republics was the relationship between popular culture and
the ideology of the state. The "Americanist" nativism, scarcely more
than nascent in the closing decades of Spanish rule, was stimulated
by the turbulent times after 1810 and abruptly blossomed as a political force. Nowhere was this more true than in the Río de la Plata.
In the years following the definitive Spanish defeat at Ayacucho,
signs of folk identity continued to be central to certain kinds of
political appeals, most often associated with conservative rural elements but hardly exclusive to them. Early nineteenth-century Latin
American nativist movements are not well understood, despite their
salient political role in countries as diverse as Argentina, Mexico,
and Brazil, and their obvious importance to any study of nationalism, popular culture, and the state in historical perspective. This
essay will use the phenomenon of social dance to look at the relationship between popular culture and the state during the transition
from colony to independent republic in the city of Buenos Aires.[1]

During the eighteenth and nineteenth centuries, social dance
constituted an increasingly important pastime in the Río de la Plata.
Most people seem to have danced, at least on special occasions,
and to one degree or another they expressed their social and personal identities in dance. This expression was partly imitative of
larger fashions that moved back and forth through the Atlantic world,
and partly expressive of the particular experience and local culture
of the dancers. The extent to which either factor predominated is
difficult to document and has been a matter of some controversy.
In nineteenth-century romantic interpretations, the dances of "common folk" were imagined to be the spontaneous expression of a
timeless ethnic essence—hence their importance as signs of national identity. In the first half of the twentieth century, Argentine
ethnomusicologist Carlos Vega argued that the great majority of
American folk dances were variants on dance fashions emanating

from Europe, copied by the colonial upper classes in their salons and then imitated by the people of mixed race who watched them. Vega's carefully documented and tightly reasoned work established an undeniable connection between Argentine popular dancing and international developments, but he was content—seemingly for ideological reasons—to dismiss all creative influence from below as mere stylistic color. Vega's approach was strongly taxonomic and essentialist, with emphasis on the individual dances as discrete species (montonero minuet, *cielito*, *pericón*, *media caña*) arranged in families ("de pareja suelta interdependiente," "de pareja suelta independiente") according to the characteristics that linked them to European dances. Though flawed, the resulting scheme[2] creates a serviceable starting point for our consideration of what Vega neglects almost totally: the ways in which the impulses of popular culture interact with the state and with those in power.

Very soon after their establishment, Latin America's colonial societies gave birth to a series of dances, the most famous of which were the *zarabanda* and the *chacona*. These dances included Iberian elements such as the fancy footwork called *zapateo*, snapping fingers, and guitar accompaniment, but an African rhythmic energy is unmistakable in body movements driven by the hips and resulting in sinuous undulations that made it appear, in Miguel de Cervantes's description of the *chacona*, as if the dancer's body became quicksilver. Sometimes performed by a sole individual, as occasionally in modern flamenco (itself indubitably influenced by these dances), the *zarabanda* and *chacona* were typically danced by a man and a woman who swept around one another (the man inevitably pursuing the woman) but did not touch, unless occasionally (and, of course, most distressingly to moralists) should they moved forward to bump their bellies together in the *ombligada*, a gesture characteristic of African-influenced popular dancing throughout America.[3] The *zarabanda* and *chacona* appear to have originated in the Caribbean during the second or third generation of Spanish settlement there, then traveled to Spain and other parts of Europe in time to be observed by Cervantes. By the 1590s, the *zarabanda* and *chacona* as well as other dances—including one with the unmistakably African name of *churumba*—were performed at the viceregal court in Lima. The elite vogue inspired a host of imitators throughout the precociously developed urban network of Spanish America, where being in touch with metropolitan fashion lent prestige to the socially competitive. By the nineteenth century, when they were still performed in many rural and provincial settings, especially in the western regions of Argentina, these dances were referred to as *bailecitos del país*; and though especially identified with peasant culture, they were often danced by provincial *gente decente*. These dances have been preserved in folklore (patriotic and otherwise) as the Chilean *cueca*, the Argentine *zamba*, and many others.[4]

Around 1700 these dances were displaced in fashionable urban settings by two newcomers: the minuet and the contradance. Both of these international dances were disseminated from Paris in all directions; and, given the accession of a Bourbon prince to the Spanish throne in 1701, Parisian styles had special new importance in Madrid. These dances are similar in that they involve a series of couples engaged in formalized evolutions, often holding hands (as in a square dance), but they contrast, too, in that the minuet is slow and delicate, not usually involving changes of partners, while the contradance is more rollicking and, in its early years, was condemned as promiscuous. The *bailecitos del país*, which acted out a pantomime of amorous pursuit, resistance, and submission, were worse from the point of view of the moralists, but the contradance introduced a new pattern of physical contact, a different sort of breach in the barriers of shame: in the course of the contradance, each dancer held hands in turn with all the other dancers in the line (or later, circle or square).[5]

The Prohibition of Dance

It was handholding that seems to have most incensed the bishop of Buenos Aires in 1746 when he drastically prohibited all dances in private houses. He issued an edict threatening the excommunication of "any person of whatever dignity, rank, character, quality, or condition" who frequented "fandangos" held in rented rooms or patios in houses on the edge of town. These impromptu fandangos attracted large numbers of people, and in his extreme condemnations of them the bishop left no doubt of the threat that they presented in his eyes. The dancing men and women "look at each other, not just in passing, but quite on purpose, and there is no barrier between them at all," he wrote. And what could one expect when lusty young men had before them "lovely maidens and married women moving their bodies with artifice, provocative expressions, and verses ringing in their ears"? "The ardor of their concupiscence" was fueled, the bishop believed, by the new element of the choreography. "Quite without hesitation," he fumed, the dancers hold hands, "lingering in that dangerous gesture just as long as they like."[6]

The bishop's blanket threat of excommunication indicates a second danger presented by dancing, at least from the imperial point of view. Social dance clearly served as an avenue of approximation among people of different skin color and social class. It had already played this role by the middle of the eighteenth century, despite the highly entrenched notion of an unbridgeable chasm separating elite from popular culture in this period. People of most classes, including artisans and black freedmen, danced some form of the minuet, resulting in natural modifications as both the minuet and contradance absorbed choreographic elements typical of the bailecitos del país. Gatherings such as those condemned by the irate bishop were habitual destinations for men of middling or higher status out to exercise what they viewed as male prerogatives. Certainly, although poor blacks, Indians, and *castas* were the most frequent targets of dance prohibitions, they alone were unlikely to inspire the insistent efforts to have the excommunication revoked. The cabildo members of Buenos Aires struggled mightily for a decade to escape ecclesiastical censure, protesting that if excommunication were taken seriously it probably applied to most residents of the city. New patterns of social intercourse surrounding dance, with its accompanying conflicts, were occurring in many parts of Spanish America during the later eighteenth century.[7]

In the discourse of social control that colonial officials applied to "dirty dancing," the central elements were issues of moral contagion and danger to the rest of society. The purity of onlookers seemed at risk to the moralists as, for example, when the slaves and free blacks of Buenos Aires—grouped according to their African origins or, in the case of the American-born, in mutual aid societies—danced publicly to drums and marimbas during the festival of San Baltazar. This sort of dancing had close links to African celebrations and often enacted a pageant presided over by royalty and various other traditional figures who wore special clothing; a staff bearer directed the evolution of the dance. The powerful drumming kept the whole group vibrating together as it watched the unfolding spectacle, in which all were also participants. By the early nineteenth century, these *candombes* took place on the edge of town or down by the riverbank on Sundays, and they became an important part of the system of black nations and societies that flourished in Buenos Aires during the period in question. However, one should not imagine that *candombes* held no attractions for *castas* and even whites. One extended explanation of their evils made clear that people of all sorts, including "decent" women, thronged to see the *candombes*.[8]

The idea of social and moral decay associated with dancing was so antithetical to the normative emphasis of the Bourbon Crown that most dances, including fandangos and even high-tone masqued balls, were usually prohibited by the state. Yet—here is the most interesting point—they all flourished anyway. The very rhythm of state prohibitions becomes the surest indication of the moralists' chronic failure to eradicate what they prohibited. Just as the bishop's decree of excommunication was finally lifted in 1765, another ban was slapped on "the indecent dances" of the blacks and on their gatherings with Indians, mulattoes, and mestizos. The ban was repeated in 1770, though with a proviso permitting black dancing that took place as part of official celebrations.[9] Even that practice was threatened by the government prosecutor of Buenos Aires in 1787–1791, who railed against the mingling of "people of all kinds" and the contagion of immorality suffered by other social groups who came in contact with the dancing. This official cited the notable new insolence, which he attributed to blacks, and the sexual misbehavior and prostitution that he saw surrounding the dances. He further bemoaned the profanation (in his eyes) of Sundays and the reinforcement of African beliefs associated with the dances, invoking the supposedly perverting power of the pounding rhythm itself. Finally, he got to the most sobering danger of all. "Everyone knows," protested this Bourbon social hygienist, that the dances sometimes attracted "two thousand blacks, and if they all acted together for any reason, who could control them?" At this time, it is well to remember, the population of Buenos Aires was one-quarter black or mulatto.[10] This antidancing campaign, like all the others, met with indifferent success. The dancing of the black nations and societies did not cease, but neither was there substantial relief from government interference. With the coming of independence, the prohibitions seem, if anything, more absolute. In 1825, for example, the police chief of Buenos Aires confirmed a resolution adopted two years earlier whereby public dancing by blacks was banned "without any exception whatsoever, not even with respect to the duly constituted societies."[11]

Nor did other kinds of dancing escape steady state censure. The 1770 ban, already cited for *candombes*, extended as well to fandangos, and the punishment prescribed for illicit dancing was no laughing matter: two years at public labor for Spaniards, and two hundred lashes for blacks, Indians, mulattoes, or mestizos.[12] As Spanish rule weakened in 1808, colonial authorities protested "the frequency with which dances are occurring, at any time of the year and involving all sorts of people." They subsequently disallowed such dancing altogether, "except when held in the houses of decent people under festive and joyous circumstances."[13] Such an escape clause usually appeared in the most resounding denunciations of delinquent dancing. Even the decree banning *candombes* "without any exception whatsoever" concluded with a proviso that "this resolution only covers dances that offend public morals," leaving the interpretation open to those charged with enforcing the law.[14]

After all, despite its dangers, dancing was indispensable on some occasions. All truly momentous celebrations—in honor of anything from military victories to royal weddings—were accompanied by the consensually recognized expression of collective joy. Surely it was this special meaning of dance that made it potentially so subversive when it occurred outside the bounds of permissible social action. The state could neither condone the apogee of collective good feeling in illicit settings nor dispense with it on occasions of officially sanctioned gaiety. Indeed, not to have danced for joy when the birth of a royal heir surmounted some long-standing dynastic impasse would have been almost treasonous. In 1664, for example, the birth of a Spanish prince inspired the cabildo of Buenos Aires to arrange a series of celebratory dances in a four-tiered arrangement to get the whole colony involved: a masqued ball for the town's elite; another for the merchants and sea captains not yet invited to rub elbows with those no richer but better born than themselves; a series of less formal dances for artisans and other town dwellers of middling status; and a series of rollicking, week-long hoedowns for the people of color at the bottom of the social heap. Participation on such occasions was emphatically not optional, and those who declined to attend these particular festivities were liable to a 50-peso fine.[15] Many years later, important patriot victories during the Wars of Independence merited similar treatment, as when in 1814 an order called for the bullring at Buenos Aires to be lit sumptuously for a dance to honor a revolutionary triumph in Salta. The order specified that the official invitations should be issued to all the ladies of Buenos Aires society, making it clear that attendance was obligatory.[16]

Dancing could not, therefore, be banished altogether from the scene, despite the sporadic fulminations of irascible prelates or governors. Most of the time it seems to have been banned, but nevertheless tolerated, at the discretion of those charged with enforcing the ban. There is, at any rate, no evidence of any execution of the dire punishments threatened by the prohibitions, before or after independence. Indeed, very few cases of arrests specifically for dancing have come to light in Buenos Aires. Those that do exist tend to reveal complicating circumstances, as in the case of a night watchman who arrested six men of color for illicit dancing in 1797. The watchman seems to have been angry because the dancers refused to open the door or stop dancing the first time that they were ordered to do so. The men were released after two weeks and fined 2 pesos apiece—more punishment than they deserved, clearly, but not the draconian sort mentioned in the edicts.[17]

Throughout the first half of the nineteenth century, enforcement was informal, or at least it involved little conflict of the kind that would be reported by the city's dozen or so police *comisarios* in messages to their superiors. A comprehensive list of reports sent by these men in the years from 1812 to 1850 (at least those that survived long enough to be catalogued at midcentury) contains many thousands of entries, trivial and grave, and seemingly all arrests as well as whatever actions had been taken as a result of someone's being found drunk and unconscious in the street, for example, or someone's falling down a well or into a latrine, or shouting slogans unfavorable to the party in power. In this list only two clearly identified police actions were found against dancing per se: one in 1827, when two black men were hauled in for dancing without permission at their mutual aid society; and another in 1830, when a woman was accused of giving a party without permission at her house. So exceptional is the case of the two men that dancing appears to have been an excuse, rather than a motive, for their arrest. The case of the woman's party probably only came to notice because a killing ended it tragically and led to police intervention. For the most part, people who intended to dance probably informed the *comisario* beforehand or enjoyed some kind of ongoing understanding with him.[18]

After 1850 the Buenos Aires police began to keep track of all establishments that hosted public dancing. To obtain a dancing license, owners usually argued that liquor was not sold on the same premises and that, as was the case for Román Gigana's establishment in the heart of the city, "the sole purpose . . . was to give dance lessons."[19] Probably because of this legal fiction, Buenos Aires dance halls acquired the name *academias*, but despite their grand title and the stringent rules governing them, they were much like dance halls anywhere.[20] The girls employed there were paid by the dance, but commercial sex was never far removed from such places. There were about ten licensed *academias*, and their special clientele were sailors from the waterfront, soldiers stationed at the barracks near what is today the Teatro Colón, rural transients who had come to the city to sell cattle or buy supplies, and thrill-seeking young males from all over town. The neighbors of one *academia* wrote angrily to the newspaper in 1855 that the dances kept them awake all night, and that the two police officials on duty there were too distracted by dark-skinned señoritas to prevent the dances from ending with bloodshed. After one such skirmish, in which the guards themselves got into a fight over one of the dancers and brought on a general mêlée that spilled out into the street, one of the neighbors claimed to have found a woman's garter inscribed "for the Señor Comisario, with thanks."[21] The toleration of prohibited activities here has the familiar ring of a vice squad on the take.

Despite the controls, the number of *academias* steadily expanded, their clientele (and the dance staff) became more diverse with the surge of European immigration, and the owners became most frequently Italian.[22] In addition to the licensed *academias*, many more operated clandestinely, with heavy quilts covering the windows and doors to muffle the music and three sentinels (one at the door and one at each corner of the block) keeping watch for the police patrol. At a silent signal from the sentinel at the corner, the man at the door hissed a warning to those inside, beginning a frantic game of musical chairs as the dancers sat down and the sweating owner prepared to greet the surprise visitors. Conversely, the patrol could be deaf to the music, since those charged with enforcing the prohibition against illicit dancing were frequently bribed to look the other way. When one operator tried to bribe the police after failing to get a license in 1881, he was able to offer the appreciable sum of 50 to 100 pesos per night; and, when the trusty officer turned him in anyway, the owner quickly (and with revealing ease) paid 1,000 pesos to stay out of jail.[23]

Prohibitions notwithstanding, the dance culture of Buenos Aires continued its fertile gestation. The dances themselves changed, as "closed couple" dances such as the waltz, polka, mazurka, and *habanera* replaced the minuet and contradance. As the closed couples of the *academias* tended to slip increasingly into tight embraces, combining kinetic elements of their local dance culture with incoming international fashions such as mazurka and *habanera*, they produced a distinctive new form that, by 1900, became known as the tango.[24]

Mention of the emerging tango—associated with prostitution and yet celebrated as an informal national symbol—constitutes a useful end point for our discussion of ineffective prohibitions and a good cue for our consideration of another matter of interest in assessing the meaning of independence: the exaltation of dance as an expression of collective identity.

Dance and Identity

Without question, certain expressions of popular culture gained greater importance for Spanish American Creoles during the struggles that led to independence. Popular music and dance led the list. Romantic notions of national identity, based on the idea of a deeply rooted folk culture, contributed to the valorization of a supposedly representative and generic "common people" whose presumably distinctive aesthetic sense found expression in dance. The nativist dances were taken for authentic expressions of the national spirit, and those who practiced and celebrated the *cielito* in the Buenos Aires of 1840 felt themselves to embody that spirit, quite literally. Given the sway that tenets of popular sovereignty held in republican discourse, nativist dance became a political resource of powerfully positive connotations. Notions of popular sovereignty and national identity worked together to legitimate the power of the newly independent states, and in so doing they drew on popular culture in novel ways.

During the Wars of Independence, patriotic nativism served as a convenient rallying point for a diverse anti-Spanish coalition, but eventually it was used to distinguish between good Americans— properly affiliated with the national culture—and bad ones. The cult of the popular appealed most to people who felt closely identified with it, a group that varied according to the context and the moment. Those who responded to nativist discourse during conflicts with *peninsular* Spaniards were not precisely those who responded to it when the Rosista regime directed it against their Unitarian enemies a generation later, and the political uses of nativism changed again in the 1870s. But whatever political appropriation of nativism was under way at any particular moment of the nineteenth century, signs of nativist identity such as dances seem to have gained wide appeal as conscious expressions of cultural affiliation, and they infallibly accompanied one side or the other (and sometimes both) in the tempestuous political struggles of the time. The *montonero* minuet offers a perfect example.

Montonero refers to the patriot guerrillas of the Wars of Independence, and the *montonero* minuet appeared in the 1820s while the fighting was still going on. It "appeared," to be more precise, in the sense of emerging into the historical record when it was announced in a Montevideo newspaper as part of an evening's theatrical program in 1829.[25] The fact is that dances such as the *montonero* had existed at least since the 1750s, when a European fashion called the *gavota* suggested the idea of combining the grave cadences of the minuet with more sprightly interludes. American dancers plainly could not resist infusing this genre with body movements reminiscent of the *bailecitos del país*. Before the Wars of Independence one might have heard this called a *minué afandangado*, but during the period of militarization and civil war that affected the Río de la Plata during the nineteenth century it received a series of new names from successive political movements. As the *montonero* minuet, it was carried by the crusading armies of Buenos Aires throughout the former viceroyalty of the Río de la Plata and on to Chile and Peru.[26] By the 1830s and 1840s, it had become the Federal minuet or the National minuet, depending upon one's political allegiance. In the dances given by the Rosas family, presided over particularly by the general's celebrated daughter Manuelita, the Federal minuet was de rigueur.

Across the Río de la Plata, many of Juan Manuel de Rosas's enemies were exiled in the walled port city of Montevideo, itself under protracted siege during the 1840s, and they entertained themselves with the same dance by a different name—the National minuet. (The besieging army, allied with and partly analogous to the Rosista party in Buenos Aires, danced the same steps but called them the Federal minuet.) The importance of this symbol of protonational identity was not limited to the mestizos, blacks, or poor Creoles to whom such dancing came most naturally. It is important to keep in mind that folk dance had precisely the same importance to many European nationalist movements of the time. During Spain's patriotic wars to expel the occupying French, folk dances such as the fandango played just this role for the Spanish resistance in Cádiz. To some extent, then, learning nativist dances was a cosmopolitan and politically engaged thing to do, even among elites of largely European cultural orientation.[27]

The *montonero*/National/Federal minuet was not the only popular dance that gained a new name and new prestige as the expression of an essential national spirit. The *cielito*, the *pericón*, and the *media caña* proved more enduring as national folk dances. All three

were contradance variations that, like the *montonero*, had incorporated elements of the preceding choreographic substratum (*bailecitos de país*). The *cielito, pericón*, and *media caña* enjoyed a vogue
in the 1820s, 1830s, and 1840s that extended from rustic festivities
in thatched-roofed ranchos lost on the pampa, at one social extreme,
to the salons of the Buenos Aires elite, at the other. The resulting
situation produced a sense of cross-class nativist affiliation aptly
exemplified by the image of Rosas, his family, and powerful supporters dancing the night away to celebrate his return to power in
1833. Outside in the patio, the common folk had the same dances
to the same music—with the addition of a guitar to spike up the
rhythm in the livelier passages.[28]

The *cielito* was the most important of the three "national" contradance variations and accompanied the dominant lyric form of
Argentine popular music in the first decades of independence. The
first positive evidence of the form's playful repetition of the word
cielo ("*Cielo, cielito, mi cielo*," for example, or "*Cielito, cielo, que
sí*") occurs in 1813, as sung by the soldiers of Manuel Belgrano on
a campaign in Potosí. Bartolomé Hidalgo, the first major poet of
the gauchesque tradition, composed *cielitos* that the patriots of the
Wars of Independence delighted in singing within earshot of Spanish fortifications: "Skinny, mangy, and sad / The Huns are all cor-
ralled," and so on.[29]

Cielitos abounded during the Rosas years. In 1830, when Pancho
Lugares, who supposedly composed the lead verse narrations appearing in the nativist sheet *El gaucho*, informed his readers that
his wife, Chanonga, was soon to join him in the city, his plans for a
celebration were predictable. He invited all his compatriots (a category that, for him, included only Federalists) to join him in dancing *cielitos* for a whole year. As for Unitarians, Lugares invited
them to sweep the streets for Chanonga's arrival. A few days later,
the paper offered a tongue-in-cheek reply to itself, framed as a
"Cielito Composed by a Unitarian Hag Drunk with Rage at Having
Been Ordered to Sweep the Street for Chanonga." These upstarts,
protested the embittered Unitarian character, her pride in tatters,
want to be served when *we* are the rightful masters. Where will the
Federalists stop? Will they next try to dance with "decent" women?[30]
Midnineteenth-century Rosista populism, it seems, used dance as
an index of class affiliation as well as cultural identity.

Even the purely black *candombe* acquired a new respectability
amid the surge of populist pride. As early as 1816, a patriotic *candombe* was officially sponsored in Montevideo's main plaza to cel-

ebrate early victories in the Wars of Independence. Rosas himself became famous for his patronage, at times attending *candombes* with his wife and daughter.[31] One nativist sheet published in Buenos Aires during the 1830s (in verse, like *El gaucho*) called itself *La negrita* and presented a black woman as its narrator: "My name is Juana Peña / And as a point of pride / Let everyone understand / There's none more Federal than I." The first quality claimed for this nativist persona in her spirited self-introduction is political correctness. The second is faithfulness. And the third? As a true daughter of Argentina, her skill at dancing the *candombe*: "In celebrations of my people / They give me pride of place / And everybody makes a space / When I step out to dance."[32] These images from the nativist press of the 1830s reflected sociopolitical realities, since rural people in general—and the black urban population of Buenos Aires in particular—strongly supported Rosas.

In addition to their importance in spontaneous social dancing and in the nativist press, distinctively American dances were featured in various kinds of performances and spectacles during the period following independence. Theatrical performances routinely closed with short farces called *sainetes* that very often included dance. A *sainete* written in 1818 represents the homecoming of a young patriot volunteer, returning from Chile with triumphant news for the American cause. After his ringing victory narrative, his parents invite everyone to dance a *cielito*.[33] In a later example, a French play announced in *El diario de la tarde* was to be followed by a *sainete* called *El gaucho, o las bodas de Chivico*, which included a *cielito* and another, lesser-known dance with the distinctly Guaraní-sounding name of *tabapuí*.[34] Dances were often presented as independent items on an evening's program, usually toward the end. "Long live the Federation! Death to the Savage, Perfidious Unitarians," began the ad for an upcoming performance by a group of Federalist theatrical aficionados scheduled for "the fourth day of the month of America" (May). The soirée opened with a "Hymn of Praise to the Magnanimous Rosas."[35]

Even more important than the theater to Buenos Aires's popular culture during the 1830s and 1840s was the circus. A number of circus companies based in the city gave regular performances in which nativist dance was prominently featured. For the most part, circus dancing was done by acrobats as part of their stunts—on a tightrope, on the top of a stack of chairs, and so on. Thus, a January 1840 show of the "Jardín del Retiro" circus promised a *media caña*, a *malambo*, a *gato*, and a Federal minuet (with a flag in each hand), all danced in exceedingly difficult situations (blindfolded, with a knife balanced on each foot, or stepping between lines of eggs). A certain athletic insouciance, rather than aesthetic refinement, was clearly the order of the day here. In this most "popular" performance venue, the nativist dances were far and away the most often advertised. Furthermore, while the actors belonging to the various repertory companies were almost invariably foreigners, the Circo Olímpico proudly called its troupe of dancing daredevils "Sons of the Country."[36]

Tightrope acts are, admittedly, not casually to be elided into social dance, but these examples illustrate clearly the nativist, populist resonances of the *cielito* or *pericón* in Buenos Aires under Rosas. Although related to the more inclusive "Americanism" that preceded it during the struggles for independence, Rosista nativism gained a heightened color from the need to discriminate among the native born. Birthplace remained of indisputable importance in the emerging collective identity, but Rosista nativism also predicated itself on a cultural option supposedly chosen by each of the general's supporters. Dance became a prime expression of that option.

Dance can be a particularly powerful sign of allegiance or identity—more so, it would appear, than many other aspects of popular culture. Perhaps its power comes from the fact that social dance is participatory. The dancer necessarily embodies the dance. Surely its spirit and the synchronization of many bodies to the same rhythms tend to move the dancers toward community of feeling.[37] Also, most dance is public, since, whether at a fandango in the patio of a tenement or at a gala celebration of state, observers watch and discuss the action. Everyone might dance the *cielito*, but the person who performed it especially well seemed more patriotic. Finally, as has already been remarked, dance is inescapably associated with joyous and significant occasions. While these observations suggest the importance of social dance in the study of cultural history, they raise questions of representativity. If dance possesses these special qualities, how much can its study reveal about broader currents of popular culture, specifically, those surrounding the advent of political independence in Buenos Aires?[38]

Conclusion

Two points emerge from this look at social dance in Argentina in the period from 1750 to 1850. The first is the striking continuity of prohibition coupled, almost invariably, with toleration; and the second is the potent new political meaning, after independence, of the popular dances created during the eighteenth century.

The first point—prohibition and toleration—suggests a familiar cultural theme, often mentioned in discussions of Hapsburg rule in Spanish America. Apparently, the behavioral prescriptions embodied in the law were not considered to be the usually enforceable standards, and yet perpetual shortcomings in living up to them did not imply the need to relax the requirements. Here we have a phenomenon related to the often-invoked expression, "Obedezco pero no cumplo"—a fragment of linguistic evidence that we commonly ask to bear entirely more interpretive weight than ought to be expected of it. The most frequent contemporary gloss on this overworked expression evokes the following rationalization: the king is far away and his legal instructions are inappropriate for local conditions. The history of social dance, combining draconian legal norms and chronically more unbridled practice, suggests a different interpretation, since the legal norms were locally instigated. We have here, perhaps, a view of human nature that is somehow more tolerant of certain shortcomings, more given to the notion that transgressions of the flesh are to be managed or held within certain bounds rather than extirpated completely. This is exactly the sort of deeply embedded cultural assumption that Richard Morse, Claudio Véliz, and others have addressed in stimulating but excessively unfettered essays.[39] If the history of social dance is any indication, the field of popular culture may offer new insights into old questions about shared assumptions and outlooks characteristic of large segments of Latin American societies.

More germane to the concerns of this volume, however, is the second point to emerge from the history of social dance in Buenos Aires. Popular dances such as the *cielito* became valuable cultural capital when insurgent forces began to construct new bases of political legitimacy through republican discourses of popular sovereignty. Republics, they alleged, were a superior form of government because they represented the collective interests of a nation. In order to make this argument persuasive, the diverse, diffuse, and fragmented caste societies of Spanish America had to be shaped (at least imaginatively) into national communities, and the invention of plausible national identities became a matter of special urgency. Just as in Europe—especially eastern Europe—traditions of popular dance were drafted into service for this purpose. As we have seen, the practice of social dance did change somewhat as middle and upper sectors of society added the *cielito* and *pericón* to their list of social graces, although European fashions continued to dominate the dance floors of the well-to-do.[40]

Whatever immediate changes occurred in people's behavior, they were overshadowed in importance by a long-term shift in the relationship between popular culture and the state. Dance is but one element of popular culture, and popular culture is but one element of a larger historical picture. The Río de la Plata is also not a microcosm of Latin America. Still, the discursive changes that occurred with regard to social dance at the time of independence in this region are sharply marked and highly suggestive. Colonial rulers had discovered no virtues at all in popular social dance—or at least none that could enter public discourse, since enjoyment on a personal level was certainly not uncommon. The salient meaning of popular dance in colonial discourse was always its moral turpitude, inevitably presented in diametrical opposition to the religious principles that, in the words of the viceroy, "raise a throne for sovereigns in the conscience of their beloved vassals, making submission and obedience into immutable principles."[41] The prosecutor who led the campaign against *candombe* in the 1780s was concerned that the black dancers seemed not to appreciate their own "lowness" (especially when they were dancing). Something had truly changed, then, by the 1820s, when *montonero* minuets and *cielitos* came to signify an authentic national spirit, something important enough to be copied and practiced in the highest social spheres. By 1850, this new discursive configuration had become one of the most salient in political life, and it has infused Argentine popular culture ever since.

To argue for a watershed at independence, however, is not to discount the value of studying a middle period in Latin American history. Historical periods, after all, are ad hoc constructions, tools forged by us to facilitate our understanding of the past, and different periodizations suit different purposes. They need not necessarily represent spans of time characterized predominantly by continuities. Most of the key insights in this volume derive precisely from the researchers' willingness to look closely at both sides of an obvious political divide. There is a great deal to be learned from studying both sides of that divide in juxtaposition. How else, after all, can one really gauge change or continuity?

Notes

1. For other studies that highlight the political significance of nineteenth-century nativism, see Adolfo Prieto, *El discurso criollista en la formación de la*

Argentina moderna (Buenos Aires: Editorial Sudamericana, 1988); Roderick J. Barman, *Brazil: The Forging of a Nation, 1798–1852* (Stanford: Stanford University Press, 1988); and John Charles Chasteen, "Cabanos and Farrapos: Brazilian Nativism in Regional Perspective, 1822–1850," *LOCUS: Local and Regional History of the Americas* 7 (1994). E. Bradford Burns's emphasis on nineteenth-century cultural politics is also valuable: *Patriarch and Folk: The Emergence of Nicaragua, 1798–1858* (Cambridge, MA: Harvard University Press, 1991).

2. The most important work on the history of eighteenth- and early nineteenth-century social dance in the Río de la Plata is that of Vega and, for Uruguay, Lauro Ayestarán. The extensive writings on dance that they produced during the midtwentieth century are collected in two carefully documented major works: Vega's *Las danzas populares argentinas*, first published in 1952, posthumously expanded with a collection of his other writings on the topic: 2 vols. (Buenos Aires: Instituto Nacional de Musicología, 1986); and Ayestarán's *La historia de la música en el Uruguay* (Montevideo: Servicio Oficial de Difusión Radio Eléctrica, 1953).

3. Vega, *El origen de las danzas folklóricas* (Buenos Aires: Ricordi Americana, 1956), 165–72. For another historical study of social dance, see Katrina Hazzard-Gordon, *Jookin': The Rise of Social Dance Formations in African American Culture* (Philadelphia: Temple University Press, 1990).

4. The best account of these early dances is found in Fernando O. Assunçao, *Orígenes de los bailes tradicionales en el Uruguay* (Montevideo: n.p., 1968). On the *bailecitos del país*, see the essays collected in vol. 2 of Vega, *Las danzas populares argentinas* (1986).

5. Vega, *El origen de la danzas folklóricas*, 85–140.

6. Quoted in José Torre Revello, "Un pleito sobre bailes entre el Cabildo y el Obispo de Buenos Aires (1746–1757)," in *Boletín del Instituto de Investigaciones Históricas* 30 (October–December 1926).

7. See, for example, Juan Pedro Viqueira Albán, *¿Relajados o reprimidos? Diversiones públicas y vida social en la ciudad de México durante el Siglo de las Luces* (Mexico City: Fondo de Cultura Económica, 1987).

8. AGN (Archivo General de la Nación, Buenos Aires), "Acuerdos del Extinguido Cabildo de Buenos Aires" (3 November 1752, 9 November 1752, 4 April 1753, 6 April 1753, 10 July 1753, 6 August 1753: Ser. 3, Vol. 1, bks. 28–29).

9. AGN, Bandos (1765, 1770) IX.8.10.3.

10. AGN, División Colonia, Cabildo de Buenos Aires: IX.19.7.2; and "Acuerdos del Extinguido Cabildo de Buenos Aires" (9 October 1788): ser. 3, vol. 8, bk. 49. On blacks in Buenos Aires, see George Reid Andrews, *The Afro-Argentines of Buenos Aires, 1800–1900* (Madison: University of Wisconsin Press, 1980); and Oscar Natale, *Buenos Aires, negros y tango* (Buenos Aires: Peña Lillo, 1984).

11. AGN, Ordenes Superiores, 21 June 1825: X.32.10.5. Much of my research on the *candombes* retraced the steps of Ricardo Rodríguez Molas, *La música y la danza de los negros en el Buenos Aires de los siglos XVIII y XIX* (Buenos Aires: Clío, 1957).

12. AGN, Bandos (1770) IX.8.10.3.

13. AGN, Bandos (1808) IX.8.10.8.

14. AGN, Ordenes Superiores, 21 June 1825: X.32.10.5.

15. Enrique H. Puccia, *Breve historia del carnaval porteño* (Buenos Aires: Municipalidad de la Ciudad de Buenos Aires, 1974), 7.

16. AGN, "Acuerdos del Extinguido Cabildo de Buenos Aires" (9 March 1813: Ser. 4, vol. 5, bk. 69).

17. AGN, División Colonia, Presidio, 16 June 1797: IX.27.5.3.

18. AGN, "Indice del Archivo de Policía" contains the following books labeled "Partes de Comisarios de Ciudad." Part 1: 1812–1830 (including books 22, 23, 24, 30, 35, 40–43) and Part 2: 1831–1850: 49–51, 65, 72–73, 77–80, 90–92, 101–3, 109–11, 116–17, 123–24, 128, 130, 132–33, 139, 141, 143–44, 147, 149, 150, 152, 156–59, 169–76, 178–80, 190–95. The two cases mentioned are 27 August 1827 (#39) and 18 May 1830 (#73): X.33.1.1.

19. AGN, "Expediente sobre Academias de Baile," Policía (Reglamentos), Permission granted to Román Gigana, 16 March 1853. An earlier usage of the term *academia*, with explicit promises of instruction offered, occurs in the ad "Academia de baile," *El diario de la tarde*, 14 March 1844.

20. See Teodoro Klein, "Las academias de baile," *Desmemoria* 2 (1995): 109–22, who gives a different derivation of the term *academia*.

21. "Bailes públicos," *El nacional*, 1 June 1855. On prostitution in Buenos Aires, see Donna J. Guy, *Sex and Danger in Buenos Aires: Prostitution, Family, and Nation in Argentina* (Lincoln: University of Nebraska Press, 1991).

22. This description is based on a survey of the petitions housed in the Archivo Histórico de la Municipalidad de Buenos Aires: Cultura, 1880–1887, cajas 20, 30–33, 41–43, 51, 109, 160. On urban transformations, see James R. Scobie, *Buenos Aires: Plaza to Suburb, 1870–1910* (New York: Oxford University Press, 1974).

23. The general description of clandestine dancing and the case involving the attempted bribe appear in "Uno de los parajes," *La pampa*, 15 December 1881.

24. On the development of the tango, see Guy, *Sex and Danger*, 141–79; and Fernando O. Assunçao, *El tango y sus circunstancias (1880–1920)* (Buenos Aires: El Ateneo Editorial, 1984).

25. Lauro Ayestarán and Flor de María Rodríguez de Ayestarán, *El minué montonero* (Montevideo: Ediciones de la Banda Oriental, 1965).

26. Vega, *Las danzas populares argentinas*, 1:375–76.

27. Ayestarán and Ayestarán, *El minué montonero*; Assunçao, *Origenes de los bailes tradicionales*, 131; Vega, *Las danzas populares argentinas*, 1:375–404.

28. Vega, *El origen de las danzas folklóricas*, 32–46.

29. Francisco Acuña de Figueroa, *Diario histórico del sitio de Montevideo en los años 1812–13–14* (Montevideo: n.p., 1890), 2: 218; quotation is from Lauro Ayestarán, "El cielito," *El día*, 23 May 1948. The first published *cielito* on record is entitled "Cielitos que con acompañamiento de guitarra cantaban los soldados del ejército patriota frente a las murallas de Montevideo" (Vega, *Las danzas populares argentinas*, 150–53).

30. *El gaucho* (Buenos Aires): "Invitación del Gaucho a sus compatriotas" and "Cielito compuesto por el Gaucho para cantar en la fiesta de Chanonga," 11 December 1830; and "Cielito compuesto por una vieja unitaria que se emborrachó de la rabia cuando le dieron la orden de barrer la calle para que pasase la Chanonga," 15 December 1830.

31. *Descripción de las fiestas cívicas celebradas en la capital de los pueblos orientales el veinte y cinco de mayo de 1816* (Montevideo: n.p., 1816), 11; Puccia, *Breve historia del carnaval porteño*, 34.

32. "Yo me llamo Juana Peña," *La negrita*, 21 July 1833.

33. Vega, *Las danzas populares argentinas*, 154.

34. "Teatro," *El diario de la tarde*, 17 February 1835.

35. "Otra función de aficionados," *El diario de la tarde*, 3 May 1842.

36. "Jardín del Retiro" and "Circo Olímpico," *El diario de la tarde,* 23 January 1840 and 1 April 1844.

37. Scholars in many fields are now using the body as a category of analysis; see Susan Leigh Foster, *Choreographing History* (Bloomington: Indiana University Press, 1995).

38. Nowhere have I found much useful theorizing on the history of social dance. The thoughts in this paragraph were inspired by W. B. Yeats: "O body swayed to music, O brightening glance, / How can we know the dancer from the dance?"

39. Richard Morse, "Claims of Political Tradition," in his *New World Soundings: Culture and Ideology in the Americas* (Baltimore: Johns Hopkins University Press, 1989); Claudio Véliz, *The Centralist Tradition in Latin America* (Princeton: Princeton University Press, 1980) and *The New World of the Gothic Fox: Culture and Economy in English and Spanish America* (Berkeley: University of California Press, 1994); and Glen Caudill Dealy, *The Public Man: An Interpretation of Latin American and Other Catholic Countries* (Amherst: University of Massachusetts Press, 1977), and *The Latin Americans: Spirit and Ethos* (Boulder: Westview Press, 1992).

40. For another application of this idea to the study of nineteenth-century Latin America, see Doris Sommer, *Foundational Fictions: The National Romances of Latin America* (Berkeley: University of California Press, 1990).

41. AGN, División Colonia, Bandos, 1790–91: IX.8.10.5.

8

Constructing the City, Constructing the State
Architecture and Political Transition in Urban Argentina, 1810–1860

Mark D. Szuchman

Mark Szuchman attempts to link the physical construction of the city to the "ideational" (ideological/cultural) construction of the Argentine state. In particular, his essay discusses some aesthetic dimensions of Buenos Aires's history during the colonial-republican transition, examining political and ideological issues in the process. Szuchman focuses on certain urban spaces, particularly the *pulperías* (combination dry-goods stores, bars, and gambling houses), which were key to both popular activities and the development of public opinion. He also pays attention to mechanisms of social control, especially the *leva* (forced recruitment) and the military draft, both of which exploited urban spaces where crowds tended to gather. These spaces included cafés and, of course, the *pulperías* themselves.

Szuchman also considers the material bases of urban life, including the economic well-being of local elites and institutions, commercial and artisanal dynamism, and the fiscal powers and capacities of public utilities. Throughout his essay, he establishes links between political beliefs and the urban aesthetic and notices the overlapping presence of, at times, contradictory patterns. For instance, he documents the coexistence of authoritarian colonial patterns with the revolutionary discourses and enlightened plans of the republican period. Here, too, Szuchman builds on his extensive research into the social, political, and cultural history of the Río de la Plata basin, about which he has published several monographs, anthologies, and articles. He is currently a professor of history and associate dean of arts and sciences at Florida International University in Miami.

This work is inspired by two sources. First, the concern on the part of political scientists with "regime transition" serves as a useful framework to study the relationships between political belief systems and nonpolitical structures. The political scientists' explanatory model of "bureaucratic-authoritarianism" was amply used in the 1970s to study the links between civilian sectors and the military, as first proposed by leading political sociologists such as Argentina's Guillermo O'Donnell. This model would undergo review as military governments yielded power to civilians in the 1980s.[1] Ironically, of all students of Latin America, historians have been involved the longest in the study of "regime transition," an area of research that has long been crucial to the exploration of nation-building, the transition from colonial to republican forms of government, and the alternations in governance systems throughout the national period. This study adds to the literature that relates matters dealing with political and governance dimensions to aspects of culture and social beliefs in the Río de la Plata. In the process, it traces the continuities that emanated from the colonial period and crossed easily—often imperceptibly—into the republican era. A key element in this study consists of assessing the forms in which revolutionary rhetoric and enlightened plans, following the establishment of independence, managed to coexist with authoritarian traits associated with the *ancien régime*.

The second factor informing this work is the lengthy list of studies on the Latin American city. Many of the political and intellectual voices speaking about the role of the city as the nation's civilizing hub, or the engine that would best distance the progressive republic from its colonial backwardness, came from Buenos Aires. This work, therefore, seeks answers in *porteño* urban forms and in *porteños'* discourse, linking avenues of progress to architectural lines that originated in and, in turn, informed political ideas.

This work will explore four dimensions of the relationship between the physical construction of the city and the ideational construction of the Argentine state: the urban basis of popular action (the city as a liberal venue), the mechanisms of social control, the material basis of urban forms, and the connections between political beliefs and aesthetics. These dimensions worked interalia in ways that fed into both the physical and ideational constructions of nineteenth-century Argentina.

The City as a Liberal Venue

A close look at Spanish American cities reveals the influence of political ideas drawn from the deep well of Iberian and Roman traditions, where we find ample evidence of the equation between urban existence and civilization. Indeed, so strongly has the city influenced the political environment and ideational universe of Latin America that we have been warned not to confuse the histories of urban centers with the histories of their nations. Still, José Luis Romero reminds us that "the decisive political influence of the cities faithfully corresponds to the peculiarities of the socioeconomic and sociocultural patterns found in the Latin American area, and for this reason it is important to establish which mechanisms unleash them and how this influence is exerted."[2] Nowhere was this relationship more true than in the region of the Río de la Plata.

Despite the historical centrality of the city in Spanish America, an explicit epistemological link between urban life and political ideas is not easily found in the historiography. Romero's works are especially strong in addressing the urban axis on which Spanish American political ideology rested. Drawing primarily from the historical record of the Southern Cone region, he noted the development of an important transition away from the aristocratic city toward the creole city in the process of gaining independence.[3]

Romero noted that this transition was facilitated by the city's naturally greater "instrumental efficacy." By this he meant that by concentrating both formal and informal institutions of power in the cities, political and social interactions were most strongly woven together in the Spanish American urban realms.[4] Romero is perhaps too close to the Argentine experience of relatively strong popular participation in different forms of political expression when he generalizes that Latin American cities effect social and political changes in part as the result of public opinion. To be sure, since the early days of republican rule, public opinion in cities such as Buenos Aires and Córdoba was taken into consideration by contenders for political office. Moreover, suffrage was exercised widely among men in the more important cities and provinces. Thus, elections took place within the city of Buenos Aires between 1810 and 1820 to select representatives to the general assembly of 1813 and to send delegates to the constitutional convention in Tucumán in 1816 and to other deliberative bodies. Similarly, the provisional regulations enacted in the province of Córdoba in 1821 gave voting rights to males over the age of 18, including freedmen. In Buenos Aires the 1821 legislation provided for the direct election of provincial assemblymen by males over the age of 20. Electoral participation increased in Buenos Aires over the course of the first two postcolonial decades: from 224 voters who participated in the *cabildo abierto* of May 22, 1810, *porteño* popular votes increased to 2,000 in the 1823 legislative election. Over 9,000 votes were cast in the election of 1829, which gave absolute powers to Juan Manuel de Rosas. To be sure, the forms taken by the electoral process often masked its insubstantial nature; still, fundamental principles of public participation were nonetheless established.[5]

The most important political novelty of the nineteenth century rested with the exteriorization of the exchanges of ideas—that is, the historically reduced space that had limited political debates to government officials within the interiors of administrative structures spilled out to street and bar. By the early 1800s, Buenos Aires's public spaces were witnesses to the heady and sometimes dangerous exchange of ideas. Thus, a "club" was established in Marco's Café, next to the Jesuit Church. This forum competed with the official venues of political discussions, where individuals *de talento* gave speeches and exchanged opinions related to the general welfare nearly every day. Both the forced tolerance on the part of authorities and the wide appeal of Marco's Café captivated popular interest. An observer noted that the revolutionary junta was "forced to ignore it."[6] Marco's Café was merely the start of the fast development of public space as a vital and most dramatic site for the unmediated broadcast of political discourse. In Buenos Aires, as in the rest of Spanish America, the primary public space was the Plaza Mayor, or central plaza. Scholars, such as Mark Harrison in the case of England, have addressed this intersection between street ritual—engaged in by either marginal or unofficial groups—and the analysis given to such spectacles by the established classes. In England, crowds formed in well-defined parts of the city. The controlling and articulate classes, unfamiliar with the culture of the street, were at once fascinated by the spectacle and fearful of its implications for social order and civic reputation. This ambivalence manifested itself in commentators' highly selective use of the terms "crowd" and "mob." What obtained in nineteenth-century England was no less true of early nineteenth-century Buenos Aires.[7]

Urban public space was more frequently used to air ideas and the will of different groups during the turbulent era that followed the fall of the Spanish monarchy to the invading French forces in 1808. However, the outdoors represented a double-edged sword;

public space offered opportunities for expression by groups on the ascendance who had seldom before experienced it with such raw energy. By contrast, to those who feared that their days in control were numbered, the outdoors became a liability while the indoors increasingly provided a refuge from turmoil. A royalist sympathizer during the time of the May Revolution of 1810 wrote: "The days have begun when the street belongs to the victors while the vanquished keep their animosities inside behind closed windows and wait for the future."[8] From such beginnings, the city became the principal venue for politics and enmity. It is significant that as early as 1801 the cabildo members of Buenos Aires had begun to confer upon the city the rhetorically subtle overtones of a nation-state when they began their meetings by pronouncing their municipal raison d'être: "a tratar y conferir lo combeniente a esta República y sus arbitadores [*sic*]."[9]

Construction and Social Control

The basic engine of the liberal state-building program was, from the start, its recruitment capability. There is little evidence that early Argentine governments garnered large-scale popular support for their foundational policies to the point of being able to rely on voluntary recruits. Indeed, the *leva*, or forced draft backed by government sanction, though hardly devoid of colonial credentials, made its greatest and most consistent presence felt *after* the start of independence. Manpower was especially critical in this part of Spanish America, noted for its sparse population. Indians in the Río de la Plata numbered far fewer than the indigenous populations of the Andean highlands or the Mesoamerican valleys. Furthermore, their seminomadic traits and fiercely effective resistance to domination placed these Indians beyond easily managed mechanisms of social control. In the Río de la Plata, the idea of eliminating Indians would gain supporters, but integrating them would seldom be considered an option.[10] There remained a considerable pool of floating rural and urban casual workers (*vagos y malentretenidos*, in the official language) to put to work on military and civilian projects.

In these endeavors, which were based on concerns for law and order, competition among political groups, who were often in violent opposition, was transcended. The *leva* took on different forms as it became an engine of frenetic activity for authorities seeking to enlarge the labor pool. Law and order became the concept and *leva* the motive force behind efforts aimed at providing the manpower for infrastructure development, urbanization, and public works.[11] The records of security officers during the first half of the 1800s contain numerous cases of men who fled from their forced assignments as workers on the city's infrastructure and beautification projects. These reluctant recruits included Argentines and foreigners alike. For example, Manuel Robleda and Joaquín Díaz, Spaniards who had been forcibly recruited to work on the city's *alameda*, the path that ran alongside the shoreline of the Río de la Plata, were declared escapees by the Buenos Aires port authorities in January 1848. Warrants were issued for their arrests. A similar process was endured by dozens of other men who, during the same period, fled to avoid serving their sentences on projects for the city's beautification.[12]

Both disjunctures and continuities characterize the issue of social control. The most obvious disjuncture is seen in the gap between the rhetoric of individual liberalism on which independence was initially predicated and the authoritarianism on which power actually rested. At the same time, continuities can be seen in the authorities' wariness of the masses, reflecting their concern regarding the culture of unruliness. To most authorities in power, the manipulable masses represented resources that political enemies could exploit, thus placing at risk urgently needed stability.[13] Frequently, the city of Buenos Aires would be the first space to experience disturbances.

The *pulpería*, a free-flowing combination of dry-goods store, bar, gambling house, information center, and hostel, also represented a venue of *liaisons dangereuses*. At the same time, the *pulpería* became a landmark of the barrio, or neighborhood, as the city grew outward and increased its density, subdividing solidarities, channeling public information, and narrowing access to goods. The urban space most coveted by *pulpería* owners was the street corner. Corner structures, which had heretofore been used typically as private dwellings, underwent structural changes over the course of the late 1700s and early 1800s. Typically, the walls at both sides of the corner property were broken through and door frames were hung to give a breezy access from the street and thus prominence to the establishment. A wooden beam often extended above ground at precisely the corner from which a sign was hung as a simple form of advertisement.[14]

The *pulpería* also represented a challenge for the authorities—in particular, for the governments of the early republican era, so susceptible to disturbances and criminal activity. The police records are filled with reports of raids, with security officers looking for members of gambling rings and men carrying weapons, or responding to complaints of drunken and disorderly behavior. Moreover, the *pulpería* was also available to the authorities as a source of forcible recruitment into the military.[15] To a European visitor, even passing by a Buenos Aires *pulpería* represented a daily hazard. As one such visitor noted, "sitting at a *pulpería* and participating in some game requiring little personal effort and, in a sudden spurt of passion, knifing some unfortunate are the most common forms of passing away the day among the lower classes of Buenos Aires."[16]

At the other end of the spectrum in matters of criminal behavior and patrons' social attributes stood the café. Its precariousness resulted less from the rowdiness of its patrons than from the sometimes dangerous political activities found within it. Cafés formed the sites of informal clubs where respectable men, some with stature in the community, gathered to discuss politics and current events. As mentioned, one such club—Marco's Café—was established in 1811, during the early stages of the revolution. After an initial period of tolerance, the revolutionary junta forced its closing. In April 1811, one month after its initial meeting, this informal club fell victim to a change in the composition of the governing junta as the result of a coup. With Cornelio Saavedra as the junta's new president, a heavy-handed policy was carried out toward suspected dissidents: "no one wished to enter [Marco's Café] for fear of a beating and a jailing."[17] Nine months later, another club would be formed to replace the previous one. The members of this new informal gathering were described as a "patriotic society consisting of wise men."[18] And so it went through the 1830s: a cat-and-mouse game between governing authorities and a political society that, when in opposition, was instinctively held to be disloyal to the state.

Thus, the *pulpería* and the *café* combined to give the city of Buenos Aires a look that included both the rough-hewn dangerous classes and the respectable *gente política*. Together, these establishments provided a combination of architectural activity and human movement unsurpassed in Spanish South America. Income from the building trades had attracted the notice of the public as early as the 1820s. In June 1827 the editors of *Crónica Política y Literaria* reported the "enormous returns" yielded by the construction trades in the city.[19] By the second half of the century, no city on the continent could compare to the commercial hubbub of Buenos Aires.

Material Basis of Urban Forms

The transition from the aristocratic city of the *ancien régime* to the creole city of republicanism took place after Europe had abandoned the baroque to embrace a newly polished classicism that carried its own ideological characteristics. Central to the new architectural style were concepts associated with rationalism, the influence of Diderot's *Encyclopedia*, and the efficient use of space. Leaving behind a visceral ornateness and a voluminous plasticity, the neoclassical spirit called for self-control, a more orderly array of lines and disposition of space, a more intellectual and less affected approach toward construction—whether for residential or public purposes—and regularized, ordered, and rigorous outlines, all of which made urban design more pliable and responsive to changing commercial and demographic conditions.

The Spanish American city had long been characterized by a nearly universal application of a regimented form. From virtually the start of Spanish settlement in the Indies, the *traza*, or plan, imposed itself with remarkable regularity, the grid pattern representing the matrix of the Crown's determinative power on spatial matters. Nicolás de Ovando's founding of the city of Santo Domingo in 1502 was based on straight lines radiating from a central plaza; quite possibly, he had been influenced by his visit to the grid-based Spanish city of Santa Fe ten years earlier during the Christians' siege of Granada. In 1513, Ferdinand enacted regulations governing the layout of urban settlements, and in 1573 Philip II's *Instrucciones* codified existing practices, many of which had sprung up irregularly. By then, however, the Spaniards had established over two hundred towns and cities in the Indies and would go on to found more.[20] The look and style of Spanish American urban construction were more widely varied, even if layouts were effectively contained within the Crown's generalized spatial formula.

The two most important determinants of a city's look included, first, the wealth of its elites and institutions; and second, the availability of materials. The income levels of a city's most prominent citizens affected construction features to the extent that these individuals' resources were channeled into both ecclesiastical complexes and their own residences. This dimension of material wealth provided each metropolitan area with an urban embroidery stitched with both the quantitative and qualitative characteristics of its elite. The political calculations of these powerful individuals and their families were expressed in the manner in which they endowed churches, subsidized public services, and donated both to the poor and to their considerably extended circles of dependents.

By the end of the eighteenth century, church-building had come to a virtual stop. New construction efforts focused on the public venue while, privately, individuals continued to dedicate attention and funds to their own dwellings, which tended to be larger in volume and stylistically different. While the end of the century also witnessed the success of the neoclassical style over the baroque in much of Western Europe's material culture, the ornate baroque, by contrast, enjoyed a considerably longer life in Spanish America.[21] In cities such as Buenos Aires, however, where neither the principal institutions propelling construction (such as the Church) nor the volume of wealth held in private hands had reached the heights of older colonial regions, the transition away from the baroque was much more easily achieved. The cities of the Atlantic regions of the Viceroyalty of the Río de la Plata had hardly undergone the embellishment traditionally encouraged by the patronage of wealthy encomenderos and well-endowed ecclesiastical orders in the sixteenth and early seventeenth centuries.

In older cities, such as Salta in the north, which had been established as extensions of the era of Peruvian conquest, wealth and contemporary aesthetic preferences were responsible for much more elaboration both in the service of the Church and the self-satisfying construction of private dwellings. The Argentine colonial style, especially in the north, was derived from Philip II's Escorial and was manifested especially by the cornices.[22] José Benito Churriguera, the architect and sculptor who was at his artistic peak in Spain in the seventeenth century, provided Argentine builders with the most imitable style. His flamboyant effects could be seen most clearly in the colonial altars of northern churches. Private dwellings, by contrast, remained unassuming.

The relative absence of quarries, wood, and iron made it impossible for Buenos Aires to take on the rich and complex urban landscape of Mexico City, Lima, Cuzco, or other metropolitan centers where the abundance of such materials enabled the construction of elaborate homes and institutional structures on a grand scale. Significant limitations in easily accessible building materials also served to limit the flamboyance of the details. The expense of forged iron, for example, restricted the use of florid designs on windows and front door gratings.[23] In the relatively few instances of ironwork on windows and doors, the gratings were imported directly from southern Spain during the 1830s. In addition, the absence of professionals in the fields of design and construction both shaped and limited external forms and decorations.

By the start of the eighteenth century, in areas of central Argentina such as the city of Córdoba, private homes began to be constructed with kiln-baked brick. Builders were usually frustrated in their desire to give monumentality to their designs and ornamentation around the main entrances; they simply had not mastered the techniques to join and turn fascia. The result was almost invariably poor and severely shortchanged imitations of the European baroque. In sum, only a modest level of novelty and minor modifications was introduced in Argentine construction by the end of the colonial era. Innovations were limited to somewhat more detailed etchings on the main entrance doors. Iron was used more frequently and became the focus of ornamentation, ceilings were finished, and more roofs on dwellings were built flat, leaving behind the historical use of tiled and pitched roofs.[24]

More significant changes came about through the multiple administrative and economic reforms of the late eighteenth century, which were most clearly represented by the sharply increased presence of the commercial sector and its effects on both the population and urban space. A trade system that had been based for more than a century on contraband was legitimated and equipped with enhanced port facilities, a cadre of customs officials, and an increased volume of exchanged goods. The number of merchants in urban areas of the Río de la Plata, especially in Buenos Aires, rose significantly starting in the late 1770s. In 1738 merchants represented about 3 percent of the city's white male population; with the Bourbon-led reforms in place in 1778, the number of merchants grew to 24 percent.[25] This significant change in the urban demographic and occupational composition was similarly reflected in the region's political matrix and spatial configuration. When added to the considerable population of artisans, the commercial and producing sectors of urban Buenos Aires accounted for just over one-half of the city's males in the late 1770s. The increased number of artisans required space for their activities, which frequently combined production and sales. The financial limitations and spatial requirements of small-time merchants, together with an economic culture that blurred distinctions between personal and occupational dimensions, meant that artisans combined living and working quarters. Seldom did they have the funds to purchase land or build separate housing for themselves. In the period between 1830 and 1850, artisans and small merchants added second floors to their combination homes and workshops, accused by climbing wooden steps; more frequently, they would add a room in the back.[26]

The growth of commercial and artisanal activities made for an increasingly busy, dangerous, and unsanitary environment that required the frequent intervention of viceregal and municipal authorities. New ordinances were enacted in 1784 to limit cart traffic in the city, establish street signage, and control the haphazard—and, in the view of some authorities, chaotic—nature of the fast-changing urban landscape of Buenos Aires.[27] Ordinances dealing with infrastructure continued to be enacted by municipal authorities well into the 1800s, an indication of their limited effect. For example, earlier attempts at providing signage had not been successful, and in 1809 city officials once again required street names and numbers to be posted on doors.[28]

In fact, urban designers had to confront the reality of a municipal administration that was unable to implement its own regulations. The historical record of failed policies followed by their reenactment is ample. This cycle included the limited collection of taxes needed to maintain and improve the infrastructure. For example, the policies and tax rates dealing with street lighting were established in 1822. Every owner of a dwelling or commercial enterprise was required to aid in the city's lighting by providing a standardized receptacle and housing for the oil lamps at each doorpost. Property owners were taxed at the rate of 2 *reales* per year per door. Yet, in November 1829, a review of the tax rolls indicated that several hundred taxpayers (*contribuyentes*) had not paid their assessments. In Census District No. 1 alone, encompassing a twelve-square-block area, the unpaid taxes amounted to 17,469 pesos. Entire city blocks had gone without tax collection for years. The list of taxpayers in arrears included people who had already died and whose estates were tied up in litigation, so that their bills continued to accumulate late charges.[29] The record of inefficient tax collection worsened the state's already difficult fiscal situation and continued to limit urban infrastructure until the export boom toward the end of the nineteenth century. The streets of Buenos Aires remained notoriously dark for many decades, the subject of periodic commentary by visitors and endless criticism by residents. Partly because of the limited success of tax collection, few residents responded to the city's invitations to submit bids to provide services such as street lighting, street maintenance, sanitation, and so on. Sometimes, not a single person would respond to the call for bids, while on other occasions, bids were won by individuals who would subsequently fail to meet their obligations.[30]

A case in 1821 illustrates the difficulties of maintaining adequate urban services in Buenos Aires. Prudencio Sagari, the *juez de policía*, or police chief, wrote to Minister Bernardino Rivadavia in February that don Manuel Collans had not fulfilled his end of the contract dealing with street lighting. A new bid was announced in April, but no one responded. At this point, don Andrés de San Pedro Galán notified the authorities of his willingness to do the job. However, after repeated and unsuccessful appeals by the municipal authorities to carry out the work, San Pedro Galán's license was rescinded in October 1822, many months after an ineffective administration had left city sidewalks in darkness at night. The lighting system hobbled along thereafter. By the end of the 1820s over 1,600 street lamps had been installed in the city. The tax, which remained at 2 *reales* per lamp, went entirely to pay the streetlighting licensee, thus, in effect, taxpayers bore the total cost, leaving no earnings for the city. In 1831 the chief of police reported to Governor Juan Manuel de Rosas that "there is not a single person in the district who does not complain of the treatment given by the street lighting system."[31]

Municipal ordinances neither dictated nor affected the aesthetics of Buenos Aires. Indeed, the Bourbon-era ordinances, which in many ways broke dramatically with the previously lax administrative philosophy, had not contemplated a redesign of the Spanish American city's architectural style. To the extent that stylistic changes took place, they originated from the relatively free marketplace of functions and needs. The clearest example of the relationship between urban forms and functions was the *pulpería*.

Nevertheless, the tax system affected the shapes and dimensions of urban structures. Throughout most of the nineteenth century, construction of buildings followed a consistent geometric pattern, known regionally as the *casa chorizo*. The structure of taxes determined physical structures, since taxes were imposed on frontage. Thus, the typical urban building had a relatively narrow front and deep interior. Although averages masked the considerable variation in the sizes of lots, it was common for frontage and depth to have a ratio of 1:3 or even 1:7.[32] This rectangular shape characterized the homes and businesses of the vast majority of *porteños*.

The erection of mansions, or *palacios*, by the elite helped to break this mold, but not until the end of the 1800s.

Politics and Aesthetics

The city of Buenos Aires became one of the principal laboratories for revolutionary intrigue and ideological experimentation. The Spanish American city was the primary venue for the expression of principles related to political emancipation. In turn, the movements that ultimately won independence in Spanish South America reflected urban roots that reached far beyond the *porteños'* debates at the *cabildo abierto* meetings of May 1810. The military arm of these principles cut a swath across nearly one-half of Spanish South American territory. Argentine forces, in effect, exported the revolution far from the confines of the port city to the other component territories of the old Viceroyalty of Río de la Plata (Paraguay, Uruguay, and Bolivia) and beyond, to Chile and Peru. The high costs of the revolution in materials and men were reflected widely in the Platine cities as well.[33]

While lives and limbs were shattered on the fields of battle, cities witnessed other forms of violence. Enemies, real and imagined, suffered the loss of reputations, estates, and worse through urban intrigue, long practiced in the colonial period and made vicious toward its demise. In the process of eliminating Spaniards from military and political power, sentiments antagonistic to Spanish culture were nowhere expressed more comprehensively and lastingly than in Buenos Aires. Such feelings were directed equally toward cultural and material notions associated with Spain; its literature, political theory, and traditions were displaced, shunned in favor of the intellectual currents blowing across the Atlantic from France and England.[34] The combined Hispanophobia and Francophilia of the revolutionaries extended to architectural forms and urban designs.

For example, one of the earliest landmarks of central Buenos Aires was the obelisk erected in the middle of the central plaza to commemorate the struggle for independence. Built along neoclassical lines, it was presented as the antinomy of the "gothic," the mocking term associated with everything Iberian. The term used by locals to refer to this obelisk, the "pyramid," resonated with the neo-Egyptian style in vogue in the French capital during the Bonapartist era. The process of Gallicizing architectural styles was reinforced by the arrival of French artists in Buenos Aires during the mid-1810s. The anti-Spanish campaign in the fields of architecture and the decorative arts was unrelenting.

When Jacob Bourdier, a French engineer who migrated to Buenos Aires, was asked in 1817 to give his opinion of a design for a structure planned around the central plaza, his response framed a set of strongly ideological and political constructs. Bourdier focused his criticism on the intended use of cups to top the building's columns, labeling the plan as retrograde and befitting more the Moorish style, which obtained in much of Spain, than the enlightened and progressive ornamentation found in France, England, and Germany.[35] Thus, while anti-Spanish propaganda drew imagery from the field of battle, republican propaganda came to include reproaches for perceived cultural and material stagnation, the consequences of a backward and imperious Spain.[36] These were the expressions attached to the psychological dimensions of colonialism noted a century later by José Ortega y Gasset who, in *The Revolution of the Masses*, observed the transitional nature of the colonial state as it led to "autochthonic life." Nineteenth-century revolutionaries and observers of aesthetic movements would have had no problem agreeing with Ortega y Gasset's conclusion that colonial periods were characterized by atrophy in refinement and complexity.[37]

One of the clearest manifestations of the cultural backlash against the Iberian heritage was the presence of artists, engineers, and architects from France and Great Britain, in contrast to the relative absence of Spaniards. The early nineteenth century was an era that, in Argentina and especially Buenos Aires, witnessed various styles in a single-minded intent to break with the past and reach beyond well-worn architectural modes. The styles that developed, however, turned out to be varied in the extreme and devoid of dominant schools. Rather, the strength of personalities and the culture of assertive individualism explain the architectural diversity found in the port city until virtually the end of the century. Broadening this diversity further was the considerable role played by empiricists, technically talented builders who were either self-taught or formed by life experiences. The so-called academicians—that is, professionals who had undergone formal training—were few. The handful of professionals in Buenos Aires were rarely trained either under the European guild system or Church patronage.

Among the earliest non-Spanish immigrants to have a say in the landscape of postindependence Buenos Aires were Santiago Bevans and Carlos Enrique Pellegrini. Not only were they not Spaniards or Spanish Americans, but neither one owned a single text on architecture or engineering written by a Spaniard or translated from the Spanish. Progressive Spanish architects and engineers had been having a difficult time in breaking the aesthetic patterns established by the baroque in Spanish America. The reason rested, in part, on the powerful role played by artisans' guilds in the form of *gremios* and *cofradías*. The earliest and most numerous ones were established first in the older and richer central areas of the Spanish Indies such as Mexico and Peru. Masons and general overseers, the *maestros de obras*, predominated among guild members; later, carpenters became prominent as well. By the sixteenth century, masons and *maestros de obras* had formed guilds in Mexico City; and by 1599, the city's *ordenanzas de albañiles* had undergone codification.[38] In the Río de la Plata, as was the case in other peripheral areas, *gremios* of carpenters and masons took on importance only after 1777, when their ranks numbered 150 members.[39]

Under the Spanish Bourbons, artists and professionals introduced new initiatives in the aesthetic movement, including the creation of new organizations: the Real Academia de las Tres Nobles Artes de San Fernando in Madrid, Mexico, Valladolid, and elsewhere between 1744 and 1752, and the Escuela de Dibujo in Salamanca and Cádiz. Here, professionally trained and progressive-minded designers came together to discuss fresh ideas that challenged the continued employment of baroque styles. In Spain, at least, the process of breaking down the dominance of the guild masters took place slowly under the strong criticisms of Spaniards such as Cean Bermúdez and Antonio Ponz, proponents of the neoclassical. In eighteenth-century Argentina, the struggle between the traditional masters and the progressive wing favored the latter. To the extent that the guilds were of much more recent vintage and relatively less entrenched, they offered weaker resistance; and insofar as the baroque had not made deep inroads in the region, the way was relatively clear for alternative designs.

Ironically, the greatest need for new construction in the Río de la Plata during the eighteenth century was found not in the cities but in the countryside, where Indian attacks posed dangers to agrarian production. The Indian frontier had undergone severe and repeated tests beginning in the 1730s through the mid-1780s. Indian raids threatened to push back the frontier to areas dangerously close to established towns and cities. The authorities responded with a militarization of the countryside that included constructing a line of fortifications, and it is here that designers and engineers concentrated their efforts.[40]

By the end of the eighteenth century, military engineers formed the largest contingent of specialists involved in public works, building fortifications, hospitals, barracks, and garrisons. They had a simplistic knowledge of civilian needs and tastes, which they learned after studying for three years at Barcelona's Academia de Matemáticas. Their training explains, in part, the flatness of buildings in this region and the absence of any ornamentation, reflecting the simplicity and essentialist functionalism associated with military design. The functional needs and the experiential nature of architecture and public building made for a curiously homegrown aesthetic form: spontaneous, not visionary, and, lasting well into the nineteenth century, almost completely alien to the academic trends prevalent in Europe. At the same time, the style reflected the contemporaneous political spirit, moved by a self-conscious unwillingness to hearken to the colonial heritage. This style represented a contradiction characterized by Alberto de Paula and Ramón Gutiérrez as a clash between ideology and reality.[41]

This duality is noticeable in the discourse dealing with architectural forms shortly after Argentina's formal declaration of independence in 1816. The opinion of Jacobo Bourdier, the French engineer who had been commissioned to study the feasibility of building *recova*, or arcade, that would span across the central Plaza de Mayo, combined aesthetics with the practical aspects of political strategies. Bourdier noted that:

> when the nation's institutions tend to erase the last traces of Spanish vassalage, public buildings ought to represent a style other than that of the Goths [Spaniards], because, in being monuments, they ought to manifest the type of public sentiment prevalent at the time of their construction. . . . This has nothing to do with the dictates of good taste, which might be mistaken, but rather with pragmatic issues, which tend to hit the mark.[42]

Bourdier, who had served in the Argentine revolutionary army and had been contracted by the Consulado de Buenos Aires to work on small projects, went so far as to suggest that "good taste" demanded the tearing down of the old cabildo building. In the end, the cabildo was not destroyed (it stands well preserved to this day) and Bourdier returned to Europe.

The *recova* was built across the Plaza de Mayo on the basis of a design by the Spaniard Francisco Cañete, a graduate of the enlightened Escuela de Dibujo in Cádiz. Cañete's design incorporated elements of similar structures in Mexico and Chile—the American components—along with Castilian traditions of old. The change from Bourdier to Cañete points to some of the reasons why ideology and praxis seldom connected: architectural patterns emanated from the idiosyncrasies of individuals in the absence of visionaries or stable leadership in either architecture or politics. The revolutionaries' ideological verve remained confined to the more nakedly political matters of appointment to office, taxation policies, personal allegiances, and so on. The material and aesthetic representations of their belief systems, by contrast, remained beyond their interests. Thus, the period's architectural dimensions were not shaped by the political elite's intellectual understanding of the relationship between material forms and the republican ethos.

One of the few times when the government took an active part in the recruitment of formally trained architects or engineers from Europe was in the case of Carlos E. Pellegrini. Born in France in 1800, Pellegrini was given a formal education by the Jesuits and went to study in Turin where, in 1821, he became involved in student activism and revolutionary politics. He was forced to flee to Geneva and eventually to Paris, where in 1825 he graduated as an engineer from the Academy of Physical and Mathematical Sciences. Juan Larrea, the Argentine minister in France, convinced him in 1827 to go to Buenos Aires and put his skills to work on behalf of the new country.

Pellegrini belonged to a small coterie of engineers and architects who came to represent the postrevolutionary generation of Romantics. The revolutionary ideology, consisting of strongly anti-Iberian sentiments, rejected intellectual and material forms that emanated from the mother country. This rejection included the Mozarabic, the Gothic, and the Spanish baroque. Preference in public structures was given instead to an ascetic Greco-Roman fashion matched in its Spartan qualities by the style found in private dwellings. In a letter written in 1828 to his father, Pellegrini described the housing of nearby Montevideo, which was indistinguishable from the style that he found in Buenos Aires: "four whitewashed walls surrounding rooms of one story, a ceiling consisting of beams cut in the grossest of fashion over which rests a smooth surface of bricks; the floors also consist of bricks, a few chairs made in the United States, a table, a bed, and on the walls, no wallpaper or pictures."[43]

The minimalist interior described by Pellegrini represented the Argentine aversion to the perceived excesses of the Spanish baroque; perhaps inevitably, this aversion gave way in the Buenos Aires of the 1830s to a Romantic revival. In either case, however,

Spanish elements simply evanesced, unlikely to return in light of the dearth of Spanish architectural manuals and treatises. Instead of works by Spaniards, Pellegrini and his contemporary, Santiago Bevans, were influenced most strongly by French and British innovators, followed by Italian stylists. In this regard, professional builders in Buenos Aires coincided with leading political liberals of the first third of the nineteenth century, such as Bernardino Rivadavia, whose considerable personal library of nearly seven hundred volumes showed a similarly clear preference for French authors (55 percent) at the expense of Iberian ones.[44]

Public Construction, Private Spaces

The classical and minimalist lines of the postrevolutionary era contained the rudimentary elements of Italian luminaries of old, such as Vincenzo Scamozzi of the late Renaissance era (1552–1616). The Scamozzi Ionic order was represented by columns with all four faces identical, usually with a rosette or flower in the center of each face of the capital. Beyond the influence felt in the early nineteenth century, the Italianizing precedents set the stage in Argentina for a lasting legacy that bore much richer fruit after 1850. Part of the reason for the long lag time rests with the slow pace of urban expansion to midcentury. The bulk of construction consisted of private and commercial dwellings while, by contrast, the business of government called for few new buildings. Typically, a government office occupied existing spaces, and thus we have few instances of bids going out for the construction of public works based on the need for bureaucratic offices. Indeed, Bourbon-era Buenos Aires offered the contradiction of an expanded bureaucracy with low levels of public construction. No new government building was erected after the designation of Buenos Aires as the capital of the Viceroyalty of Río de la Plata in 1776; existing property was typically rented and refurbished to suit the needs of the bureaucrats, as when the old slave-auction house became the customs house in 1785. The old cabildo building retained the offices of the municipal government, and various rooms in existing buildings became ministries and secretariats.[45]

By contrast, bids for public infrastructure works took place with considerable frequency. Among the most important of these dealt with plans for improved and expanded port facilities. Buenos Aires's port in the early nineteenth century consisted of little more than a long wooden pier. On January 14, 1822, a major storm blew away the dock, which was eventually replaced by two long wharves in the early 1830s. The need for port facilities, however, did not bring about any special architectural design; instead, it represented the ad hoc functionalism typical of the era.

Paving and maintaining city streets also called for a regular bidding process. The city contracted for the laying down of stones along the central streets in 1822 and 1823, a job that was ultimately carried out by self-taught individuals who fulfilled their contracts with a minimum of effort or sophistication. Years later, Santiago Bevans, in an unusually understated comment for the era, noted that "it is necessary to admit that the streets of Buenos Ayres present a very bad aspect."[46]

The slow progress of public construction and the few incidences of government-sponsored projects reflected a cultural definition of the outdoors and public space during the first half of the nineteenth century. The outdoors was characterized as an environment unsuited for decent society. In the daytime, it was considered the stage for strange and untrustworthy hawkers to ply their trades, a meeting place for all those people who had no fixed and relevant purpose in society, a spawning ground for troublemakers—the so-called *vagos y malentretenidos*—and the domain of women who, instead of following the norms of decent society by keeping themselves under wraps (literally and otherwise), idled their lives away in gossip. At night, the outdoors represented the venue for superstitious characters, macabre figures, and the spirits of evildoers.[47] The outdoors and the indoors were polar opposites: "in contrast to the [ideal of] deserted streets, domestic life is intense and encompasses the era's small amount of *porteño* social life."[48] While the association between public space and unwholesomeness formed part of the cultural norms, the antinomous relationship was made clearer still during the long period of *rosista* domination when, during bursts of political crises, dead bodies were inexplicably found in some of the city's public spaces. Indeed, novels written by anti-Rosas literati have been interpreted as highlighting the stark duality of an unsafe outdoors and a confined indoors, which, while not guaranteeing security, was at least a refuge from political evil.[49]

The fall of Juan Manuel de Rosas in 1852, after a dictatorial rule that lasted nearly one quarter-century, signaled the opening for a more grizzled and exclusivist version of the liberalism that had permeated the thinking of the radical revolutionaries of 1810. The arrival of midcentury liberalism was accompanied by a clearly articulated distrust of the masses. To be sure, the masses never held an especially laudable place among Argentine conservatives. In this, they were not alone. In Mexico historical distrust of the masses was quickly transformed into fear after the Indian rebellions led by José María Morelos and Miguel Hidalgo.[50] Similar attitudes could be found in the Andean regions.[51] In Argentina, Rosas's brand of conservatism was supported by an *estanciero* class wary of rural laborers who responded all too easily to personal affinities and thus could play into the hands of the *estancieros'* enemies. In addition, early nineteenth-century conservatism in Argentina was imbued with a sense of corporatism that included the assumption of a natural order of leadership by elites and deference by the masses. The prerevolutionary era was extolled for being stable and for providing an environment in which each person knew his place.[52] Rosas had declared himself the strongest supporter of the status quo ante. "I believed it important," he wrote, "to accustom the people always to regard with respect the upper classes of the country."[53]

The liberals who ruled after the fall of Rosas in 1852 also had deeply rooted suspicions of the masses. Their concerns were based, first, on identifying them as a class rather than as partisans of one caudillo or another, and second, on characterizing the gaucho as representative of the Iberian legacies of ignorance, routine, and inertia. For liberals, therefore, the masses were considered a troublesome residue of colonialism that first had to be marginalized and, ultimately, eliminated through assimilation to avowedly better peoples, such as immigrants from Europe. This liberal generation was certainly more restrictive than either its liberal predecessors or conservative allies in opposition to Rosas. In September 1852 the city's charter was altered. Municipal reforms for the city of Buenos Aires were decreed by General Justo José de Urquiza, a federalist who became disillusioned with Rosas and went on to remove him from power. Urquiza, a native of Entre Ríos Province and less aristocratic than many of his political peers in the city of Buenos Aires, defined notions of urban citizenship and participation very amply:

> Art. 2. The Municipality, considered to be an association of families united by the interests, goods, and rights common to all its members, forms a civil entity: it is capable of contracting, acquiring, owning, and working toward justice in the same way as individuals.
> Art. 3. Members of the Municipality will be residents of the city of Buenos Aires, fathers of families, known to be honest and respectable in their dealings.[54]

Two years later, after the split between Urquiza's federalists and the leaders of Buenos Aires, the region's centralists and liberals rewrote the municipal charter. On October 11, 1854, participation in city affairs was significantly narrowed:

> Art. 3. Members of the Municipality will be residents of the city of Buenos Aires, older than 25 years of age or free from parental supervision, and with a minimum capital of 10,000 pesos, or instead, a profession or occupation that provides the equivalent income.[55]

The strong anticolonial and anti-Iberian sentiments of the time were nowhere more clearly presented than in the writings of Domingo F. Sarmiento, one of the most prolific exponents of the new generation of liberals, the Generation of '37, who came to power in the 1850s. Sarmiento linked the perceived national malaise with the state of the country's material culture, specifically its architectural traditions. In Buenos Aires the prevailing flat-roofed houses, the majority of which were single-story boxes of brick and masonry (*casas de azotea*), represented for Sarmiento all the retrograde aspects of Argentina, both in terms of its material culture and its political essence. Writing in the 1880s, Sarmiento noted that by the 1860s:

> the flat-roofed house definitively begins to lose its authoritativeness, and begins to be considered unworthy of the living space of a free people. We will stop being oven-birds [*horneros*], and show ourselves to have the human faculty of diversity with respect to housing forms, since we have already seen that the teepee, the shack, and *casas de azotea* represent the material forms of the savage, of the Arab, in the same way that the nest is an invariable form of housing for the oven-bird. Only foreign immigration, the architect from other countries, the Italian mason, could break the archaic traditions from the East that Rosas had established in an apparently irrevocable manner.[56]

Sarmiento lived to see significant changes in the architectural and urban layout of Buenos Aires. The mixture of elite liberalism and commercial progress of the second half of the nineteenth century effected widespread changes in the city's material culture. Relatively few new private dwellings had been erected during the 1840s, but beginning in the 1850s the number of building permits rose significantly, a reflection of much-improved economic conditions.[57] The extraordinary export boom of the last third of the 1800s facilitated capital, encouraged a significant increase in population (largely through European immigration), enlarged the scope of the state, and raised demand for both public and private construction. In the area of public construction, an unusual degree of academic eclecticism dominated the urban scene, drawing from British, German, French, and Italian fashions in a mélange that, on the one hand, purposely avoided any Iberian traces and, on the other, accumulated all other "civilized" European influences under the precepts of universal liberalism.

Conclusion

Commenting on the material construction of the liberal state in Argentina, historians of architecture Daniel Schávelzon and Héctor Karp note that the styles that followed the fall of Rosas and that continued through the 1920s were not independent of the economic and political moments in which they developed. They reflected the political architecture of the state and reified the oligarchy's theory of governance and its economic principles. A comprehensive architectural style was transplanted from Europe, leaving aside the region's historical antecedents. The ensuing construction demonstrated that behind this asserted universalization was a teleological vision of power by the country's dominant sectors, which attempted through architecture to obscure reality by transforming the historic nation into an ideal Gallicized variant.[58]

No longer a modest renter of existing space, the fast-growing post-1852 state now took it upon itself to become the primary designer and coordinator of urban infrastructure and public buildings, including schools, museums, theaters, ministries, parliaments, courthouses, and a comprehensive array of other urban structures. In the event, the scope of construction in Argentina was enlarged at the cost of the simpler lines common during the relatively impoverished colonial and early republican periods. The functional-minded, mostly dilettante-designed, stoic architecture of the past was eliminated, making way for the massive scale of an eclecticism that spoke of European derivative aesthetics. If radical change characterized the material environment of the new liberal state, which would dominate Argentine governments until the Great Depression, authoritarian traditions dating to the late colonial period continued to underlie important segments of the political culture.

Notes

1. Rubén M. Perina, "The Performance and Consequences of Military Rule in Argentina, 1966–1973" (Ph.D. diss., University of Pennsylvania, 1981); Guillermo O'Donnell, "Reflections on the Patterns of Change in the Bureaucratic-Authoritarian State," *Latin American Research Review* 13, no. 1 (1978): 3–38; and O'Donnell, *Modernization and Bureaucratic-Authoritarianism: Stud-*

ies in South American Politics (Berkeley: University of California, 1973). For an alternative to O'Donnell's views, see William C. Smith, *Authoritarianism and the Crisis of the Argentine Political Economy* (Stanford: Stanford University Press, 1991).

2. José Luis Romero, "La ciudad latinoamericana y los movimientos políticos," in *La urbanización en América Latina*, ed. Jorge Hardoy and Carlos Tobar (Buenos Aires: Editorial del Instituto Torcuato Di Tella, 1969), 297.

3. Romero, "La ciudad latinoamericana," 297–310; José Luis Romero, *Latinoamérica: Las ciudades y las ideas* (Buenos Aires: Siglo Veintiuno Editores, 1976).

4. Romero, "La ciudad latinoamericana," 297.

5. Félix Luna, *Fuerzas hegemónicas y partidos políticos* (Buenos Aires: Editorial Sudamericana, 1989), 27–30.

6. Juan Manuel Beruti, "Memorias curiosas," in Senado de la Nación (República Argentina), *Biblioteca de Mayo*, vol. 4, *Diarios y crónicas* (Buenos Aires, 1960), 3784.

7. Mark Harrison, *Crowds and History: Mass Phenomena in English Towns, 1790–1835* (New York: Cambridge University Press, 1988).

8. Reprinted by Roberto H. Marfany, *El pronunciamiento de Mayo* (Buenos Aires, 1958), 87 et seq., and quoted in Tulio Halperín Donghi, *Historia argentina. De la revolución de independencia a la confederación rosista* (Buenos Aires: Paidós, 1989), 49.

9. Archivo General de la Nación (hereafter AGN), Acuerdos del extinguido cabildo de Buenos Aires, Serie IV, Tomo I, Libros LVII–LIX, Años 1801 a 1804, passim.

10. T. Cañedo-Argüelles Fabrega, "Efectos de Potosí sobre la población indígena del Alto Perú. Pacajes a mediados del siglo XVII," *Revista de Indias* 48 (January–August 1988): 237–56; Kris Jones, "Indian-Creole Negotiations in the Southern Frontier," in *Revolution and Restoration: The Rearrangement of Power in Argentina, 1776–1860*, ed. Mark D. Szuchman and Jonathan C. Brown (Lincoln: University of Nebraska Press, 1994); James Schofield Saeger, "Another View of the Mission as a Frontier Institution: The Guaycuruan Reductions of Santa Fe, 1743–1810," *Hispanic American Historical Review* 65, no. 3 (1985): 493–517; Susan Migden Socolow, "Spanish Captives in Indian Societies: Cultural Contact along the Argentine Frontier, 1600–1835," *Hispanic American Historical Review* 72, no. 1 (1991): 73–99.

11. Donna J. Guy, "Women, Peonage, and Industrialization: Argentina, 1810–1914," *Latin American Research Review* 16, no. 3 (1981): 65–89.

12. AGN X-17-8-6, Casas embargadas a unitarios, 1848.

13. David Bushnell and Neill Macaulay, *The Emergence of Latin America in the Nineteenth Century* (New York: Oxford University Press, 1988), 19 and passim; elsewhere, Bushnell, Macaulay, and other historians point to the need to note the elites' internal divisions. For the Argentine case in the nineteenth century, see Roberto Etcheparreborda, "La estructura socio-política argentina y la Generación del Ochenta," *Latin American Research Review* 13, no. 1 (1978): 127–34. See also Susan Calvert and Peter Calvert, *Argentina: Political Culture and Instability* (Pittsburgh: University of Pittsburgh Press, 1989); Howard J. Wiarda, "Toward a Theory of Spanish American Government," in *Politics and Social Change in Latin America: The Distinct Tradition*, ed. Howard J. Wiarda (Amherst: University of Massachusetts Press, 1982), 109–31; Natalio Botana, *La tradición republicana. Alberdi, Sarmiento y las ideas políticas de su tiempo* (Buenos Aires: Editorial Sudamericana, 1984); and Alberto Flores Galindo, *Aristocracia y plebe. Lima, 1760–1830* (Lima: Mosca Azul Editores, 1984).

14. Juan Kronfuss, *Arquitectura colonial de la Argentina* (Córdoba: Biffig-nandi, 1930), 17–18.

15. On the use of the *leva*, see Mark D. Szuchman, *Order, Family, and Community in Buenos Aires, 1810–1860* (Stanford: Stanford University Press, 1988), 16–65. On the *pulpería*, see Richard W. Slatta, "Pulperías and Contraband Capitalism in Nineteenth-Century Buenos Aires Province," *Americas* 38 (January 1982): 347–62; and John Charles Chasteen, "Violence for Show: Knife Dueling on a Nineteenth-Century Cattle Frontier," in *The Problem of Order in Changing Societies: Essays on Crime and Policing in Argentina and Uruguay, 1750–1940*, ed. Lyman L. Johnson (Albuquerque: University of New Mexico Press, 1990), 47–64.

16. Alexander Caldeclaugh, *Travels in South America* (London, 1825), 1:180.

17. Beruti, "Memorias curiosas," 3784–87.

18. Ibid., 3822.

19. *Crónica Política y Literaria*, June 2, 1827.

20. For an overview of different architectural styles and configurations during the seventeenth and eighteenth centuries as reflections of the colonial mentality, see George Kubler, "El urbanismo colonial iberoamericano, 1600–1820," in *Historia y futuro de la ciudad iberoamericana*, ed. Francisco de Solano (Madrid: Consejo Superior de Investigaciones Científicas, Universidad Internacional Menéndez Pelayo, 1986), 27–45.

21. Irving Leonard, *Baroque Times in Old Mexico: Seventeenth-Century Persons, Places, and Practices* (Ann Arbor: University of Michigan Press, 1959).

22. Kronfuss, *Arquitectura colonial*, 16.

23. Blas Matamoro, *La casa porteña* (Buenos Aires: Centro Editor de América Latina, 1972), 14.

24. Juan Kronfuss pointed out that the flat-roofed structure (*techo de azotea*) is not a native design; moreover, given the frequency of rain in the region, the sloped roof with tiles is appropriate to the area. The flattening of the roof was the result of imported styles and did not respond to the utilitarian needs of the region. Kronfuss, *Arquitectura colonial*, 71.

25. Susan Migden Socolow, *The Merchants of Buenos Aires, 1778–1810: Family and Commerce* (Cambridge: Cambridge University Press, 1978), 13; Facultad de Filosofía y Letras (Universidad de Buenos Aires), *Documentos para la historia argentina*, vol. 10, *Padrones de la Ciudad y Campaña de Buenos Aires (1725–1810)* (Buenos Aires, 1920); ibid., vol. 11, *Territorio y población: padrón de la Ciudad de Buenos Aires (1778)* (Buenos Aires, 1919).

26. Kronfuss, *Arquitectura colonial*, 156.

27. See Facultad de Filosofía y Letras (Universidad de Buenos Aires), *Documentos para la historia argentina, Administración edilicia (1776–1805)*, vol. 9, introduction by Luis María Torres (Buenos Aires, 1918), 101–7.

28. Beruti, "Memorias curiosas," 3730.

29. AGN X-31-9-1, Policía, Alumbrado Público, Empedrado y Conservación, Calles y caminos, Títulos de celadores, de carretillas.

30. Ibid.

31. Ibid.

32. James R. Scobie, "Changing Urban Patterns: The *Porteño* Case, 1880–1910," in *El proceso de urbanización en América desde sus orígenes hasta nuestros días*, ed. Jorge Hardoy and Richard Schaedel (Buenos Aires: Editorial del Instituto Torcuato Di Tella, 1969), 323–38; James R. Scobie, "Buenos Aires as a Commercial-Bureaucratic City, 1880–1910," *American Historical Review* 77 (October 1972): 1035–73; James R. Scobie, *Buenos Aires: From Plaza to Suburb,*

1870–1910 (New York: Oxford University Press, 1971), 45; Szuchman, *Order, Family, and Community*, 8–9.

33. Tulio Halperín Donghi, "Gastos militares y economía regional: El Ejército del Norte (1810–1817)," *Desarrollo Económico* 41 (April–June 1971): 87–99; Tulio Halperín Donghi, *Guerra y finanzas en los orígenes del Estado argentino, 1791–1850* (Buenos Aires: Editorial del Belgrano, 1982).

34. E. Bradford Burns, "Ideology in Nineteenth-Century Latin American Historiography," *Hispanic American Historical Review* 58, no. 3 (1978): 409–31.

35. Alberto S. J. de Paula, "Neoclasicismo y romanticismo en la arquitectura argentina," in *Documentos para una historia de la arquitectura argentina*, ed. Marina Waisman (Buenos Aires: Ediciones Summa, 1991), 57.

36. Burns, "Ideology in Nineteenth-Century Latin American Historiography," 409–31.

37. José Ortega y Gasset, *La rebelión de las masas* (Madrid: Prensa de Occidente, 1930). See Kubler, "El urbanismo colonial iberoamericano," 27–45.

38. See Francisco del Barrio Lorenzot, *El trabajo en México durante la época colonial. Ordenanzas de gremios de la Nueva España* (Mexico: Secretaria de Gobernación, 1921).

39. Lyman L. Johnson provides a look into guild membership in eighteenth-century Buenos Aires in "The Racial Limits of Guild Solidarity: An Example from Colonial Buenos Aires," *Revista de Historia de América* 99 (January–June 1985); Alberto S. J de Paula and Ramón Gutiérrez, *La encrucijada de la arquitectura argentina, 1822–1875: Santiago Bevans, Carlos E. Pellegrini* (Resistencia: Universidad Nacional del Nordeste, 1974), 14.

40. Carlos A. Mayo, "Landed But Not Powerful: The Colonial Estancieros of Buenos Aires," *Hispanic American Historical Review* 71, no. 4 (1991): 776.

41. De Paula and Gutiérrez, *La encrucijada de la arquitectura argentina*, 16.

42. José Antonio Pillado, *Buenos Aires colonial* (Buenos Aires: Compañía Sudamericana de Billetes de Banca, 1910), 106.

43. Alejo B. González Garaño, *Carlos E. Pellegrini, 1800–1875* (Buenos Aires: Imprenta Busnelli, 1939), 35–36.

44. Ricardo Piccirilli, *Rivadavia y su tiempo* (Buenos Aires: Editores Peuser, 1960), 105.

45. Susan M. Socolow, "Buenos Aires at the Time of Independence," in *Buenos Aires, 400 Years*, ed. Stanley R. Ross and Thomas F. McGann (Austin: University of Texas Press, 1982), 32.

46. De Paula and Gutiérrez, *La encrucijada de la arquitectura argentina*. The state of the streets of the city of Buenos Aires was the subject of commentary by government officials and visitors; see José A. Wilde, *Buenos Aires desde setenta años atrás, 1810–1880* (Buenos Aires: Editorial Universitaria, 1960); John Miers, *Viaje al Plata, 1819–1824* (Buenos Aires: Solar/Hachette, 1968); and Concolorcorvo, *El lazarillo de ciegos caminantes* (Buenos Aires: Ediciones Argentinas Solar, 1942).

47. Mark D. Szuchman, "Disorder and Social Control in Buenos Aires, 1810–1860," *Journal of Interdisciplinary History* 15 (Summer 1984): 83–110; Szuchman, *Order, Family, and Community*, chap. 4; Matamoro, *La casa porteña*, 24; Beruti, "Memorias curiosas," 3800, 3812.

48. Matamoro, *La casa porteña*, 24.

49. Doris Sommer, "*Amalia*: Homebodies as Heroes," paper presented at Latin American Studies Congress, New Orleans, 1988.

50. For a fine overview of urban tensions in the streets of other Latin American cities, see R. Douglas Cope, *The Limits of Racial Domination: Plebeian*

Society in Colonial Mexico City, 1660–1720 (Madison: University of Wisconsin Press, 1994); and Sandra Lauderdale Graham, *House and Street: The Domestic World of Servants and Masters in Nineteenth-Century Rio de Janeiro* (Cambridge: Cambridge University Press, 1988).

51. Bushnell and Macaulay, *The Emergence of Latin America in the Nineteenth Century*, 16–19.

52. John Lynch, *Argentine Dictator: Juan Manuel de Rosas, 1829–1852* (New York: Oxford University Press, 1981), 98. For an alternative view, see Jorge Myers, *Orden y virtud. El discurso republicano en el régimen rosista* (Bernal, Buenos Aires: Universidad Nacional de Quilmes, 1995).

53. Ernesto H. Celesia, *Rosas, aportes para su historia*, 2d ed. (Buenos Aires: Ediciones Peuser, 1968), 1:530, quoted in Lynch, *Argentine Dictator*, 99–100.

54. "Constitución de la Municipalidad de Buenos Aires. Decreto del Director Provisorio de la Confederación Argentina," in *Recopilación de los Debates de Leyes Orgánicas Municipales y sus textos definitivos. I (1821–1876)*, Honorable Concejo Deliberante de la Ciudad de Buenos Aires (Buenos Aires: H. Consejo de la Ciudad, 1938), 18.

55. Ibid., 60.

56. Domingo F. Sarmiento, "Arquitectura doméstica," *Anales del Instituto de Arte Americano e Investigaciones Estéticas* 11 (1958): 101.

57. Ibid., 101.

58. Daniel Schávelzon and Héctor Karp, "La arquitectura del estado liberal," in *Documentos para una historia de la arquitectura argentina*, ed. Marina Waisman (Buenos Aires: Ediciones Summa, 1991), 84.

Conclusion—Was There an
Age of Revolution in Spanish America?

Eric Van Young

Eric Van Young chairs the Department of History at the University of California, San Diego. He has written extensively on the social, economic, political, and cultural history of late colonial and early modern Mexico. His insightful conclusion raises a number of critical issues concerning the convenience of periodizations such as the one advocated in this volume. First, he hints at the Eurocentric nature of the concept of an "Age of Revolution." Next, he argues that the linguistic/cultural turn now dominant in our discipline reduces the utility of this and other large-scale periodizations or, at the very least, renders them tentative and fluid. Ultimately, however, he implies that there may indeed be good reasons to create discrete narratives for certain aspects of Age of Revolution Spanish America, albeit with adjustments to give the notion more heuristic weight. Specifically, he proposes the need for a "loose model of multiple but interrelated time frames moving at different rates." Van Young's thought-provoking remarks should prompt contributors and readers alike to develop a more nuanced understanding of some of the themes addressed in this anthology.

Human beings are hard-wired to tell stories, it seems. We do it constantly, and in many different ways. Most often the mode of telling is diachronic, unfolding over time—as in dreams, memories, jokes, confessions, biographies (and autobiographies), novels, collective and public histories, myths, films, or even pieces of music. Sometimes the mode is synchronic, and the story meant to be captured in a single *gestalt*—as in paintings, inscriptions, monuments, or even buildings.[1] Whether conscious or unconscious, the act of paring down and organizing reality through narrative in this fashion has many ends: to entertain, to explain, to admonish, to justify or rationalize, to awe. Furthermore, stories may be internal to other stories, bend back upon themselves, run parallel to each other along different axes, and/or move at different speeds.[2] The impulse to periodize long spans of history may be seen as a sub-genre (or sub-sub-genre) of storytelling, or narrative representation, of which history itself is one of the most ancient forms. From this point of view, the periodizing to which historians and other historically minded practitioners of the human sciences are so given, at least in the West, is little more than the creation of a sort of mythic framework within which smaller stories are set as morality plays that both derive meaning from, and impart it to, the grander narrative. By this I mean that the "Age of Revolution" might be seen as an encompassing framework, and the "failure to develop economically," the "continuity of a Catholic tradition in civic life," the "rise of caudillismo," or the "growth of a native belletristic tradition," for instance, as the embedded morality plays. What story does the Age of Revolution narrative tell for Spanish America?

Narrative and Periodization

I began to read these chapters, in one form or another, as long ago as late 1995. My first encounter with them was through an essay by Susan Socolow, not published in the present collection but part of one of the original conference sessions, organized by Victor Uribe, that produced the volume. I read Socolow's paper on a rainy night at La Rábida, near Seville, in close proximity to the famous Franciscan monastery there. Just up the road is the little river-port town of Palos de la Frontera, whence Christopher Columbus set out in 1492, thus marking as much as any event in world history an epochal point of inflection between one era and another. Feeling in a reflective and slightly mystical mood, I was prompted to some thoughts on periodization as an intellectual and heuristic exercise by Socolow's opening statement that "chronological divisions in history are always somewhat artificial."[3] I suppose this to be true of the chronological divisions themselves, and even of periodization (the labeling of historical epochs) as an early postmillennial employment practice of professional historians, but not necessarily of the impulse to storytelling (narration) as a way of making sense of things. Even from the viewpoint of a universe blandly indifferent to the human compulsion to narrate, as one anonymous aphorist has noted, time is nature's way of making sure that everything does not happen all at once. Narrative representation is therefore in a very real sense built into the way we exist in the world.

While it may be true that historical periodization and the cognitive formation that gives rise to it are not exclusively Western characteristics, they certainly have about them a flavor of the commodification so typical of the "modernity" that worked its way outward from the West. This commodifying mode is historical flotsam borne to the shore of the present by a sustaining cognitive tide. One aspect of commodification is to reduce the recalcitrant outer world to a representation that we agree then corresponds to a readily manipulable, modular sort of reality. We do this with both time and space.[4] Commodification is a process to which not only individuals but also states are notably prone.[5] The periodizing impulse is underwritten not just by a certain phenomenological/descriptive tendency in conjunction with the building of temporal boundaries —that is, we say that "this is different from that, and therefore this era from another"—but also by some typically unexamined assumptions about causality. These assumptions are epitomized at their most reductionist in the formulation "post hoc, ergo propter hoc," the classic statement of the fallacy that the succession in time of two phenomena implies them to be linked causally, oldest to youngest. On the other hand, the blunt statement "shit happens," as an alternative model to assumptions about causality and periodization, is not very useful in helping us to fight off entropic doom. At any rate, the important points here are two. First, the periodizing impulse arises from a basic cognitive formation—the impulse to storytelling, of which it is one of a series of culturally and historically modeled manifestations. Second, the impulse itself and the outcomes it produces in terms of the imposed architecture of historical time, whatever intellectual work they may do for us in understanding the past, are shaped very much by cultural logics internal as much to our present circumstances as to the history we are dividing up.

In keeping with the latter point, I want to suggest that the structure of this book—the sequence of the essays, their relationship to each other, and the cumulative story they tell—actually seems to follow much the same course as the evolution of the field of Latin American history itself over the last several decades. The point where Latin American historians find themselves now does not mark the end of the tale, for instance, in the same way that our arrival at the final lines (p. 568) of Mario Vargas Llosa's *The War of the End of the World* (" 'Archangels took him up to heaven,' she says, clacking her tongue. 'I saw them.' ") brings us to the end of his epic tale of Canudos. Rather, it represents a plateau, an open-ended historiographical moment (and a quite interesting one, at that).[6] In this sense the essays move, *grosso modo*, from older-style studies of politics and economic life, which generally work at a high level of aggregation, to the emerging microhistory of popular and political culture, much in the way the field itself has shown a tendency to move. Less a matter of increasing sophistication (since the more "traditional" essays here are very sophisticated), or of following a vulgarly Marxist formula (from structure to superstructure), this shift in register in the course of the volume has more to do with changing approaches within the human sciences generally and history more particularly, for which both positive and negative claims are being loudly and insistently debated these days.[7] As much historical writing moves from synoptic description to the reconstruction of local knowledge, and from grand narrative to exemplary tale, we may be losing in breadth of vision what we are gaining in depth of focus. But whether that self-induced myopia is a good or a bad thing, it does seem somewhat incompatible with the sweeping time cuts required by large-scale periodization. The unabashedly localist epistemologies and relentlessly pointillist techniques of the newer forms of cultural history tend to undermine our confidence in assertions about what large groups of people were doing over long stretches of time. In this way, perhaps, periodization itself in the restricted sense, with its scientist drive to generalization and parsimony, is becoming an obsolete function, the cognitive equivalent of a prehensile tail.

In thinking about revising the conventional periodization scheme of Latin American history—typically, colonial/national—in favor of one that spans the creation of the new nation-states (the Age of Revolution scenario), we may be creating a paradox: the very lack of fit between the sorts of history many of us are doing and the older grand narrative (periodizing) framework stimulates a revisionist yearning, but the newer-style history reduces the utility of periodization itself as an intellectual technology for approximating the very historical realities whose representation we find most compelling. As a practical matter this does not mean that the effort to periodize should be abandoned, but at the very least it suggests that large periodizations should be seen as indicative and highly tentative, fluid, and responding to different purposes—as "heuristic" devices, perhaps—rather than as final answers in themselves, and that they should never be reified into general characterizations, still less into explanations.

If the conventional colonial/national periodization rests on the supposition of some sort of Euro-Atlantic "bourgeois revolution" clearing the path for capitalist development, it is clearly impossible to make this argument for Spanish America until fifty or one hundred years later (depending upon where one is looking), although ideological and political liberalism are sometimes taken as a proxy for such a development in the early decades of independent nationhood. The colonial/national divide might be more compelling if history were seen solely as "public history," as I have suggested above and will expand upon below. In such a narrative, the broadening of the political nation, the reconfiguration of the state, and the expansion of the public sphere might be seen as transcendent effects of independence. But even assuming that such a sea change occurred in Spanish America, what would then become methodologically of the downward displacement, in social and cultural terms, so characteristic of the gaze of historians in recent years? Either the underlying assumptions of the conventional periodization are retrogressive, or we need to develop a much more sophisticated sort of theoretical understanding to integrate them with revisionist social and cultural history.

The issue under discussion should probably not be whether there is sufficient political, social, economic, or cultural continuity in a given period to justify setting it off from other eras, but whether it is illuminating to study it as a period or not. These are somewhat different questions, whose resolution depends less upon the nature of continuity than upon the nature of periodization. Whether limited to its Euro-Atlantic setting or extended to Spanish America, the Age of Revolution scenario assumes the utility of seeing disjunction as a process with origins and implications. In a thoughtful and widely cited essay published about fifteen years ago, William Taylor made a strong case for rehabilitating the independence break as an epochal point of inflection in Latin American social history, an argument that looks progressively less convincing in scholarly terms the more we advance into that social history.[8] Even from a strictly political perspective, disaggregating *ancien régime* from successor state surely makes the understanding of either much more difficult. Moreover, in terms of illuminating the lives of the ordinary people who constituted the mass of the population in Spanish America and whose experience has so recently moved to center stage in historians' work, the very slippage between "public" history and "infrahistory" explains much about the relationship among dominant and subaltern groups, state and civil society, the public sphere and the private, and so forth.[9] Splitting the history of Latin or Spanish America in twain at independence may be the historiographical equivalent of an economist's breaking a Kondratieff cycle in two at the point of inflection between the A and B phases. More broadly, these considerations raise the interesting question of how periodization does what it does—that is, how it explains change over time in a convincing way. Is this done by excluding vital points of inflection, or by including them? In this sense, employing the Wars of Independence as a point of separation between colonial and early national experiences in Spanish America creates misgivings, because it tends to sound like one hand clapping.

To develop this point further, briefly, let me suggest that these developments in history as a discipline have converged with a major change within Latin American historiography specifically to undermine the conventional periodization of the region's post-1492 centuries into colonial and national eras, with a neat break at about 1820. On the one hand, as I have suggested, historians have turned away from political chronicle toward economic, then social, and more recently cultural history. Not only do economic and social structures, and cultural understandings, arguably take longer to change than political arrangements, but they also may not be dependent upon politics to shape them. The influence of Annales-school historiography is obvious here, with its multilevel model of historical development positing different time streams concurrently moving at different rates beneath the epiphenomena of the history of "events."[10] On the other hand, critiques of dependency theory have shown that we may unhitch international economic asymmetry from political subordination in large measure, so that the "colonial heritage" of Latin America outlined in the canonical *dependentista* text by Stanley and Barbara Stein about thirty years ago becomes less an effect of regime change or cryptoimperialism on the part of nineteenth-century developed economies (Europe and the United States) than of long-term economic forces explained more compellingly within a neoclassical framework.[11] After independence, this revisionist scholarship suggests, Latin America's terms of trade with external economies responded less reflexively to political changes than we had thought, demonstrating little consistent tendency toward massive decapitalization over the long term.[12] Thus, the dismantling of the old Spanish imperial structures may have mattered a good deal less than the conventional wisdom of dependency theory suggested, and therefore the crisis of independence itself may be de-emphasized as a major point of inflection in Latin American history.

To return to my initial question: What story does the Age of Revolution scenario tell for Spanish America? What smaller narratives does it enfold? How does it contradict the received wisdom about the history of Spain's former empire in the New World, and how is its adoption by historians likely to change our view of the region's development? Finally, what are some potentially productive ways of thinking that might help us consolidate the Age of Revolution periodization or, if necessary, adjust it so that it bears more heuristic weight? These are some of the questions touched upon explicitly or implicitly in the essays in this volume, and I hope to revisit them in a moment. But first, as a preliminary step to addressing these issues as an intellectual cluster, we might propose four broadly arguable propositions—not profoundly original, but perhaps useful nonetheless. These are: 1) that the Spanish American Wars of Independence constitute a serious historical as well as historiographical problem; 2) that schemes of political, economic, and cultural periodization may or may not be in sync with each other, and are therefore debatable as desiderata for marking off one epoch from another; 3) that schemes of sociocultural change have generally not assumed major importance in discussions about periodization but might well be imported to the center of the issue if we consider them to have a significant degree of explanatory suggestiveness; and 4) that perhaps we should be less concerned with resolving whether the "traditional" or "revisionist" periodization better fits the facts than with constructing a loose model of multiple but interrelated time frames moving at different rates.[13]

The Family Romance of the Nation-State

In considering why periodization as such and the newer forms of social and cultural history now becoming fashionable may be incompatible, I suggested that our construction of historical time is likely to be shaped as much by the contemporary preoccupations of the historians doing the constructing as it is by the inherent characteristics of the period(s) under scrutiny. This introjection of the present into the past certainly shows up in the Age of Revolution scenario proposed in this volume and elsewhere and mostly advocated, unless I am mistaken, by Anglo-American scholars. Victor Uribe's bracketing of the 1780–1850 period would seem to correspond in large measure to an "age of revolution" or even "industrial revolution" model for North Atlantic Euro-America. Aside from

de-attributing to the Wars of Independence their traditional importance, the Age of Revolution in Spanish America would thus be
identified with an essentially European historical chronology, with
the era of enlightened European despotism, imperial reform, and
the American and French Revolutions ushering it on stage, the Revolutions of 1848 escorting it off, and the late scientific and industrial revolutions singing the choral part. The delimitation of these
vast world-historical trends into a "period" also accounts for the
attractiveness of the Age of Revolution to those scholars working
in or near a dependency paradigm (ironically enough, given what
has already been said above), since it encompasses the reconfiguration of Latin America's linkage to the developed world and takes
the region to the eve of export-led development.[14] Yet, we need to
ask ourselves whether this periodization makes sense of the Latin
American experience, or simply drags it along willy-nilly in the
wake of the North Atlantic world. What scholars are often really
looking for in slicing up large slabs of history in this way are the
avatars of modernity, into which Latin America entered in a distinctly disadvantaged position.[15] That is to say, the Age of Revolution periodization represents an anachronism produced by late
twentieth-century attempts to think about a putative series of absences, or failures, in Latin America: the failure to industrialize, to
institutionalize stable democratic regimes, to establish secular-
modernist mental frameworks until quite late, and so forth. So we
are faced with another paradox here: we abandon one set of essentially political criteria for another; and in attempting to cut Latin
America loose from the European world to enjoy its own historical
fate, we bind it even more tightly.

The conventional periodization of Latin American history, with
a break at independence (effectively at about 1825 or so) dividing
the colonial and national eras, is predicated upon the romance of
the nation-state.[16] Of these there have actually been rather few successful exemplars, several of them sheltering empires (formal or
informal) in their shadows: Britain, France, the United States. Other
nation-states have had a rather bumpier road to existence, much
higher maintenance costs (which in the case of the big winners are
shifted to other players), and altogether more ambiguous histories.
Diminutive nations are still coming into being (or re-emerging),
their births sometimes witnessed by a great deal of poisonous rhetoric and worse practice. Spanish Americans were dragged along (or
dragged themselves along) in the van of this powerful historical
engine, so it is not so easy to discount the teleological element in

the traditional periodization, the invention of nationhood with its "Big Bang" at independence and the working out of its ideological and political implications during the succeeding nearly two centuries.[17] But the *volkisch* nineteenth-century sentiments that spawned and reinforced nationalism in many parts of the globe (most particularly in the West) were absent from many of the former colonial nations of Spanish America, which lacked the ethnic coherence to make of the cult of nationality and the attendant expansion of the political nation much of a success except as the covering myth for actually much more fragmented polities.[18] Official and unofficial *indigenismo*, rooted as an element of creole patriotism in the eighteenth century and flowering more fully in the twentieth in places such as Peru and Mexico, has proved a difficult and volatile substitute, not least because it can give rise to embarrassing political and welfare claims that modern states are loath to satisfy, even when they are clothed in a populist fig leaf.[19] The nation-as-subject, therefore, has become so integral to the modern experience of the citizen-as-subject—indeed, the introjection of the former into the latter is identified as a hallmark of modern state- and nation-building—that denaturalizing it, even well into the era of globalization, often proves exceedingly difficult.[20]

Exemplars of recent historical works that cross the national divide in some fashion, muting or even ignoring the "Big Bang" as a historical marker and opting for other temporal boundaries more appropriate to their topics, are increasingly common. Themes whose treatment lends itself to this approach include a number of slower-evolving human (and natural) phenomena not easily captured by political periodizations, many of them "cultural" in a somewhat restricted sense of the term; in other words, factors that anthropologists study in the world of the living. These include gender relations, forms of religious sensibility, ethnohistory, agrarian structures, and so forth. To take but a single genre of work pertaining to the area of Latin America with which I happen to be most familiar, the history of ethnic groups in Mexico (most prominently indigenous peoples) has readily lent itself to study within time cuts transcending the traditional colonial/national divide. Several interesting examples are recent works by David Frye and Cynthia Radding on near- and far-northern Mexico, respectively; Antonio Escobar Ohmstede on the Huastecas; and Pedro Bracamonte on Yucatán.[21] One reason these studies work so well to denaturalize in some measure the conventional periodization is that they are not set on doing so—that is, they tend to pursue the inner logic of ethnohistories across traditional temporal boundaries, to whatever points of historical inflection they may lead.[22] In contrast, anthologies that consciously set out to bridge the gap often end up as well-intentioned assemblages of essays exploring themes on either side of the continental divide that is independence, without ever actually descending to the terrain on the other side, although they may spy it from afar.[23] Textbooks in general also tend to keep to the old periodization. Perhaps most of us are just prisoners of teaching on the semester system.

Continuities and Discontinuities in Spanish America's Age of Revolution

Like estimates of gross domestic product or other exercises in aggregation, historical periodizations are useful in helping us make sense of the buzz of experience. But they are also highly generalizing and therefore problematic in many respects, not least spatiotemporally and analytically. In thus aggregating a manifestly more fragmentary and idiopathic range of historical experiences, we need to acknowledge that large-scale periodization tends to blur or even erase the local or regional rhythms that might subvert the larger model, a point I have made in a somewhat different context above. Certainly this is true if we look at Spanish America in the Age of Revolution (or any other age) as a bloc, a point to which Richard Salvucci alludes in his essay in this volume. Thus, we often say that certain localities, culture areas, or entire nations "become modern" or approach the lifeways of the developed Euro-Atlantic center at different rates, even if one critiques on its very face as imperialistic, self-serving, hegemonically nearsighted, or even immoral the assumption of a unilinear, mimetic progression in human affairs upon which such a scenario is often built.[24] Paraguay seems a fly in amber, for example, next to an Argentina hectically torn by the process of modernization; the latter's history molds to the Age of Revolution template fairly well (creation of the Viceroyalty of the Río de la Plata/fall of Juan Manuel de Rosas), while the former's is somewhat out of sync with it, as if marching to its own drummer.

Another way in which large-scale historical periodizations blur rather than clarify the picture is by tending to ignore the slippages between major modes of social analysis. Thus, for example, political events such as the creation of states and their institutional structures may overtake by some generations political culture (people's attitudes about what politics are about, and the ground rules for political life). This seems to be what Victor Uribe is telling us in his essay on New Granadan/Colombian public life between the end of the colonial regime and the first few decades of the republican era. Viewed from another angle, this disjunction among the political, economic, social, and cultural registers—the fact that different sorts of beliefs and activities change at different rates and may therefore be out of phase with each other—also accounts for apparent continuities across epochal divisions of historical time, as in the business practices of the Chilean merchants described by Marti Lamar in her essay. The larger lesson to be learned about periodization from these essays is perhaps that continuity does not necessarily imply stasis but may embrace ongoing, uninflected change in the same direction over a long period of time. To return yet once more to my initial question, then (and given these caveats), what story do these fine essays tell about the Age of Revolution narrative for Spanish America?

In general terms, as Victor Uribe points out in his skillful gloss in the Introduction, continuity over the period 1750/1780–1850 seems to be the *leitmotiv* of the volume, thus reinforcing the case for unity in the period in the conventional sense. Within this general tendency, however, there are significant differences among the scholars whose views are represented. At one end of the spectrum, the essay by Samuel Amaral and Richard Doringo lends clear support to the continuity thesis (that is, that independence from Spain did little fundamentally to alter economic life). Salvucci plumps for overall continuity as well, while toward the other extreme Mark Szuchman finds a mixed picture, Sonya Lipsett-Rivera slow and subtle changes over the period, and John Chasteen considerable change over a relatively short time span, ascribable mostly to political independence. The distinctions are hardly coincidental, but linked in ways I have already suggested to the different realms of social life under examination by each author and the historical approaches appropriate to them. What is surprising about some of these conclusions is that they seem to find cultural formations and their expressions (in the limited sense of the term "culture") more malleable and sensitive to political change, and over shorter periods of time, than one would have thought. Most of the authors point to the considerable ambiguity of the period, at best. Lamar, who finds a good deal of continuity in the business practices of Chilean merchants across the independence divide, nonetheless points out that "specificity in periodization requires operating at the level of 'events' and always implies discontinuity"; while Chasteen, who seems to want to argue for a watershed at independence, notes that large-scale periodizations "need not necessarily represent spans of time characterized predominantly by continuities" (that is, they can embrace points of inflection).

Elizabeth Kuznesof's essay interestingly compounds the ambiguity of the Age of Revolution scenario by raising the question as to whether and when Latin America, and specifically Mexico, were ever truly "colonial" in the first place, and therefore (implicitly) as to whether the formal political independence of most of the region won during the years 1810–1825 constitutes a point of historical inflection worth debating at all. In her acute short review of the periodization debate she cites Richard Morse to the effect that Mexico became a "true colony" only with the Bourbon reforms (that is, from about 1760), and Latin America as a whole truly colonized only between then and about 1920. While this theory has the gratifyingly truculent snap of all engaging revisionist reformulations, it begs the large question of just what was going on in the New World possessions of the Iberian metropoli in the preceding 250 years, if not colonization. Historically, colonization took many forms and had just as many motives, sometimes all in play at once and linked to one another: strategic, demographic, economic, religious, cultural, and so forth. But one thing most European colonial regimes did in the process of at least partially realizing their goals was to try to impose a perfect stasis on the colonized peoples—to make of them museums of unmodernity by disfranchising them historically as well as politically. From this point of view, the Bourbon reforms initiated the Age of Revolution through an ill-starred modernization project bent on containing two contradictory reformist impulses within a long-established colonial system: one embracing economic expansion, the other increased rates of fiscal extraction, political control, and *étatisme*. If we concede for the moment (*pace* Morse) that Latin America had long been colonized by the time the Bourbon and Pombaline reforms began, it is the nature of late colonial social change that warrants our attention rather than any attempt to find the origins of colonial rule under enlightened despotism. Here, Kuznesof's suggestion that the periodization debate opened by Morse, among others, might best be illuminated by reference to changes in the systems of gender, race, and family relations (and, I would interject, by attention to cultural phenomena more broadly), makes a good deal of sense. This is precisely what several of the essays in the volume attempt. But there are also other themes that unify the 1750–1850 period: economic life, political culture, the development of the public sphere, cultural life in the more restricted sense of the concept, and so forth. Let me briefly touch upon some of these.

There are several areas of inquiry in which the case for a meaningful continuity during the Age of Revolution can be made, one of which is gender and family relations (including the demographic regime). As the essays on Mexico by Lipsett-Rivera and Kuznesof demonstrate, by the late eighteenth century changes were already afoot in this intimate sphere of social relationships, with its rich and complex cultural resonances, and continued into the next century largely oblivious of the independence process. Among the changes cited by the two authors as unifying the Age of Revolution rather than breaking it in two at 1821 were slow population growth, legal changes favoring women's education and work opportunities (most notable among the urban population), declining rates of illegitimacy for all ethnicities, increasing incidence of legitimate marriage and marriage across ethnic lines in places such as Mexico City, high proportions of female-headed households in many Latin American cities more generally, and changes in the model of marriage, especially for elite groups. Yet, Lipsett-Rivera points out that the Wars of Independence did not significantly alter the nature of marital problems, many ideas about marriage, or the language of reciprocity within it.[25]

Another area of inquiry in which continuing change during the period 1750–1850 is in evidence, with little in the way of substantial inflection at independence, is that of state social policy under the Bourbons, which bears the signs of the secular-utilitarian philosophy typically associated only with the postindependence Spanish American successor states. Turning again to New Spain, this policy is demonstrated by the history of Mexico City's Poor House (1774–1871), recently studied by Silvia Arrom. Her remarks are worth quoting at length:

Studies of Latin America, still dominated by a strong tradition of patriotic historiography, generally assume that enlightened ideas about poverty and poor relief only appeared after independence. . . . Most studies of Mexico correlate the "modern" attitudes with nineteenth-century liberalism. Some note that the secularization of welfare institutions was a two-step process that began with independence in 1821 and ended with the Reform Laws of 1856–59. But the shift in ideology from traditional religious notions of charity to modern ideas of secular social welfare . . . is usually linked to the triumph of the Liberal Reform in the middle of the century. The continuities between colonial and republican policies have been obscured by the tendency of Mexican historians to begin or end their studies in 1821, for students of the national period failed to follow through on the hints in brief seminal studies of the colonial period that the Bourbon period brought important innovations in social welfare policies. In contrast . . . [the history of] the Poor House suggests that a true watershed occurred in the late eighteenth century. The desire to substitute indiscriminate almsgiving (*la caridad mal reglada*) with "well-regulated" charity that disciplined the poor is embodied in the first paragraph of the 1769 bylaws.[26]

So in the cases of gender and family relationships, and in certain areas of public policy, one would need to acknowledge that important changes under way in ideology, attitude, and practice tend more to unify the period than inflect it internally.

Moving to yet a third broad theme of inquiry, how well does the Age of Revolution scenario map onto the economic life of Spanish America between the Bourbon reforms and the midnineteenth century? Certainly there were costs to independence in terms of population loss and dislocation, the disruption of internal markets and the loss of protected (if constraining and increasingly unpredictable) external markets, the ruin of mining in many areas, the deep wounding (if not collapse) of domestic agricultural production, capital flight, and so forth. But deeper, less contingent forces were in play over the century 1750–1850, so that, as Kuznesof points out for the case of Mexico, the "down from colonialism" thesis is not as compelling as it once seemed.[27] Many of these factors, such as stagnation in domestic-use agriculture, were already in evidence in the Latin American region as a whole well before the advent of independence, as Salvucci points out; nor does he find independence to have affected commercial trends as fundamentally as we used to think. Amaral and Doringo characterize their own essay as offering no clear evidence to support the counterfactual proposition that after independence Latin America had the potential to develop along the lines of Western Europe, so that for them the Age of Revolution scenario is largely one of failure, or a series of absences. In her case study of Chilean merchants, Lamar notes that despite some turnover in the personnel of the elite merchant group (from *peninsular* to Chilean creole and British), prevailing business practices remained much the same after independence from Spain as before, including risk-aversive strategies of diversification, familism (the tendency to rely on kinship bonds to structure business relationships), the role of large merchants as financiers of mining enterprises, and so forth. Comments Lamar: "Beneath the political drama of independence, economic and social continuities characterized the 'middle period' in Chilean history."

Finally, another interesting way to approach the issue of continuity and change in the economic realm during the period 1750–1850 is along the axis of material culture: what Latin Americans ate, how they dressed, what their homes were like, and to what manufactured items they had access; and, more generally, why they spent their money on certain material items rather than others, what the cultural value of these items was as well as their economic cost, how goods were differentially distributed over space, time, ethnic boundaries, and class, and how consumption was related (or unrelated) to patterns of advancing modernity. Here we have little to go on in the secondary literature; although there exists a mountain of historical studies of systems of production and exchange, material culture as such has received little sustained attention. Arnold Bauer's work on material culture in Latin America between 1500 and 2000 promises in this respect virtually to open a field already well cultivated by historians and anthropologists for the Euro-Atlantic world.[28] Bauer does break the history of material culture at independence in his scheme, presumably on the grounds that this political rupture opened Latin American markets as never before to an influx of foreign goods either prohibited or inhibited by colonial commercial regulations,[29] a point on which Amaral and Doringo find themselves in agreement. While this is certainly a reasonable assumption and may in the end prove correct, it should be kept in mind that consumption patterns—the culture of consumption, if you will—depend not only upon the availability of goods but also upon income levels, effective disposable income, prices, and a host of social desiderata. It is credible that better-off city dwellers generally, members of elite groups, and the burgeoning but tiny middle class might change their tastes and consumption patterns, but how widely diffused could any such alteration have been? Although we still know relatively little about levels of welfare and real income for working people even in cities (where the data are likely to be most dense) in the first decades after independence, what we do know suggests that for most people material conditions did not improve significantly until late in the century (see, for example, Kuznesof's essay). From this point of view, it is difficult to imagine that material culture for the vast majority of Latin Americans, particularly laboring people in the countryside, could have changed much before the mid- or late nineteenth century.

Amaral and Doringo as well as Salvucci in their wide-ranging essays place considerable emphasis on institutional arrangements in the new states in explaining the generally poor economic performance of the Latin American countries after independence. Salvucci specifies what he means by institutional factors, citing among them property rights, state legitimacy, bureaucracy, and the distribution, exercise, and limits of coercive power. The insistence of the three authors on such factors seems well placed, even though Salvucci's rather rueful aside that "explanations that depend on institutions are often substitutes for explanations, not explanations themselves," with its aphoristic pithiness, sounds suspiciously like a disclaimer. This is an important issue because the play of institutional factors is often indirect, their role one of mediating or intervening variables in social and political—or as here, economic —processes. Thus, for example, institutional instability creates uncertainty in the economic sphere by increasing the variability of return on investments, which in turn dampens growth. But the role of institutional arrangements is not necessarily so obvious, since they can themselves be effects of deeper cultural formations. We need to look *behind* such arrangements, since behind them may lie not only the play of interests in the neoclassical sense but also the conflicting (or consensual) "interests" of culture—that is, enduring representations of the world and prescriptions for the Good.

In this sense the institutional "instability" described by Amaral and Doringo as well as Salvucci for the first half of the nineteenth century (Amaral and Doringo characterize it as "bedlam") can be seen not only as the direct outgrowth of the destructive effects of independence in the realms of foregone income flow, loss of economies of scale, capital flight, and so forth, but also as symptoms of the institutionalized instability of a burgeoning liberal order.[30] Although these institutional arrangements themselves (for example, forms of republican government, monarchical projects, federalism and regionalism as expressed in political structures, and taxation systems) have been relatively well studied for the new states, their meaning as expressions of political culture (for example, in terms of ethnic relationships, forms of citizenship, the claims of paternalistic and clientelistic modes of political power in the postcolonial context, and state-civil society relations) have until recently been less well served.[31] Here, indeed, independence may introduce a significant discontinuity. Let us briefly take a closer look, then, at what our authors have to say about continuities and disjunctions in politics and political culture in the Age of Revolution.

Political structure and practice, especially at the "national" level (comparisons across the independence divide are obviously anachronistic here), represent a clear and oft-studied disjunction with independence: from universal Catholic monarchy to increasingly secularized nation-states, from sacral legitimacy for the state to popular sovereignty, from bureaucratic-patrimonial to at least nominally elective forms of rule, and so forth. Yet another clear outgrowth of independence in the early nineteenth century was the political fragmentation of larger colonial entities into smaller ones along lines of competing regional elites; Victor Uribe has much of interest to say on this theme for the transition of Nueva Granada through Gran Colombia to Colombia, and some years ago Brian Hamnett described a similar process at work behind, and reinforced by, Mexican independence.[32] Absent entirely coherent class groupings and the restraining influence of imperial state structures, this spatio-political fragmentation explains much about the apparently chaotic politics of the last third of the Age of Revolution throughout much of Spanish America.[33] On the other hand, important clusters of elite-held ideas about political life and the social compact were remarkably stable across the divide of independence. As Chasteen points out in his essay, for example, elite ideas about the essential degradation and volatility of the masses changed little even as elements of popular culture were appropriated as signifiers of emergent national identities. This was certainly true of Indo-America (the Andean region and Mesoamerica), where elite attitudes about indigenous people remained at best disdainful well beyond the end of the Age of Revolution, and where "the problem of the Indian" was indissolubly linked to that of modernization and its blockages.

Well worth a much deeper exploration than I can possibly afford it here is the question of political culture, on which the essays of Uribe, Chasteen, and Szuchman, especially, have much to say. As with others of the major issues touched upon in this volume, there is hardly any postindependence innovation without some colonial antecedent, or any continuing thread of thought or behavior without a new twist after the achievement of nationhood; but on the whole, much of the story of the period 1750–1850 is one of continuity within changing political circumstances. We have already looked briefly into one of the most basic areas of social mores, that of gender relations and the status of women, and seen that change was already afoot before independence. Another basic (and related) cultural feature of the newly decolonized Spanish American societies was the relationship between honor, defined essentially by birth and untainted European ethnicity, and social status. Many historians have noted a shift in this relationship more in the direction of a class—that is, wealth-based—model even during the late eighteenth century, though the transition was to be a long and problematic one. Uribe underlines this in the case of Colombia, particularly, pointing to a tendency for what he calls intra-elite "status-honor" rivalries to be carried over into the life of the new nation as a sort of cultural hangover, while admitting that this "Weberian striving after honor" and the social status attached to it might well be mixed with ambition for material gain, an interpretation shared by Lamar for her Chilean elite merchant groups. Under these circumstances, proximity to the state became a surrogate source of honor, power, prestige, and patronage, and the sociopolitical turmoil in Colombia and elsewhere a medium of "status-honor" conflict over access to the means of administration, rather than a class conflict over the means of production. Nor, given the preoccupation of upper-status groups all over the Spanish New World with the destabilizing proclivities of the ignorant and irresponsible *populacho*, were democratic forms of accessing the state apparatus appealing to those members of the partially reconstituted elite who came to form the political nation in the new republics.

Obvious changes did occur with independence in the nature and extent of what Jurgen Habermas called the "public sphere"; in the advent of universalizing claims of republican citizenship and their effects on other realms of life; and in the emergence of public discourses and cultural usages linked to emergent national identities.[34] Thus, where Szuchman speaks in his essay of his interest in "regime transition" with independence, it might be even more useful to embrace civil society along with the state. Szuchman's account of the construction of a public sphere in Buenos Aires is eloquent enough to warrant quotation:

> the most important political novelty of the nineteenth century rested with the exteriorization of the exchanges of ideas—that is, the historically reduced space that had limited political debates to government officials within the interiors of administrative structures spilled on to street and bar, estancia and *pulpería. By the early 1800s*, Buenos Aires's public spaces were witnesses to the heady and sometimes dangerous exchange of ideas [emphasis added].

As the decibel level of public discussion rose in the republican era and its venues proliferated, elite concerns with social control grew in tandem with them. But the new claims of citizenship and common people's metabolization of liberal thought, especially in the cities, made plebeians much more uppity vis-à-vis power holders than they had ever been during the colonial period outside the context of outright violence in the form of riots or insurrections. As Szuchman notes in this volume, in newly independent Argentina there was "a gap between the rhetoric of individual liberalism [and also the claims of citizenship] on which independence was initially predicated and the authoritarianism on which power actually rested." Sarah Chambers's work on Arequipa during the Age of Revolution makes much the same point in terms of common citizens' dealings with the judicial system and their voluble denials, when hailed before the authorities, that they were criminals or vagrants. Something of the same can be seen among resisters to incarceration in Mexico City's Poor House in the early nineteenth century.[35] Nor were public behaviors, such as systems of social control and direct citizen interactions with the state, the only areas to be colonized by changed understandings about the political world. Lipsett-Rivera's essay on newly independent Mexico links new forms of citizenship to child-rearing through emergent ideas about "republican motherhood," in which mothers were seen as responsible for religious instruction, civic education, and the inculcation of patriotism in their children, while reciprocally, motherhood became "not only a sacred duty but a state that conveyed rights."[36]

Both Szuchman and Chasteen in their essays deal interestingly with developing public discourses and cultural usages associated with emerging national identities, but even here the story was mixed, embodying elements both new and old. In describing the raising of an obelisk in the central plaza of Buenos Aires to commemorate the struggle for independence, for example, Szuchman remarks that the monument was designed along neoclassical lines as opposed to the Gothic style said to be characteristic of Spanish colonial times. Domestic architecture remained linked stylistically to the older aesthetic, however, so that the transformation of architecture as a political discourse was suggestive but incomplete, divided into public and private levels later to be compressed into one as the character of Spanish American cities changed from "aristocratic" to "creole." Along somewhat similar lines, Chasteen evokes in some detail the schizoid history of popular dance forms in the Río de la Plata. He finds that over the period 1750–1850 there existed a "striking continuity of prohibition coupled, almost invariably, with toleration," even while those popular cultural expressions acquired potent new political meanings in the wake of independence, becoming avatars of a new national identity struggling to be born. Remarks Chasteen of the transition:

Colonial rulers had discovered no virtues at all in popular social dance—
or at least none that could enter public discourse. . . . The salient meaning of popular dance in colonial discourse was always its moral turpitude,
inevitably presented in diametrical opposition to the religious principles
that, in the words of the viceroy, "raise a throne for sovereigns in the
conscience of their beloved vassals, making submission and obedience
into immutable principles.". . . Something had truly changed, then, by
the 1820s, when *montonero* minuets and *cielitos* came to signify an authentic national spirit. . . . By 1850, this new discursive configuration
had become one of the most salient in political life.

Popular dances had had their signs reversed, then, starting as
emblems of the social forces the colonial order had sought to contain, and being transformed into signatures of the very nation-state
whose existence was predicated on the destruction of that same
colonial order. This sign reversal (or appropriation) was accomplished in less than a generation or so, testimony to the rapidity
with which cultural inventories can change.[37]

Although neither Szuchman nor Chasteen is by any means na-
ive in his appreciation of emerging forms of public expression in
politics and social life, there is some danger as we pursue this
anatomy of the Age of Revolution that we may confect by indirec-
tion a Black Legend of colonial repression, thus assuming that the
expression of political ideas was an invention of the post-1808 era.
Szuchman implies, however ("by the early 1800s"), that not only in
Buenos Aires but also in other new national capitals, provincial
cities, and towns, a new freedom of expression in public life was
actually antecedent to the severance of political ties with the colonial metropolis, not only among elite groups but among common
people as well. Nor was colonial society, particularly in its last half-
century or so, devoid of a muted or shadowy public sphere (in ritual
forms, for example, in elite literary salons, or in the internal politics of indigenous communities), or of forms of political socializa-
tion (the colonial court system, for instance, at whose manipulation
indigenous communities became quite adept). Although some of
its more focused agencies of repression—the Inquisition, for example—could be extremely nasty and terroristic, the colonial regime never even approached totalitarian efficiency, but instead its
apparatus leaked like a sieve. This is one reason why the universalizing claims of religious belief and its institutional supports were
so important—and why they clashed so violently with the tenets of
liberalism, state-building, and the ostensibly universalizing claims
of republican citizenship after independence.

Final Iteration

Was there an Age of Revolution in Spanish America, embracing the latter half of the eighteenth century and the first half of the nineteenth? On the evidence of the essays in this volume and other work stretching back a decade and more, one would have to say "yes." Thinking about Spanish American history within this periodizing framework does not mean denying to the independence movements their importance either in Latin American or world history, respectively, as the moments of origin of most of the nation-states of the modern Western Hemisphere, or as avatars of subsequent decolonization and wars of national liberation in the later nineteenth and twentieth centuries. But it does mean de-emphasizing political events in the more traditional sense as boundaries of the large narratives in which national or multinational histories are told and made sense of. The displacement from center stage of political chronicle, and of the venerable and fruitful traditions of teleological *historia patria* and hagiography that long served as its vehicles, certainly seems to be in keeping with more modern trends in the discipline of history, especially with the downward and outward refocusing of the historian's gaze to social and cultural themes in explaining the fate of peoples.

It is possible, of course, to see the Age of Revolution periodization, like the more traditional colonial/national one, as marked off by purely political desiderata—Bourbon reforms on one end, triumph of liberal state-building and the emergence of some regime stability (admittedly a little fuzzier as a benchmark) on the other. The chief heuristic advantage the Age of Revolution framework offers, however, is the identification of substantial continuity over the century 1750–1850 in economic trends, certain repertoires of basic and intimate cultural beliefs, and behaviors such as gender relations and family life (and religious sensibility, which, interestingly, is hardly discussed in this volume), and the underside (the less public side) of political culture, all of which I have inventoried briefly in this essay. Some of the elements of Spanish American society that did change substantially with independence, such as institutional arrangements embracing political and economic life, the expansion of the public sphere, and certain forms of cultural expression reconfigured into emblems of nationalist sensibility, were precisely parts of the cultural inventory most vulnerable to rapid political manipulation within the changing context of state formation and nation-building. Can the case be made, in the end, for the

importation of a cultural problematic to the center of the periodization discussion? I believe that it can. From this point of view, the
Age of Revolution takes on a hitherto unsuspected internal unity
pivoting less, perhaps, on the fall of the colonial order and the advent of national successor states than on the advent of modernity.

Notes

1. Such artifacts of simultaneity have their serial-temporal aspects, too, since
the human eye takes time to travel over a bounded, flat surface of even limited
size, and buildings are experienced in a temporal fashion as our bodies move
through them.

2. For a playful, ingenious, and haunting treatment of the nature of stories
and the way they may be nested one within another, see A. S. Byatt's fairy tale/
novella of the same title, the central piece in her collection *The Djinn in the
Nightingale's Eye* (New York: Vintage Books, 1994), 95–272. Byatt's protago-
nist, a middle-aged English "narratologist," finds the central narrative of her own
bourgeois academic life coming unraveled after her separation from her husband;
and while attending a scholarly meeting in Turkey, she in a sense "invents" herself into a different narrative in which she uncorks a bottle and falls in love with
the ageless genie who emerges.

3. "(Some Random Thoughts on) Continuity and Change in Latin American
Social History, 1780–1850," annual meeting of the Conference on Latin American History, Atlanta, January 1996. From the same CLAH session, see also Victor Uribe's extensive unpublished paper, "Continuities and Changes in Latin
American Political History, 1780–1850," a tour-de-force effort to organize, gloss,
and place in an overall historiographical framework much of the major Anglophone
scholarly work on the political history of Latin America from the end of the eighteenth century through the middle of the nineteenth. I would note in passing that
both Socolow and Uribe cite me as one of the early exponents of this revisionist
periodization, especially my article, "Recent Anglophone Historiography on
Mexico and Central America in the Age of Revolution (1750–1850)," *Hispanic
American Historical Review* 65 (1985): 725–43. Indeed, Socolow ventures in a
footnote to her paper that I "picked it up" from my late teacher Woodrow Borah,
as though it were a disease. I plead guilty, since I have in my own work attempted
to get away from purely politically driven periodizations and thus undermine for
earlier eras the "statolatry" Alan Knight identified as underlying much of the
teleological approach to histories of the Mexican Revolution; Knight, *The Mexican Revolution* (Cambridge: Cambridge University Press, 1986), 1:559, note 386.
Both Borah and David Brading, among others, were at this long before I;
see, for example, Woodrow W. Borah, "Discontinuity and Continuity in Mexican
History," *Pacific Historical Review* 48 (1979): 1–25; and, among David Brading's
works, *Haciendas and Ranchos in the Mexican Bajío: León, 1700–1860* (Cambridge: Cambridge University Press, 1978). Nor is it entirely accurate to assert,
as Socolow does in her unpublished paper, that this revisionist periodization of
the transition from the colonial era to that of modern states and export economies
has not caught on except as a program for anthologies (some of which I cite
below). Historian Stewart Voss, for example, is at present completing a book
based on a cognate, or even more extended, chronological cut that he calls the
"middle period" in Latin American history; Stewart Voss, *Latin America's Middle*

Age: From Imperial Reform to World Depression (Chapel Hill: University of North Carolina Press, forthcoming). About a decade ago Mark Szuchman adopted a similarly broad (admittedly vague) usage of this "middle period" in his edited anthology, *The Middle Period in Latin America: Values and Attitudes in the 17th–19th Centuries* (Boulder: Lynne Rienner, 1989), especially the editor's introduction, 1–18. Doctoral dissertations tend increasingly to adopt some form of this periodization, and a glance at the *Hispanic American Historical Review* or other Latin American history journals will reveal that it is often employed by scholars. Interestingly enough, what seems at issue in discussions of the revisionist periodization is not so much the nether endpoint—whether to begin it in 1780, 1750, or even earlier—but the upper endpoint, and specifically the significance of the span 1808–1825.

4. Paradoxically, commodification swallows up a smaller narration within a larger one, since the very aim of commodification is to efface particularity and history through reduction to homogeneous units. There are parallels here to the effects of periodization.

5. Thus, to parallel James Scott's *Seeing Like a State: How Certain Schemes to Improve the Human Condition Have Failed* (New Haven: Yale University Press, 1998), we may add "remembering like a state," since even when they claim conservative credentials ("we are preserving the traditional"), states like to fracture time to justify their own continuity ("before us, after us"). The public cultural traditions that mark continuity may also be "invented," as we were powerfully reminded by Eric Hobsbawm and Terence Ranger, eds., *The Invention of Tradition* (Cambridge: Cambridge University Press, 1983).

6. Mario Vargas Llosa, *The War of the End of the World*, translated by Helen R. Lane (New York: Penguin Books, 1997).

7. For some airing of this trend within the discipline more broadly, which began with a linguistic turn off the main highway of grand narrative and landed many of us in the dark forest of postmodernism (where there is no forest, properly speaking, but only trees), see among other recent works Joyce Appleby, Lynn Hunt, and Margaret Jacob, *Telling the Truth about History* (New York: Norton, 1994); Robert F. Berkhofer, Jr., *Beyond the Great Story: History as Text and Discourse* (Cambridge, MA: Harvard University Press, 1995); and Brian Fay, Philip Pomper, and Richard T. Vann, eds., *History and Theory: Contemporary Readings* (Malden and Oxford: Blackwell, 1998). For an example of the way these questions are playing out in one major subfield of Latin American history, see the special issue of the *Hispanic American Historical Review* (79:2, May 1999) devoted to "Mexico's New Cultural History: ¿Una lucha libre?"

8. William B. Taylor, "Between Global Process and Local Knowledge: An Inquiry into Early Latin American Social History, 1500–1900," in Olivier Zunz, ed., *Reliving the Past: The Worlds of Social History* (Chapel Hill: University of North Carolina Press, 1985), 115–90.

9. I have borrowed the term "infrahistory" from James C. Scott, *Domination and the Arts of Resistance: Hidden Transcripts* (New Haven: Yale University Press, 1990), who uses it in a somewhat more restricted sense than I intend here.

10. This begs for the moment the issue of the "stickiness" of political *culture* as a subset of culture in the broader sense—that is, in attitudes about politics, the rules of the political game, the relationship of politics to "the Good" in the minds of most people, and the linkage between politics and other primary social parameters, such as kinship, gender arrangements, and class—as opposed to their everyday practice or the sheer contingencies of political life. I think it is possible to make this distinction because of the way political activity as a power

system—in defining and enforcing property rights, for example, or in collecting taxes, making war, or settling conflicts—affects immediately the action-stream of so many individuals simultaneously, even in very localized political venues, since its action is so hierarchically organized and so concentrated temporally and structurally.

11. Stanley J. and Barbara H. Stein, *The Colonial Heritage of Latin America: Essays on Economic Dependence in Perspective* (New York: Oxford University Press, 1970). For a recent, withering (and largely convincing) critique of dependency theory, see Stephen Haber, "Introduction: Economic Growth and Latin American Economic Historiography," in Haber, ed., *How Latin America Fell Behind: Essays on the Economic Histories of Brazil and Mexico, 1800–1914* (Stanford: Stanford University Press, 1997), 1–33. A propos the periodization under discussion here, Richard Salvucci notes of Mexico in his essay in the same volume: "The economic history of the later eighteenth century surely begins with the fiscal consequences of the Seven Years' War and Spain's 'defensive modernization' of its empire. . . . Perhaps the 'Independence Era' [a.k.a. the "Age of Revolution"] in Mexico began in 1759 and ended with the war of 1847." Salvucci, "Mexican National Income in the Era of Independence, 1800–40," in Haber, *Why Latin America Fell Behind*, 216–42, at p. 235.

12. In critiquing the central tenet of dependency theory—that over time the Latin American economies were bled into underdevelopment—Haber comments: "The weight of the evidence points to the conclusion that there has been no secular deterioration in Latin America's terms of trade, but rather there have been cyclical swings with no discernible long-term trend." Haber, "Introduction," 12.

13. I am myself agnostic about whether to abandon wholly the old colonial/ national division in favor of an Age of Revolution scenario, although I think the issue well worth discussing; it all depends upon what sorts of questions one wants to answer by periodizing. The present essay is just as much or more an extended critical exercise—if we understand the function of criticism to be the denaturalization of prevailing practice: to make practice look strange, or have it justify itself—as it is a prescription for a revisionist point of view.

14. For a recent example, see the excellent anthology edited by Steven C. Topik and Allen Wells, *The Second Conquest of Latin America: Coffee, Henequen, and Oil during the Export Boom, 1850–1930* (Austin: University of Texas Press, 1998).

15. Some pundits have even suggested that Latin America as a whole passed directly from a premodern to a postmodern condition without ever experiencing modernity. On these issues, see John Beverly, Jose Oviedo, and Michael Aronna, eds., *The Postmodernism Debate in Latin America* (Durham: Duke University Press, 1995).

16. Paul Johnson, *The Birth of the Modern: World Society, 1815–1830* (New York: HarperCollins, 1992), in many respects convincingly locates the advent of modernity more generally in the second and third decades of the nineteenth century, but he typically devotes little attention to events or trends in Latin America. Benedict Anderson, on the other hand, in his widely influential essay on nation-building, *Imagined Communities: Reflections on the Origin and Spread of Nationalism*, rev. ed. (London: Verso, 1991), highlights the role of nationalism imported from the New World to the Old during the early nineteenth century; for a critical gloss on Anderson in relation to Mexico, see the highly suggestive essays of Claudio Lomnitz, *Deep Mexico, Silent Mexico: Essays on Nationalism and the Public Sphere* (Minneapolis: University of Minnesota Press, 2000), esp. Chapter 2.

17. In one way or another this is the central theme of a large part of post-independence historiography for Latin America as a whole. One of the most wide-ranging and eloquent treatments of the process of state- and nation-building in Spanish America is David A. Brading's *The First America: The Spanish Monarchy, Creole Patriots, and the Liberal State, 1492–1867* (Cambridge: Cambridge University Press, 1991), and Brading's well-known works on Mexico that lie behind it. But these processes have been traced in detail for individual countries as well, especially on the level of high politics and ideology. See, for example, Hans-Joachim König, *En el camino hacia la nación: Nacionalismo en el proceso de formación del Estado y Nación de la Nueva Granada, 1750–1856* (Bogotá: Banco de la República, 1994); and on Mexico, the essays by Lomnitz, *Deep Mexico, Silent Mexico*. What is interesting about works structured like König's is that for the sake of building a more or less purely political genealogy of state and nation they adopt the Age of Revolution periodization, but for different ends than I will be advocating here. For a recent magisterial overview of the political processes of independence, see Jaime E. Rodríguez O., *The Independence of Spanish America* (Cambridge: Cambridge University Press, 1998).

18. The issue of ethnocultural conflict as a central dynamic in the Mexican Wars of Independence, and specifically the failure of large comparative/theoretical works in historical sociology to take such intranational fissures into account in tracing the genealogies of nation-state building in the West, are dealt with at some length especially in the Introduction to Eric Van Young, *The Other Rebellion: Popular Violence, Ideology, and the Struggle for Mexican Independence, 1810–1821* (Stanford: Stanford University Press, 2000). Samuel Amaral and Richard Doringo note in passing in their demographic statistics the ethnic heterogeneity of Latin America in comparison with contemporaneous European societies. This is important, since it suggests the difficulty of applying a set of basically Euro-Atlantic desiderata in assessing the potential for rapid social and economic change in the former Iberian colonies.

19. On creole patriotism, see Brading, *The First America*. For a useful survey of indigenist rhetoric and policy in Mexico in the postrevolutionary era, see Alan Knight, "Racism, Revolution, and *Indigenismo*: Mexico, 1910–1940," in Richard Graham, ed., *The Idea of Race in Latin America, 1870–1940* (Austin: University of Texas Press, 1990), 71–113; and for a suggestive essay on ethnic identity and *indigenismo* in the Andean republics, Brooke Larson, "Andean Highland Peasants and the Trials of Nation-Making during the Nineteenth Century," in *Cambridge History of the Native Peoples of the Americas*, vol. 4: *South America*, edited by Frank Salomon and Stuart Schwartz (Cambridge: Cambridge University Press, 2000).

20. See, for example, Philip Corrigan and Derek Sayer, *The Great Arch: English State Formation as Cultural Revolution* (Oxford: Oxford University Press, 1985).

21. David L. Frye, *Indians into Mexicans: History and Identity in a Mexican Town* (Austin: University of Texas Press, 1996); Cynthia Radding, *Wandering Peoples: Colonialism, Ethnic Spaces, and Ecological Frontiers in Northwestern Mexico, 1700–1850* (Durham: Duke University Press, 1997); Antonio Escobar Ohmstede, *Da la costa a la sierra: Los pueblos indios de las huastecas, 1750–1900* (Mexico City: Centro de Investigaciones y Estudios Superiores en Antropología Social/Instituto Nacional Indigenista, 1999); and Pedro Bracamonte y Sosa, *La memoria enclaustrada: Historia indígena de Yucatán, 1750–1915* (Mexico City: Centro de Investigaciones y Estudios Superiores en Antropología Social/Instituto Nacional Indigenista, 1994).

On the other hand, it goes without saying that some of the monumental works on indigenous peoples of the last several decades have kept closely to the colonial/national divide in terms of their temporal scope; for example, Charles Gibson, *The Aztecs under Spanish Rule: A History of the Indians of the Valley of Mexico, 1519–1810* (Stanford: Stanford University Press, 1964); Nancy M. Farriss, *Maya Society under Spanish Colonial Rule: The Collective Enterprise of Survival* (Princeton: Princeton University Press, 1984); and James Lockhart, *The Nahuas after the Conquest: A Social and Cultural History of the Indians of Central Mexico, Sixteenth through Eighteenth Centuries* (Stanford: Stanford University Press, 1992). Less technically ethnohistorical than these works on Mexico, but cognate to them and employing the same rough time frame as the Frye, Radding, Escobar, and Bracamonte studies, are a group of recent books on nation-building processes and their relationship to indigenous peoples in the Andean area. Among the best of such studies are Charles F. Walker, *Smoldering Ashes: Cuzco and the Creation of Republican Peru, 1780–1840* (Durham: Duke University Press, 1999); and Mark Thurner, *From Two Republics to One Divided: Contradictions of Postcolonial Nation-making in Andean Peru* (Durham: Duke University Press, 1996).

22. The "inner logic" of ethnohistory may not correspond to the logic of state discourse, however, making this approach harder than it might appear at first glance. In writing an ethnohistorical survey of the indigenous peoples of western-central Mexico, for example, I found that after independence the national state's ostensibly inclusionist policies made formerly "Indian" populations virtually invisible in the post-1821 documentation and the historiography based upon it. See Eric Van Young, "The Indigenous Peoples of Central-Western Mexico from the Spanish Invasion to the Present," in *Cambridge History of the Native Peoples of the Americas*, vol. 2, *Mesoamerica*, edited by R. E. W. Adams and Murdo J. MacLeod (Cambridge: Cambridge University Press, 2000), especially the essay on sources.

23. See, for example, Jaime E. Rodríguez O., ed., *Mexico in the Age of Democratic Revolutions, 1750–1850* (Boulder: Lynne Rienner, 1994); and Kenneth J. Andrien and Lyman L. Johnson, eds., *The Political Economy of Spanish America in the Age of Revolution, 1750–1850* (Albuquerque: University of New Mexico Press, 1994). To be fair, the individual essays in some influential recent collected works that have followed thematic rather than temporal logics do not work across the continental divide, either. For some examples, see Friedrich Katz, ed., *Riot, Rebellion, and Revolution: Rural Social Conflict in Mexico* (Princeton: Princeton University Press, 1988); Jaime E. Rodríguez O., ed., *Patterns of Contention in Mexican History* (Wilmington, DE: Scholarly Resources, 1992); and William H. Beezley, Cheryl English Martin, and William E. French, eds., *Rituals of Rule, Rituals of Resistance: Public Celebrations and Popular Culture in Mexico* (Wilmington, DE: Scholarly Resources, 1994).

24. For a compelling, still unsurpassed critique of this tendency, see Eric R. Wolf, *Europe and the People without History* (Berkeley: University of California Press, 1983).

25. See also Steve J. Stern, *The Secret History of Gender: Women, Men, and Power in Late Colonial Mexico* (Chapel Hill: University of North Carolina Press, 1995).

26. Silvia M. Arrom, *Containing the Poor: The Mexico City Poor House, 1774–1871* (Durham: Duke University Press, 2000; manuscript), 84. On the history of psychiatry, the medicalization of madness, and the treatment of the insane in the late colonial period, see María Cristina Sacristán, *Locura y disidencia*

en el México ilustrado, 1760–1810 (Zamora: El Colegio de Michoacán; Mexico City: Instituto Mora, 1994); although Sacristán keeps to the traditional periodization, she demonstrates a clear trend toward the secularization of attitudes in the eighteenth century.

27. See, for example, Richard Garner, with Spiro E. Stefanou, *Economic Growth and Change in Bourbon Mexico* (Gainesville: University Press of Florida, 1993). While Garner resolutely refrains from discussing the postindependence period in Mexico (the latter third or so of our Age of Revolution), he does paint a picture of a colonial economy already losing much of its earlier dynamism, so that the slow or even negative growth rates and developmental stagnation of the decades after 1821 seem more a continuation of the preceding period than a reversal of previous prosperity. Along the same lines for Mexico, see Eric Van Young, *La crisis del orden colonial: Estructura agraria y rebeliones populares de la Nueva España, 1750–1821* (Mexico City: Alianza Editorial, 1992); John H. Coatsworth, *Los orígenes del atraso: Nueve ensayos de historia económica de México en los siglos XVIII y XIX* (Mexico City: Alianza Editorial, 1990); Arij Ouweneel, *Shadows over Anahuac: An Ecological Interpretation of Crisis and Development in Central Mexico, 1730–1800* (Albuquerque: University of New Mexico Press, 1996); and numerous essays by Pedro Pérez Herrero, among them "Regional Conformation in Mexico, 1700–1850: Models and Hypotheses," in Eric Van Young, ed., *Mexico's Regions: Comparative History and Development* (La Jolla: Center for U.S.-Mexican Studies, University of California, San Diego, 1992), 117–44, and "El México borbónico: Un 'éxito' fracasado?," in Josefa Zoraida Vázquez, coord., *Interpretaciones del siglo XVIII mexicano: El impacto de las reformas borbónicas* (Mexico City: Editorial Patria, 1992), 109–51. For Latin America more generally, see Haber, ed., *How Latin America Fell Behind*.

28. Arnold J. Bauer, *Goods, Power, History in Latin America, 1500–2000* (Cambridge: Cambridge University Press, 2000). I thank the author for making an outline and part of his text available to me in manuscript.

29. In addition to Bauer's much more detailed work, see my essay, "Material Life," in Louisa Schell Hoberman and Susan Migden Socolow, eds., *The Countryside in Colonial Latin America* (Albuquerque: University of New Mexico Press, 1996), 49–74 (embracing all of Latin America); and in conjunction with it my article on real wages and standards of living in late colonial Mexico, "Los ricos se vuelven más ricos y los pobres más pobres: Salarios reales y estándares populares de vida a fines de la Colonia en México," in Van Young, *La crisis del orden colonial*, 51–123.

30. For an extremely impressive study of the fiscal and political economy side of these new arrangements in Mexico, see Araceli Ibarra Bellón, *El comercio y el poder en México, 1821–1864* (Mexico City: Fondo de Cultura Económica, 1998).

31. For some recent exemplars of this type of work for Mexico, see Enrique Florescano, *Etnia, estado y nación: Ensayo sobre las identidades colectivas en México* (Mexico City: Aguilar, 1997); Fernando Escalante Gonzalbo, *Ciudadanos imaginarios. Memorial de los afanes y desventuras de la virtud y apologia del vicio triunfante en la República Mexicana: Tratado de moral pública* (Mexico City: El Colegio de México, 1992); Peter F. Guardino, *Peasants, Politics, and the Formation of Mexico's National State: Guerrero, 1800–1857* (Stanford: Stanford University Press, 1996); and Cheryl E. Martin, *Governance and Society in Colonial Mexico: Chihuahua in the Eighteenth Century* (Stanford: Stanford University Press, 1996). For some examples for the Andean region, focusing on ethnicity and nation-building, see Walker, *Smoldering Ashes*; Thurner, *From Two*

Republics to One Divided; and from an even longer-term perspective, Thomas A. Abercrombie, *Pathways of Memory and Power: Ethnography and History among an Andean People* (Madison: University of Wisconsin Press, 1998).

32. Brian R. Hamnett, *Roots of Insurgency: Mexican Regions, 1750–1824* (Cambridge: Cambridge University Press, 1986).

33. None of this is to say that a marked regionalism had not existed before independence, but simply that afterward regions gained a greater degree of political autonomy vis-à-vis much weakened central states. In much of Spanish America, the nineteenth century saw a prolonged struggle to weaken a strong regional structure and strengthen a weak class structure; see Eric Van Young, "Introduction: Are Regions Good to Think?" in Van Young, ed., *Mexico's Regions*, 1–36; and my essay (a slightly more developed version of an earlier Spanish original), "Doing Regional History: Methodological and Theoretical Considerations," in David Robinson, ed., *Conference of Latin Americanist Geographers Yearbook* 1994 (20): 21–34.

34. On the development of the public sphere in nineteenth-century Mexico, see Carlos Forment, "Civil Society and the Invention of Associative Democracy in Mexico, 1830–1880," conference on "Mexican Popular Political Culture, 1800–2000," Center for U.S.-Mexican Studies, University of California, San Diego, April 1998. From the same conference, see Richard Warren's paper, "The Discourse of Masses and the Masses of Discourse: Crowds and Popular Political Culture in Mexico City from Independence to the Reform"; the same author's soon-to-be-published book, *Vagrants and Citizens: Political Culture and the Urban Masses in Mexico City from Colony to Republic* (Durham: Duke University Press, 2000); and for Colombia, Victor Uribe-Uran, *"Honorable Lives": Lawyers, Family, and Politics in Colombia, 1780–1850* (Pittsburgh: University of Pittsburgh Press, 2000), and "The Birth of a Public Sphere in Latin America during the Age of Revolution," *Comparative Studies in Society and History* 42, no. 3 (April 2000): 425–57.

35. Sarah C. Chambers, "Crime and Citizenship: Judicial Practice in Arequipa, Peru, during the Transition from Colony to Republic," in Carlos A. Aguirre and Robert Buffington, eds., *Reconstructing Criminality in Latin America* (Wilmington, DE: Scholarly Resources, 2000); Arrom, *Containing the Poor*.

36. For two other recent investigations that explore an emergent political culture, ideas about liberalism, and gender relations, see Sarah C. Chambers, *From Subjects to Citizens: Honor, Gender, and Politics in Arequipa, Peru, 1780–1854* (University Park: Pennsylvania State University Press, 2000); and Christine Hunefeldt, *Liberalism in the Bedroom* (University Park: Pennsylvania State University Press, 1999).

37. Even in the face of this cultural malleability, however, one would want to establish more subtle nuances among the social venues in which the cultural manifestation in question was taking place. Thus, we might want to distinguish the more openly "textual" sorts of behaviors like dance, taking place in the consciously performative/public realm, from cultural expressions in the familial/semi-public or interior/individual realm, and think about a correlation between their publicness and the rapidity with which they might change.

Index

About the Contributors

SAMUEL AMARAL is a professor of history, formerly at Northern Illinois University, De Kalb, and currently at the University of Tres de Febrero, Buenos Aires, Argentina. His most recent book is *The Rise of Capitalism on the Pampas: The Estancias of Buenos Aires, 1785–1870* (1998). With Marta Valencia, he edited *Argentina: El país nuevo* (1999); with Leandro Prados de la Escosura, *La independencia americana: Consecuencias económicas* (1993); and with William E. Ratcliff, *Juan D. Perón: Cartas del exilio* (1993). His current research focuses on Peronism and Argentine politics from 1955 to 1976.

JOHN CHARLES CHASTEEN has taught Latin American history at the University of North Carolina, Chapel Hill, since 1990. He is the author of *Born in Blood and Fire: A Concise History of Latin America* (2001). An early practitioner of Latin America's "New Cultural History," he published *Heroes on Horseback: A Life and Times of the Last Gaucho Caudillos* (1995), and numerous essays in the field. He has translated major Spanish- and Portuguese-language works by Tulio Halperín Donghi, Angel Rama, and Hermano Vianna. With Joseph S. Tulchin he edited *Problems in Modern Latin American History: A Reader* (1994). More recently he has turned his attention to the social history of Latin American popular dance and has published several contributions to that field.

RICHARD DORINGO is a Ph.D. candidate at Northern Illinois University, De Kalb. He is finishing a dissertation on collective welfare in Mexican economic thought between 1821 and 1917. He currently teaches history at The Andrews School in Willoughby, Ohio, and at Cleveland State University. His latest research deals with Mexican and U.S. labor history.

ELIZABETH ANNE KUZNESOF is a professor of Latin American and Brazilian history at the University of Kansas, Lawrence. She is the author of *Household Economy and Urban Development: São Paulo, 1765–1836* (1986) as well as numerous articles on Brazilian social history and on the history of family, childhood, and domestic service in Latin America.

MARTI LAMAR is an assistant professor of Latin American history at Saint Norbert College, De Pere, Wisconsin. She received her Ph.D. from the University of Texas at Austin where she wrote a dissertation on Chilean merchants in the period 1795–1823. She has published on the topic of colonial inheritance laws and women in the *Journal of Social History* and is currently working on a faculty-student collaborative project that investigates contemporary Chilean women.

SONYA LIPSETT-RIVERA received her Ph.D. from Tulane University in 1988. She is the author of *To Defend Our Water with the Blood of Our Veins: The Struggle for Resources in Colonial Puebla* (1999) as well as many related articles and chapters. With Lyman Johnson she is the co-editor of *The Faces of Honor: Sex, Shame, and Violence in Colonial Latin America* (1998). She also co-translated Juan Pedro Viqueira Albán's *Propriety and Permissiveness in Bourbon Mexico* (1999). Professor Lipsett-Rivera has been awarded the Tibezar Prize (1992) and honorable mention for the Conference Prize of the Conference on Latin American History (1998). Currently, she is an associate professor at Carleton University in Ottawa, Canada.

RICHARD J. SALVUCCI teaches economics at Trinity University in San Antonio, Texas. He is the author of *Textiles and Capitalism in Mexico: An Economic History of the Obrajes, 1539–1840* (1987). He has published numerous articles and book chapters on the economic history of Latin America and the Caribbean, the most recent (jointly with Linda Salvucci) being "Cuba and the Latin American Terms of Trade: Old Theories, New Evidence," in the *Journal of Interdisciplinary History* (2000). His current projects include a financial history of Mexico's "London Debt" in the nineteenth century and a book on Mexican foreign trade in the nineteenth century.

MARK D. SZUCHMAN is a professor of history and associate dean of arts and sciences at Florida International University, Miami. He has written books on nineteenth-century Argentine history, including *Mobility and Integration in Urban Argentina: Córdoba in the*

Liberal Era (1976) and *Order, Family, and Community in Buenos Aires, 1810–1860* (1988). With Gilbert M. Joseph he edited *I Saw a City Invincible: Urban Portraits of Latin America* (1996); and with Jonathan C. Brown, *Revolution and Restoration: The Rearrangement of Power in Argentina, 1776–1860* (1994). He is the sole editor of *The Middle Period in Latin America: Values and Attitudes in the 17th–19th Centuries* (1989). Professor Szuchman was the managing editor of the *Hispanic American Historical Review* from 1991 to 1997. His current research concerns the material and ideological representation of power and citizenship.

ERIC VAN YOUNG is a professor in and the chair of the Department of History, and the associate director of the Center for U.S.-Mexican Studies, at the University of California, San Diego. His published work includes *Hacienda and Market in Eighteenth-Century Mexico: The Rural Economy of the Guadalajara Region, 1675–1820* (1981); *La crisis del orden colonial: Estructura agraria y rebeliones populares de la Nueva España, 1750–1821* (1992); and *The Other Rebellion: Popular Violence, Ideology, and the Mexican Independence Struggle, 1810–1821* (2000). He has published numerous articles on related topics and influential historiographical essays and critiques on economic, social, and cultural history.

Latin American Silhouettes
Studies in History and Culture

William H. Beezley and
Judith Ewell
Editors

Volumes Published

Silvia Marina Arrom and Servando Ortoll, eds., *Riots in the Cities: Popular Politics and the Urban Poor in Latin America, 1765–1910* (1996). Cloth ISBN 0-8420-2580-4 Paper ISBN 0-8420-2581-2

Roderic Ai Camp, ed., *Polling for Democracy: Public Opinion and Political Liberalization in Mexico* (1996). ISBN 0-8420-2583-9

Brian Loveman and Thomas M. Davies, Jr., eds., *The Politics of Antipolitics: The Military in Latin America*, 3d ed., revised and updated (1996). Cloth ISBN 0-8420-2609-6 Paper ISBN 0-8420-2611-8

Joseph S. Tulchin, Andrés Serbín, and Rafael Hernández, eds., *Cuba and the Caribbean: Regional Issues and Trends in the Post-Cold War Era* (1997). ISBN 0-8420-2652-5

Thomas W. Walker, ed., *Nicaragua without Illusions: Regime Transition and Structural Adjustment in the 1990s* (1997). Cloth ISBN 0-8420-2578-2 Paper ISBN 0-8420-2579-0

Dianne Walta Hart, *Undocumented in L.A.: An Immigrant's Story* (1997). Cloth ISBN 0-8420-2648-7 Paper ISBN 0-8420-2649-5

Jaime E. Rodríguez O. and Kathryn Vincent, eds., *Myths, Misdeeds, and Misunderstandings: The Roots of Conflict in U.S.-Mexican Relations* (1997). ISBN 0-8420-2662-2

Jaime E. Rodríguez O. and Kathryn Vincent, eds., *Common Border, Uncommon Paths: Race, Culture, and National Identity in U.S.-Mexican Relations* (1997). ISBN 0-8420-2673-8

William H. Beezley and Judith Ewell, eds., *The Human Tradition in Modern Latin America* (1997). Cloth ISBN 0-8420-2612-6 Paper ISBN 0-8420-2613-4

Donald F. Stevens, ed., *Based on a True Story: Latin American History at the Movies* (1997). Cloth ISBN 0-8420-2582-0 Paper ISBN 0-8420-2781-5

Jaime E. Rodríguez O., ed., *The Origins of Mexican National Politics, 1808–1847* (1997). Paper ISBN 0-8420-2723-8

Che Guevara, *Guerrilla Warfare*, with revised and updated introduction and case studies by Brian Loveman and Thomas M. Davies, Jr., 3d ed. (1997). Cloth ISBN 0-8420-2677-0 Paper ISBN 0-8420-2678-9

Adrian A. Bantjes, *As If Jesus Walked on Earth: Cardenismo, Sonora, and the Mexican Revolution* (1998; rev. ed., 2000). Cloth ISBN 0-8420-2653-3 Paper ISBN 0-8420-2751-3

Henry A. Dietz and Gil Shidlo, eds., *Urban Elections in Democratic Latin America* (1998). Cloth ISBN 0-8420-2627-4 Paper ISBN 0-8420-2628-2

A. Kim Clark, *The Redemptive Work: Railway and Nation in Ecuador, 1895–1930* (1998). Cloth ISBN 0-8420-2674-6 Paper ISBN 0-8420-5013-2

Joseph S. Tulchin, ed., with Allison M. Garland, *Argentina: The Challenges of Modernization* (1998). ISBN 0-8420-2721-1

Louis A. Pérez, Jr., ed., *Impressions of Cuba in the Nineteenth Century: The Travel Diary of Joseph J. Dimock* (1998). Cloth ISBN 0-8420-2657-6 Paper ISBN 0-8420-2658-4

June E. Hahner, ed., *Women through Women's Eyes: Latin American Women in Nineteenth-Century Travel Accounts* (1998). Cloth ISBN 0-8420-2633-9 Paper ISBN 0-8420-2634-7

James P. Brennan, ed., *Peronism and Argentina* (1998). ISBN 0-8420-2706-8

John Mason Hart, ed., *Border Crossings: Mexican and Mexican-American Workers*

(1998). Cloth ISBN 0-8420-2716-5
Paper ISBN 0-8420-2717-3

Brian Loveman, *For* la Patria: *Politics and the Armed Forces in Latin America* (1999). Cloth ISBN 0-8420-2772-6
Paper ISBN 0-8420-2773-4

Guy P. C. Thomson, with David G. LaFrance, *Patriotism, Politics, and Popular Liberalism in Nineteenth-Century Mexico: Juan Francisco Lucas and the Puebla Sierra* (1999).
ISBN 0-8420-2683-5

Robert Woodmansee Herr, in collaboration with Richard Herr, *An American Family in the Mexican Revolution* (1999).
ISBN 0-8420-2724-6

Juan Pedro Viqueira Albán, trans. Sonya Lipsett-Rivera and Sergio Rivera Ayala, *Propriety and Permissiveness in Bourbon Mexico* (1999).
Cloth ISBN 0-8420-2466-2
Paper ISBN 0-8420-2467-0

Stephen R. Niblo, *Mexico in the 1940s: Modernity, Politics, and Corruption* (1999).
Cloth ISBN 0-8420-2794-7
Paper (2001) ISBN 0-8420-2795-5

David E. Lorey, *The U.S.-Mexican Border in the Twentieth Century* (1999).
Cloth ISBN 0-8420-2755-6
Paper ISBN 0-8420-2756-4

Joanne Hershfield and David R. Maciel, eds., *Mexico's Cinema: A Century of Films and Filmmakers* (2000). Cloth ISBN 0-8420-2681-9 Paper ISBN 0-8420-2682-7

Peter V. N. Henderson, *In the Absence of Don Porfirio: Francisco León de la Barra and the Mexican Revolution* (2000).
ISBN 0-8420-2774-2

Mark T. Gilderhus, *The Second Century: U.S.-Latin American Relations since 1889* (2000). Cloth ISBN 0-8420-2413-1
Paper ISBN 0-8420-2414-X

Catherine Moses, *Real Life in Castro's Cuba* (2000). Cloth ISBN 0-8420-2836-6
Paper ISBN 0-8420-2837-4

K. Lynn Stoner, ed./comp., with Luis Hipólito Scriano Pérez, *Cuban and Cuban-American Women: An Annotated Bibliography* (2000).
ISBN 0-8420-2643-6

Thomas D. Schoonover, *The French in Central America: Culture and*

Commerce, *1820–1930* (2000).
ISBN 0-8420-2792-0

Enrique C. Ochoa, *Feeding Mexico: The Political Uses of Food since 1910* (2000). ISBN 0-8420-2812-9

Thomas W. Walker and Ariel C. Armony, eds., *Repression, Resistance, and Democratic Transition in Central America* (2000). Cloth ISBN 0-8420-2766-1   Paper ISBN 0-8420-2768-8

William H. Beezley and David E. Lorey, eds., *¡Viva México! ¡Viva la Independencia! Celebrations of September 16* (2001).
Cloth ISBN 0-8420-2914-1
Paper ISBN 0-8420-2915-X

Jeffrey M. Pilcher, *Cantinflas and the Chaos of Mexican Modernity* (2001).
Cloth ISBN 0-8420-2769-6
Paper ISBN 0-8420-2771-8

Victor M. Uribe-Uran, ed., *State and Society in Spanish America during the Age of Revolution* (2001). Cloth ISBN 0-8420-2873-0   Paper ISBN 0-8420-2874-9

Andrew Grant Wood, *Revolution in the Street: Women, Workers, and Urban Protest in Veracruz, 1870–1927* (2001).
ISBN 0-8420-2879-X

Charles Bergquist, Ricardo Peñaranda, and Gonzalo Sánchez G., eds., *Violence in Colombia, 1990–2000: Waging War and Negotiating Peace* (2001).
Cloth ISBN 0-8420-2869-2
Paper ISBN 0-8420-2870-6

William Schell, Jr., *Integral Outsiders: The American Colony in Mexico City, 1876–1911* (2001). ISBN 0-8420-2838-2

John Lynch, *Argentine Caudillo: Juan Manuel de Rosas* (2001).
Cloth ISBN 0-8420-2897-8
Paper ISBN 0-8420-2898-6

Samuel Basch, M.D., ed. and trans. Fred D. Ullman, *Recollections of Mexico: The Last Ten Months of Maximilian's Empire* (2001). ISBN 0-8420-2962-1

Sowell, David, *The Tale of Healer Miguel Perdomo Neira: Medicine, Ideologies, and Power in the Nineteenth-Century Andes* (2001).
Cloth ISBN 0-8420-2826-9
Paper ISBN 0-8420-2827-7